How to Transform Workplace Bullies Into Allies

A volume in
Ethics in Practice
Carole L. Jurkiewicz and Robert A. Giacalone, *Series Editors*

How to Transform Workplace Bullies Into Allies

Jacqueline A. Gilbert

Middle Tennessee State University

INFORMATION AGE PUBLISHING, INC.
Charlotte, NC • www.infoagepub.com

Library of Congress Cataloging-in-Publication Data

A CIP record for this book is available from the Library of Congress
http://www.loc.gov

ISBN: 978-164113-960-1 (Paperback)
     978-164113-961-8 (Hardcover)
     978-164113-962-5 (E-Book)

Disclaimer

All scenario vignettes, companies, places, projects, people, and employee names
within this manuscript are fictitious. Any resemblance to existing entities
or people is coincidental.

Printed in the United States of America

To Jack Ivancevich, Bette Stead, Norma Carr-Ruffino,
Joe White, and Gary Namie, who taught me to persevere,
make a difference, and move mountains.

And to my mother, Johanna Gilbert, who made everything possible.

Contents

SECTION **I**

Overview of Bullying

SECTION **II**

What's Behind It?

SECTION **III**

How to Fix It? Communication

Foreword

The book in your hands is bursting with relevant information, thanks to Jacqueline Gilbert's commitment to eradicate bullying in all workplaces. Her voice is effusive. She starts the reader on a journey toward mastery. And as a veteran educator, she knows that the book is only the beginning. There are recommendations aplenty for managers and leaders craving to learn beyond the minimum. Of course, learning about bullying is not for self-interest alone. Do it for the sake of your organization's sustainability.

Contemporary workers, led by workers raised on anti-bullying programs in primary and secondary school, are the least tolerant of all generations toward abusive bullying misconduct. Managers and leaders who remain ignorant about, or indifferent to, bullying risk personal and organizational failure. Work doesn't get done without people. It is futile to manage without understanding the zero-tolerance expectations of the newest workers. Being aware of bullying and its deleterious effects on employee health and productivity is not optional; it is mandatory.

I cannot overstate the comprehensiveness of Gilbert's coverage of the bullying phenomenon in this book. She leads readers through profiles of bullies—the perpetrators—and targeted individuals, the workplace culture that enables bullying, bystanders, top management support for eradication, and aspirational features of an ideal "people-centered" culture. Breadth is coupled with a realistic touch certain to appeal to modern readers accustomed primarily to truncated social media communication and visually appealing stimuli. She does not preach or over-teach.

How to Transform Workplace Bullies Into Allies, pages ix–xii

A variety of features attracts readers with graphical depictions of several phenomena, tables and charts comparing aspects of bullying and incivility, moral development, destructiveness of shame, family tree charting (a guided tour of your family of origin and socialization patterns, characteristics of a community-centered culture, bystander continuum, mature assertiveness, how to think before posting on the web, and a four-dimensional view of diversity. The pages employ vivid visual messaging techniques to optimize absorption of the information.

The book, at first glance, looks like a quick read. After all, Gilbert identifies all the resources for readers. She found the research. But don't be fooled by the ease of access to information. Take the deep dive into each bullying sub-topic masterfully designed for you in the study and rehearsal exercises. Only then will readers glean the best outcomes from the book. Slow down. Incorporate the lessons taught to the practitioner-readers eager to stop bullying. There's more inside than is first apparent.

To me, the challenges that immerse readers in the ideas under discussion in each chapter are key deliverables. Frequent self-assessments force readers to confront personal beliefs that may lead to misperceptions and misunderstandings at work. Readers have the chance to gauge the role of personal envy, toxicity of your workplace culture, bystander status, problem-solving orientation, flawed unilateral communication styles, cyberbullying experiences, organizational inclusivity, and styles of conflict resolution.

Our Workplace Bullying Institute education is "evidence-based." I know of no other non-academic book written about the prevention and correction of workplace bullying that cites research as meticulously as does Gilbert's. She makes references (sneakily) painless for her lay audience of managers and leaders in the field not familiar with academic studies. It is an amazing accomplishment. Look for the Web Quest sections. They are great reads.

As with all self-assessments, descriptive scenarios among workplace actors, suggestions to read materials at their source, and tutorials that characterize workplace bullying in a new light, the author brings readers back to the necessity of applying that new-found knowledge to realistic situations. It all comes down to the question of "What Would You Do?" in each chapter. Gilbert asks us how we would react when faced with opportunities to bully, witness, or get involved. Experiencing the phenomenon from the inside fosters empathy for targeted coworkers and colleagues.

The author also makes several points not found in other books on the topic. Among the bully types are stalkers—the creepy ones who invade a person's life at work and off-site. They are responsible for genuine paranoia by targets. Stalking or "gang stalking" appears to be on the rise. Gilbert wisely acknowledges its emergent presence.

In Chapter 3 the author posits a significant role for past family dysfunction. It may help explain being a bullied target in adulthood. Thankfully breaking free from our destructive histories is encouraged.

Gilbert tackles the topics of multiculturalism and diversity in organizations. Diversity, as a practicable extension of the hard-won civil rights laws and inculcation of the movement from decades past, was thought to be widely accepted. But I was an academic. Diversity was once non-contentious on campuses.

However, the election of America's first black president obviously generated fear and resentment by whites who felt threatened. The election of 2016 revealed those hidden fears. It was in the college town of Charlottesville, Virginia, in 2017 that marching white supremacists dared us to wage the Civil War again.

I thank Gilbert for Chapter 8 to remind us that work free from discrimination is not yet our reality. We know that Hispanics and African Americans suffer bullying at higher rates than whites despite legal "protections." We learn in this chapter about the routinization of negative acts against others, dubbed "cultural stoning"—micro-inequities and microaggressions that recipients easily detect, but witnesses who do not share the others' status normalize and miss. Extrapolating from the dyadic interaction to the dichotomous organizational response—as either reactive/apathetic or proactive/unifying—is brilliant.

Too many employers treat diversity as a legal obligation. Managers nod to the need to comply with laws and policies begrudgingly, undermining organizational commitment to doing the right thing.

We should consider indifference toward diversity and denial of bullying to be two indicators of troubled workplaces. Ignoring the former will eventually land employers in court. The latter will drain valuable resources that sustain the employer—highly skilled employees, a healthy and present work force, and productivity requisite to remain competitive. Stupidity about diversity belies the very public lessons learned by defiant companies that for too long defended harassers and abusers on the payroll. By now, wise employers have shifted gears into proactive mode, pushed by the #MeToo movement.

In an accordion-like demonstration of intellectual range, each chapter flexes from teaching to extended study before collapsing back to the focus on what can be done practically. The outcome is the biggest take-away from each chapter and the book in total. The book helps answer the "So what?" questioning by those skeptical that bullying matters.

I've read all the books written in recent decades about workplace bullying. *How to Transform Workplace Bullies Into Allies* rises above other titles on several dimensions. It uniquely backs every idea and suggestion with evidence. Its methodology is multi-modal. It not only teaches; it assesses, challenges, and inspires. This single volume delivers the comprehensive toolkit that an internal organizational champion needs to plan, implement, and sustain an anti-bullying initiative. The timing is opportune. After two decades of denial, American organizations are more ready than ever to address their long-ignored bullying problems. This book tells them how.

I'm proud to call Dr. Gilbert a colleague and friend.

—Gary Namie, PhD
Workplace Bullying Institute

INTRODUCTION

A New Organizational Mandate

Have you been targeted by a toxic, nasty, or obsessive person at work? Did their mean-spiritedness catch you off guard and leave you isolated from former on-the-job friends? If companies don't know how to adequately address abusive conduct or how to instigate and maintain civil cultures, they can inadvertently foster additional confusion and dysfunction at work. Disrespectful treatment produces psychological angst, like PTSD, hypervigilance, depression/anxiety, and an overall reduced ability to contribute. It also manifests in physical ailments such as insomnia, irritable bowel syndrome, hypertension, stomachaches, ulcers, and headaches. Running for cover within firms is unfortunately common. When bosses fail to address toxic politics, workers may spend more time sparring with their perceived enemies than they do learning, growing, developing, innovating, and productively engaging with other people. Hurtful cultures (and the bad publicity they generate) may cause benefactors and corporate investors to withdraw their business.

Although numerous books and articles have been written to describe bullying, no comprehensive resource exists that

- explains the multifaceted nature of abuse,
- provides examples of when and how it occurs, and
- gives learners guided exercises to promote awareness, to cultivate civility, and to improve their emotional intelligence.

One reason that incivility and abusive conduct continue is that people don't recognize it when they see it, and they don't know it when they do it.

How to Transform Workplace Bullies Into Allies supplies readers with a framework to assess their workplaces and/or schools, to learn about the fallout from acts that dishonor their peers, and to develop an action plan derived from resources that promote civil discourse. It includes:

- Inventories and activities to gauge knowledge and skill development in the areas of abusive conduct, bully typologies, target background, mobbing, effective dialogue at work, cyberbullying, diversity/microaggression, interpersonal conflict, and change management.
- Summaries of research that supports a mandate for good behavior and illuminates company deficiencies.
- Rich bits of what civility experts, management researchers, and ethics practitioners say about abusive conduct to help readers learn why it's important for businesses to examine their culture, and the consequences for continuing status quo.
- Case studies, scenarios, and exercises designed to reinforce key concepts and to stimulate critical thinking about workplace misbehavior.
- Examples of firms that proactively modified culture to minimize (and eliminate) toxic practices.
- Concrete steps for changing organizational policies and "the way we do things" to honor and respect people's spirits. Recognizing unconscious norms is a first step to promoting a positive environment.

By navigating web quests, learning modules, and teachable moments, readers will develop a keen awareness of what it takes to be a respectful contributor in any setting. Moreover, they will gain expertise in what has been deemed a critical skill set by many organizations, including the Society for Human Resource Management. *How to Transform Workplace Bullies Into Allies* supplies readers with the tools to

- recognize conditions that contribute to abusive conduct,
- deter schoolyard/workplace bullies by suggesting alternative behavior,

- develop a program for recovery, and
- behave as proactive change agents.

Through reflection and assessment, you will learn what to do when faced with behavioral dilemmas and how to be a first responder when you see an explosive situation. Community-centered companies can diminish peer aggression and promote collegial support. Organizations that hold workers to a higher standard create respectful cultures, competitive advantages, and ideal places to work.

Acknowledgments

This book represents the culmination of my personal experience and previous work. A sincere thanks to Jeff Cornwall (professor and master blogger) for his encouragement, and continued gratitude to my MTSU Write mentors Dr. Jennifer Kates and Dr. Linda Busby Parker for their patience, guidance, suggestions, and directive critique. A special thank you to my editors—Dr. Bob Giacalone and Dr. Carole Jurkiewicz—for their support and for their insights, to Jennifer Goode Stevens for her superb copyediting, and to Kara Hooper, Kathryn Bowlin, and Micah Loyed for their guidance and custom artwork.

Most of all, I wish to acknowledge the targets of bullying who inspire me to write. The downtrodden have a unique perspective—one that gets shuffled to the bottom of the stack when they are sidelined, discredited, verbally smeared, and questioned as to their very sanity—all the while stoically attempting to do their jobs. Incidents of workplace abuse must be recognized for what they are. They are not joking, entitlement of rank, or put downs in the guise of "just playing around." Respect as mandate (over time) can morph into a larger anti-bullying resistance movement.

I am grateful to my management students for creating awareness. They have educated corporate executives, Oakland High School freshmen, and the YouTube community. All of you teach me something new every day.

To the unsung heroes at RFID journal (and especially editor Mark Roberti) who provide extraordinary, cutting edge material on topics that

How to Transform Workplace Bullies Into Allies, pages xvii–xviii
Copyright © 2020 by Information Age Publishing

profoundly impact our lives, I am grateful. You do a herculean job at describing nascent technology.

I hope that continued workplace bullying education will make stories of ridicule, contempt, disbelief, and public smear non-existent. To all those who rally in support of this cause (including Drs. Gary and Ruth Namie, co-founders of the Workplace Bullying Institute), and the network of Healthy Workplace Advocates who create momentum to do more, I am indebted.

SECTION I

Overview of Bullying

1

Introduction to Bullying—Impact

Recognizing Our Part in Problem Creation

Courage is fire, and bullying is smoke.
—Benjamin Disraeli

The Problem and Definition

In 2013, two university student teams stood nervously inside a multinational headquarters. Each team was about to present its version of a civility policy before executives in a head-to-head competition. The stakes were high: winners would receive media coverage, prominence, extra credit, and a donation made to their college on behalf of the winning team. When the master of ceremonies introduced them, he said:

> "I'd never even heard of workplace bullying before, I had no idea what it was..."

Many people feel the same way. Even though my students have presented on topics of mobbing, cyberbullying, stalking, hazing, and corporate bullying for school and corporate audiences, the reason for audience

How to Transform Workplace Bullies Into Allies, pages 3–23
Copyright © 2020 by Information Age Publishing

surprise is always the same: "We didn't realize this was a problem." The elephant in the room of unaddressed abuse can morph into something much worse, and it can permeate company corridors until it creates a toxic culture and an unstated norm of incivility. Employees who appear mean-spirited may be casualties of cultures where ostracism, industry blackballing, and months (if not years) of unemployment occur for people who side with their "marked" coworkers.

A survey of several hundred employees and leaders within 17 industries revealed that targets of incivility quit in approximately 12% of cases.[1] Christine M. Pearson and Christine Porath, authors of *The Cost of Bad Behavior: How Incivility Is Damaging Your Business and What to Do About It*, estimate that a single bullying incident experienced by half of a 10,000-person workforce can result in millions of dollars in damages, including health claims, absenteeism, and time spent worrying about the incident. Bullying can also increase employee turnover and "presenteeism": sickness and disengagement due to poor treatment, along with litigation, mediation/arbitration, and workers' compensation/disability claims.[2]

Bullies have been described as

> people who are willing to cross the boundaries of civilized behavior that inhibit others. They value the rewards brought by aggression and generally lack guilt, believing their victims provoked the attacks and deserve the consequences.[3]

Why Should We Pay Attention?

Targets can feel they have lost control of their lives, particularly if they experience obsessions, compulsions, and hypervigilance, or an overpowering, constant need to avoid danger. In *A Life Interrupted: The Story of My Battle With Bullying and Obsessive-Compulsive Disorder*,[4] author Sumi Mukherjee describes the mental torment and repetitive behaviors he suffered as a result of unrelenting school bullies. People with OCD may feel an urge to check and recheck what they have done to escape potential punishment.

Scene: An employee describes how she feels in the wake of prolonged psychological abuse.

OCD muscled out positive thought. My new mental warden, my own personal conveyor belt of anxiety, panic, fear, and intrusive thought, allowed for only short-lived periods of relief. Things spiraled out of control when I got home. At night the unwanted Others, like a never-ending amusement park carousel ride, made their appearance: Had I locked my office door? Did I shred the documents from our client meeting? Had I thrown something valuable into my garbage? Were the papers correctly placed in my report? Turning my office key to go home unlocked a Pandora's Box of potential disasters, mistakes, and gargantuan liabilities in the making. *I just had to check one more time.*

Because psychic turmoil is not always evident, bullying may seem like a victimless crime. What observers fail to realize is the profound and lasting impact of abusive behavior. Targets have described their tormenters as "devils," "witches," "demons," and "owners" and have depicted their coworkers as wildly cheering, bloodthirsty spectators.[5] Their willingness to "tough it out" only exacerbates their symptoms of high blood pressure, social isolation, obsessive thinking, anxiety, embarrassment, shame, and missed days from work. Correspondingly, the "John Wayne" individualistic norm within the United States mandates stoicism and moving ahead.

Bullying can leave permanent physical marks. Nobel Prize-winning research has found that stress shortens telomeres—the protective encasings at either end of a DNA strand. Reduction of these end caps is associated with an increased chance of disease and an abbreviated life span.

A bully can literally shorten your life.

Abuse that is severe, or that continues over an extended period, can shrink the brain's mnemonic center, or hippocampus, and make it difficult for targets to distinguish the past from recent occurrences or to place events in contextual perspective.[6]

Scene: Dave, who was humiliated in a company meeting, talks about being terrified of expressing himself.

We all bring our respective baggage to the office. A lifetime of trauma can leave us silenced, banging our fists against the walls of a soundproofed plexiglass cube. I've learned the costs of free speech can far exceed its benefits, so I keep my mouth shut.

Electronic encephalograph (EEG) research found that after people read shame-inducing scenarios they experienced desynchronization, or an interruption of coherent activity that occurs in relaxed individuals' alpha brain waves.[7] Targets may feel overwhelmed from the OCD/PTSD/hypervigilance and/or depression they experience after an attack, and from the embarrassment, shame, and humiliation they feel at work.

> You can kill a person only once, but when you humiliate him, you kill him many times over.
> —The Talmud

Abuse can also contribute to hippocampal hyperactivity, which is associated with intrusive and unwanted thought.[8]

Reflection

Think of a time when you felt bullied or disrespected by another person. What were your feelings toward the aggressor? Toward yourself? What action did you want to take?

_____

_____

_____

_____

The Workplace Bullying Institute reports that "29% of bullied targets considered suicide; 16% actually had a plan to execute."[9] Inability to cope with a life-altering event (and resulting fallout) can be fatal. Consider what happened to:

Kevin Morrissey: former managing editor of *Virginia Quarterly Review* who made multiple attempts to contact university officials regarding a perceived hostile work environment, and who later died by suicide. According to Ted Genoways (Morrissey's former boss), the University of Virginia found Morrissey's complaints of supervisor abuse without merit. An employee at the magazine stated that people may perceive bullying as something that happens on school playgrounds.[10]

and

Tyler Clementi: talented, award-winning musician and freshman at Rutgers University, who experienced mental torment after his roommate secretly filmed and posted to the Internet an intimate encounter of Clementi with another young man. Clementi later died from jumping off the George Washington Bridge.[1]

Christopher Boehm, author of *Moral Origins: The Evolution of Virtue, Altruism, and Shame,* argues that a Cro-Magnon resides within each of us. Although people may know in their rational, thinking brains that bullying is wrong, the experience born of thousands of years of hand-to-hand combat suggests that appearing bigger and badder may increase opportunity.[11] The inner beast can, however, antagonize and profoundly hurt other people. Belligerent leadership styles can produce short-term gains, but they leave employees unmotivated. A Center for Creative Leadership study found that supervisors who had problems with people skills, team building, adapting to change, and maintaining a big-picture view of their functional specialty found their career trajectories derailed as they failed to ascend the ranks like their more-people-savvy peers.[12] Moreover, a study of 51,836 leaders showed the chance of being rated as both *highly unlikable* and *highly competent* was about 1 in 2,000.[13] Persona can thus influence perceptions of job competence. Positively rated leaders solicited feedback, encouraged give and take, and changed direction as a result.[14] To succeed, leaders must bring something additional to the table—a complementary set of soft skills for interacting with coworkers.

> Who would you rather work for? Someone who is continually disgruntled, or someone who possesses superior people skills?

The Behavioral Continuum

Not all abuse appears as over-the-top, in-your-face onslaughts. Abuse resides on a continuum, one ranging from willful intention to sniper attacks, to unawareness or ignorance. The most egregious abusers physically injure other people.

Overt bullying > **Covert bullying** > **Incivility**

Overt Bullying: (Physical Abuse, Hazing, Emotional, and Mental Abuse)

Physical Bullying

The strikingly uncivil blatant bullies engage in physical assault. In the schoolyard, physical abuse manifests as kicking, pushing, shoving, punching, hair-pulling, and yanking. Although these behaviors rarely appear at work, acts of screaming, overpowering by standing too close, and intimidating individuals with a hostile stare (or staring them down until they look away) do occur. The dirty look, hairy eyeball, eye roll, or sneer with upper lip curled are all ways to show signs of physical disapproval and disdain.

Sexual harassment—defined as gender discrimination via unwelcome sexual overture—can also have an element of physical abuse. Examples include cornering someone against a desk, wall, or copy machine so that it is impossible to escape, ogling with elevator eyes, leaning against someone, hovering over another person's desk, unwanted touching or requests for touching, caressing, or "coming on" to someone in an overtly sexual way.

Hazing

Hazing occurs when pledges in school organizations like sports teams, bands, fraternities, and sororities, or when new employees in organizations like the NFL, fire and police departments, and other large companies endure rituals during their probationary period—ones that consist of danger/suffering and/or humiliation. At one Houston fire department, five firefighters were dismissed for waterboarding a rookie employee with substances like mustard, flour, chocolate, and ice cream until he started to cry. Stophazing.org describes violent, physical hazing as branding, spanking, kidnapping, and forced intoxication. Harassment and intimidation hazing are more frequent, but they are less-recognized forms of abuse (see the "Hazing Continuum" below). At work, hazing does not usually progress past the intimidation phase. Examples of intimidation include coercing new or probationary employees into doing favors for senior members, demanding credit on projects to which senior members contributed minimally, and/or assigning newbies undesirable tasks. Hazing at work stems from cultures of fear and/or suspicion. Mary Wilfert, who compiled the "NCAA Building New Traditions: Hazing Prevention in College Athletics Report" explains that individuals who are on "power trips" may exercise their authority inappropriately. They may physically or emotionally abuse other people.[15]

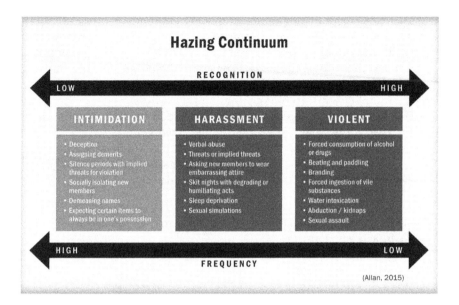

Source: Used with permission of Allan, E. J. (2015). Stophazing.org. Retrieved from http://www.stophazing.org/wp-content/uploads/2016/03/HazingPreventionEDITED.pdf

Emotional/Mental Bullying

Nonphysical aggression can take several forms. Abusive tactics range from overpowering attacks to subtler, almost subliminal microaggressions. Emotional abuse may be unspoken, as in the Jonathan Martin case where the presumed straw that "broke the camel's back" was when his teammates stood up with their lunch trays and moved when he sat down. After the incident, Martin quit the NFL. He alleges a string of hazing incidents as a rookie player, including offensive phone and text messages from teammates.

Nonphysical bullying may also consist of purposely mean-spirited comments, such as

Backhanded compliments: failing to whole-heartedly praise. An example is a comment like "You've excelled at everything you've ever tried except shorthand."

Chronic invalidation: negating or dismissing someone's thoughts or feelings. "No, no, that's not what happened," or "You're silly to feel that way." Recipients may learn to doubt the importance of their reactions.

Command and control: demanding that people comply with requests instead of engaging them in dialogue. An example: "We're going to have the party on Friday. Period."

Cursing: using foul, degrading language to intimidate, overpower, put down, ridicule, or shame someone. Displacing anger or blowing things out of proportion is abuse. Words live on in perpetuity, far past their initial utterance. They have the power to choke and wound the self-esteem of another person. People can avoid oral minefields by carefully calibrating their words.

Degrading within earshot: discussing someone in the third person when they are present: "She's a miserable coworker."

Demands and ultimatums: "Do this or else! I'm not kidding." Workers may initially comply but later may retaliate or sabotage the manager.

Denial of responsibility/scapegoating: "You made me real mad!"

> Relational culprits fail to take responsibility for their thoughts, feelings, and emotions.[16]

Gaslighting: trying to make someone else feel bad, at fault, guilty, or wrong by manipulating them. Movies like *Gaslight* and *Suddenly, Last Summer* demonstrate worst-case scenarios, where targets felt like they were losing their minds. Signs of psychological manipulation include coercion (raising one's voice, combined with threatening language and/or gestures and body stance),[17] negative surprises that keep others guessing and simultaneously place bullies in the relational driver's seat, sarcasm, belittling another person's achievements and/or behavior, and nonstop criticism that elevates the manipulator's status by comparison. Gaslighters shift reality to maintain control. If the gaslighters are in a powerful position, such as parent or boss, targets may experience unease, anxiety, and fear.

Getting people on stage: purposefully creating havoc or uproar in which abusers enjoy seeing other people upset. Low self-esteem bullies use this tactic to avoid giving other people credit and to cast themselves as the center of attention.

Mercurial moods: making people test the waters before they can approach. To avoid inadvertently inflicting mercurial moods on others, wait a few seconds, respond (don't react), and engage in simple stress-management techniques (in terms of sleep, exercise, yoga, and meditation) so that other people don't pay for your personal ill humor.

> "Speak as if everyone is listening," with the corollary: "The less said, the better."

See the Why am I Talking schematic.

Moralistic judgements: contrasting yourself with someone else, implying they are somehow lacking, and that you are superior by comparison. Saying things like "I hate it when people gossip," suggests that you never gossip and that the other person is flawed in so doing. Judgments create in-group/out-group distinctions, and colleagues are unfairly labeled.

Marshall Rosenberg, in the book *Non-Violent Communication: A Language of Life,*[18] suggests instead using language that concentrates on needs and how those needs can be met.

> Example: My spouse refuses to work this summer; how can she be so lazy?

> Rephrase: My spouse needs some time off from her teaching. What are some things she can do from home that will generate income, and how can I help her find these?

Name-calling: the verbal equivalent of mudslinging. The Pygmalion effect suggests that people grow to behave the way they are treated. Verbal abuse may result in recipients who are unwilling to speak for themselves.

Passive aggressiveness: expressing displeasure in a roundabout manner. Passive-aggressive people rarely get what they want because others have trouble figuring out what it is.

> Example: Your coworker pouts when they feel wounded instead of engaging peers in a frank discussion.

Rapid fire: saying whatever bubbles to the top of their minds and feeling doggone good about it in the moment—although they may regret their choice later.[19] Author Lindsay Gibson suggests "detaching" by refusing to become enmeshed in someone else's drama. Find a different, alternative viewpoint for a response—one that puts the onus back on contentious parties.

> Example: If your boss says, "You need to be more poised, like Derrick," you can choose to interpret her statement in a more positive light.

> "Many people admire Derrick's speaking skills."

A simple interpretation does not attack, defend, or evaluate, but instead leaves prickly comments with their respective sender.

Schoolmarm scolding: speaking in a chiding, authoritarian fashion.

Examples:
- I had to bite my tongue.
- I don't know why it didn't occur to you.

High-handed statements put naysayers in the role of judge and jury and leave recipients in a deflated one-down position.

Sanctimonious tongue-lashing: denouncing someone who stepped on a bully's toes.

> **Example:** I let them have it!

Doctors Gary and Ruth Namie, in *The Bully at Work: What You Can Do to Stop the Hurt and Reclaim Your Dignity on the Job,*[20] describe "constant critics" as fastidious nitpickers who carp about others' shortcomings to mask their own and who engage in nonstop castigation and negative critique of targets' job competence.

In face-to-face forums, one tactic that may inhibit a bully's aggression is to repeat their name several times slowly,[21] to delay and to interrupt their outbursts.

> **Example:**
>
> Bully: I think Trudie needs to keep her big mouth shut. Every time I turn around that hot air flap is polluting this office, talking nonsense that nobody cares anything about. She needs to go back to where she came from.
>
> Intervener: Sarah Jane, Sarah Jane, Sarah Jane . . .
>
> Bully: What? You trying to say something to me?
>
> Intervener: Why are you saying those things about Trudie? What you're saying is hurtful and untrue.

The above tactic slows bullies' momentum and might cause them to reconsider their statements.

Talking "at" someone: delivering a fault-finding lecture, unaccompanied by mutual conversation or follow-up discussion.

Threatening: either physical violence or emotional abandonment.

> **Examples:**
> - I'll be your friend if you do X, Y, and Z.
> - I'm going to make things warm for you.

Bullies may threaten people they perceive as weak or passive or people who have few options because of their position within a group. If this tactic works, perpetrators may become repeat offenders.

Why Am I Talking? Framework Suggests Using Circumspection Before Speaking

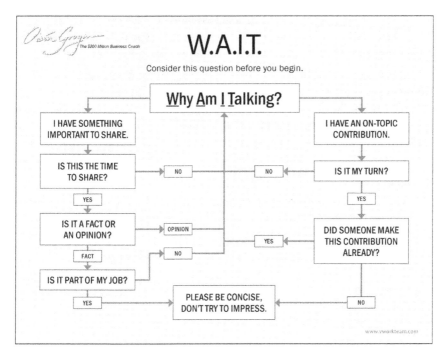

Covert Bullying: (Bypassing/Tattling, Cyberbullying, and Gossip)

Aggression can be either overt or covert. Overt bullying happens in the line of sight, up close and personal. Covert bullying occurs behind the scenes and is best accomplished by individuals who are capable of "licking upward" and "kicking downward."[22] Slime-factor bullies behave deferentially to those with power and duplicitously to peers and subordinates. Two-faced peers are more difficult to detect than the ones who wear their hearts on their sleeves. Covert bullying methods include:

Bypassing

Bypassing is going over someone's head, when a face-to-face meeting would be more appropriate. If a coworker does something hurtful that could potentially result in physical/psychological injury or is against the law, then consulting a manager is the suggested course of action.[23] If an issue can easily be resolved between coworkers, then notifying a manager may create unnecessary conflict. Patty McCord, former chief talent officer at Netflix and author of *Powerful: Building a Culture of Freedom and Responsibility* shares that unless ethical or legal violations (like sexual harassment) have occurred, workers at Netflix are expected to speak with one another. Mutual sharing ceases when employees believe their coworkers are spies.

Snitching, or "tattling," occurs more frequently when supervisors are friends with the office bully/mole and reward them with protection and/or perks. In the book *Snitch Culture,* Jim Redden describes snitching as "the lowest form of human behavior" and as subterfuge in which people try to make someone else look bad. Managers abet tattling when they bad-mouth targets to in-group members.

Scenario

Angie has complained to her team leader, Anne, about Susan. Afterward Anne scheduled a meeting with Susan to discuss her inappropriate behavior and to issue a warning.

What did Anne do incorrectly? What should she have done instead?

_____

_____

_____

_____

[See page 22 for an explanation]

Cyberbullying

Cyberbulling is posting intentionally hurtful, thoughtless opinions on the Internet or posing as a cyber frenemy to lure information from unsuspecting parties (see Chapter 7 for a more detailed explanation on cyber concepts).

Gossip

Gossip is churning information about colleagues or peers. By the time misinformation makes the rounds, targets might not even recognize the fantastical story being circulated. Gossipers share information that had been conveyed in confidence before an audience, almost invariably in a less-flattering light.

Reflection

In which of the above overt or covert bullying behaviors have you engaged? What was the effect on recipients? How do you think your behavior made them feel, and what was the impact on your relationship?

_____

_____

_____

_____

▬▬▬▬

Incivility: Poor Manners, Ignorance of Social Norms, Lack of Pleasantries

Bullying differs from incivility in the degree of intent. People who are unaware of office etiquette may display off-putting behavior, but they may not always know what they did wrong. Bullying, on the other hand, implies a deliberate attempt to debase or weaken an opponent. Bullies know the correct course of action, and they choose to do otherwise.

The uncivil can be educated, but bullies may need to experience consequences along with training to reverse course.

Examples of Bullying Versus Incivility	
Bullying	**Incivility**
Verbal put-downs and physical abuse	Looking at an electronic device during a meeting
Undermining someone's work performance	Interrupting someone while they are talking; contradicting them
Coercing another person to allow them to cheat	Unexplained tardiness or early departure from a meeting
Humiliating someone in a group setting	Incessant bragging
Posting negative information or embarrassing videos online	Forwarding e-mail without asking
Vicious gossip	Making culturally inappropriate, ignorant remarks
Threatening someone with negative consequences	Encroachment
Tattling	Using other people's belongings without asking
Yelling, shouting, and screaming[2]	Barging into someone's office without first knocking and waiting for an invitation to enter

Bullies and the Uncivil May Both Lack a Fundamental Set of Core Traits

Lawrence Kohlberg explains that moral development—or the journey toward honoring the highest level of behavioral principles—exists within three separate levels:

Level 1 Pre-Conventional	Level 2 Conventional	Level 3 Post-Conventional
Focus on doing what's "right" to avoid punishment	Following norms of society (or the group) to blend in	Commitment to immutable principles of freedom, justice, and human rights through willingness to stand up for other people and endure personal difficulty
Self-interested concern	Conformance to societal or crowd expectations	Transformative behavior that empowers others

Although individuals at the post-conventional level are the most likely to make decisions that benefit their organizations, managers who allow themselves to be influenced by peers may not always operate from a higher-order perspective.

Moral development consists of the following four components:

1. *Cultural intelligence* (CI): effectively interacting within a diverse environment, appreciating new ways of doing things, valuing contributions of other cultures, and modifying perspectives;
2. *Emotional intelligence* (EI): displaying persistence, empathy, positive attitude, and authentic emotions by transforming anger into social action, disconnecting from "useless" emotions like bitterness and frustration, and recognizing when one's own emotions and the emotions of other people are inaccurate or dishonest[24];
3. *Relational intelligence* (RI): behaving as a team player by tactfully disagreeing with other people, and acting as a liaison between disparate groups to facilitate conflict resolution; and
4. *Spiritual intelligence* (SI): creating synergy, offering intuitive insights, and connecting with coworkers by focusing on love, forgiveness, compassion, and peace.

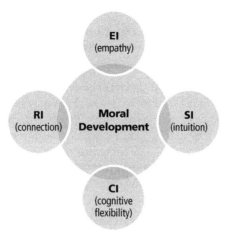

Confronting disinhibited and disrespectful coworkers takes courage, but sometimes it takes only a single voice to stop the abuse. Proactive change agents can develop their skills through:

1. *Seeking* opportunities to make personal and societal improvements.
2. *Speaking* their minds in a respectful manner.
3. *Getting* involved in nonviolent actions that disrupt the status quo.
4. *Taking* a stand despite the perceived consequence.
5. *Gathering* followers who create momentum, who contribute to a larger movement.
6. *Moving* toward bullied targets. Change agents triumph despite obstacles,[25] persevere even if the cost of nonconformance is high, and sacrifice for other people.[26]

Companies that tolerate, instigate, and participate in abuse can experience negative repercussions. Learning more about the problem (and how we create it) is a first step toward changing organizational culture. Developing talents to create community-centered culture is a gift to our peers.

Silence purchases the continuance of poor behavior.[27]

**Scene: The first day experience and expectations
of Catug*n's newest employee, Blanche.**

The day I arrived at headquarters, Catug*n gleamed like the Emerald City—fifteen stories of reflective glass encircled by meticulous, manicured lawns. This was corporate's mother ship—a place where financial minds did numerical wizardry and where industry captains crafted mind-blowing, cross-border megadeals. Catug*n was by far the tallest building for miles. I sat in my office chair, spinning first one way then the other in an office that overlooked the rotating company emblem. As I ran my hand across the faux wood surface I saw my reflection—an ear-to-ear grin about ready to break my face.

Exercise

If you had free rein to redesign your workplace/school, what would communication with your colleagues and interaction with your boss look like? How is it representative of your current position, and did you expect something different when you first started?

Online Resources

- Gilbert, J. A. (2011, May 15). How to spot a snitch [Blog post]. Retrieved from https://organizedforefficiency.com/how-to-spot-a-snitch/
- Gilbert, J. A. (2011, September 12). Narcissism unwrapped [Blog post]. Retrieved from https://organizedforefficiency.com/narcissism-unwrapped/
- Gilbert, J. A. (2013, May 7). Cataloguing the chronically uncivil [Blog post]. Retrieved from https://organizedforefficiency.com/cataloging-the-chronically-uncivil

- Gilbert, J. A. (2015, January 31). Employment and emotional terrorism [Blog post]. Retrieved from https://organized forefficiency.com/employment-and-emotional-terrorism/
- Gilbert, J. A. (2017, May 26). How to prevent hazing [Blog post]. Retrieved from https://organizedforefficiency.com/how-to -prevent-hazing/
- Gillpatrick, S. (2011, March 9). The workplace bully: More than a simple stressor [Blog post]. Retrieved from https://organizedfor efficiency.com/the-workplace-bully-more-than-a-simple-stressor
- Gillpatrick, S. (2011, May 3). Can bullying be workplace violence? [Blog post]. Retrieved from https://organizedforefficiency.com/ can-bullying-be-workplace-violence?
- Hazing prevention guide & fact sheet. (n.d.). *StopHazing.* Retrieved from http://www.stophazing.org/wp-content/uploads/ 2016/03/HazingPreventionEDITED.pdf

Web Quests

1. Search the web for ways to positively affect other people through positive attitude and altruistic behavior. How can you use at least three of these techniques to cheer someone who has been bullied?

_____

_____

_____

_____

2. Research companies that fall within the definition of *negligent employer*: those that enable bad behavior (at work) through inept policy and lack of employee-centered procedures. What are the consequences for employee morale and for the company's image?

_____

_____

_____

_____

3. Explore the topic of *positive leadership* and explain at least three ways you can demonstrate exemplary behavior.

_____

_____

_____

_____

What Would You Do?

1. You are taking a course with all seven types the article "Coping With Seven Disruptive Personality Types in the Classroom" [28] describes. These include explosive, antisocial, passive-aggressive, narcissistic, paranoid, litigious, and compulsive. As a manager, how should you react to each of these when you see them creating a disturbance?

_____

_____

_____

_____

_____

_____

_____

_____

_____

_____

Assessment

Label the following statements with one or more of the categories that you think best represents them: (a) hazing, (b) passive-aggressive bullying, (c) physical bullying, (d) emotional abuse, (e) cyberbullying, (f) tattling, (g) gossip, (h) incivility, and (i) proactive change.

1. _____ I sometimes stand too close to people just to see how they react.
2. _____ If I see bullying, I actively intervene to help targets.
3. _____ I sometimes give people the "cold shoulder" when I am displeased with their behavior.
4. _____ If I see someone at work doing something I don't like, I immediately tell the supervisor.
5. _____ I forward emails without asking for permission first.
6. _____ I call out the new kid if he or she makes me angry.
7. _____ I sometimes interrupt other people when they are talking to make my point.
8. _____ I post anonymous negative feedback on the Internet.
9. _____ I go out of my way to be nice to someone who is having a bad time at work or at school.
10. _____ I shout at people when I think they are inappropriate.
11. _____ I refuse to look at or talk to people I don't like.
12. _____ I think of devious ways to "get back" at someone who hurt me.
13. _____ I contradict people when I think they are wrong.
14. _____ I am a peacemaker.
15. _____ I am a member of a workforce clique that enjoys making non-clique members feel uncomfortable.
16. _____ I do volunteer work in the community.
17. _____ I feel entitled to speak my mind, especially if it's in a public forum and embarrasses someone who is unfamiliar with group norms.
18. _____ I try to improve my demeanor by asking for feedback.
19. _____ I introduce myself to new people at work and/or school and try to become their friend.
20. _____ I support my friends and colleagues if I see people abuse them.
21. _____ I try to change policies, systems, and ways of practice that I know are ineffective.
22. _____ I follow the bully's lead in taunting people they don't like so that I can stay on their good side.
23. _____ I laugh with people (not at them).

24. _____ I coerce the "new kid on the block" into doing things for me in exchange for my protection or my friendship.
25. _____ I join in verbal group smear or remain silent, even if the target has been kind to me.
26. _____ I raise my voice and blame people to get my way.
27. _____ I don't apologize when I hurt someone. I just pretend like nothing happened.
28. _____ I sometimes shove people out of my way.
29. _____ I roll my eyes when I disagree with what someone says.
30. _____ I hide other people's resources (or refuse to share information) so that they will look bad, and I will look better by comparison.[3]
31. _____ I blame other people when I do something wrong.
32. _____ I look at my cell phone during a conversation.
33. _____ I try to give other people compliments, either in person or electronically.
34. _____ I protect and support coworkers who bring me gossip.
35. _____ If I am displeased with someone, I think that it's okay to talk about them behind their back.
36. _____ When I am angry, I point my finger at people to whom I'm speaking.
37. _____ I mockingly repeat what someone else says if I don't like it.
38. _____ I point out colleagues' mistakes in a public forum.
39. _____ I talk "at" people when I want to get my own way, and I quickly end the conversation.

―――――

Explanation for the "Snitching" Scenario on Page 14

All parties in a dispute deserve the right to state their case so that final decisions are not one-sided, and a perception of favoritism does not occur. Managers need to consider the following caveat: What is the complainant's motivation? Could it be envy—trying to make someone else look bad while enhancing their own status? Or revenge against someone who hurt them or whom they consider a professional threat? Or perfectionism and obsession (OCPD[29] that manifests as policing behavior and exaggerated claims of wrongdoing)? Or sadistic pleasure gained at the expense of getting someone in trouble?

Assessment Key

1. c; 2. i; 3. b; 4. f; 5. e or h; 6. a; 7. h; 8. e; 9. i; 10. d; 11. b; 12. b; 13. h; 14. i; 15. a; 16. i; 17. a; 18. i; 19. i; 20. i; 21. i; 22. a, d; 23. i; 24. a; 25. g; 26. d; 27. d; 28. c; 29. b; 30. b; 31. d; 32. h; 33. i; 34. d or f; 35. g; 36. c or h; 37. b; 38. d; 39. d

---

Notes

1. The National Center for Education Statistics reported that in 2017, approximately 20% of school-aged children 12–18 experienced bullying. In a study of over 130,000 sixth, ninth, and 12th grade students, 29% of bullied targets, 22% of perpetrators, and 38% of people who were both targets and perpetrators reported thinking about suicide or attempting suicide.

    National Center for Education Statistics (NCES). (n.d.). *Fast Facts. Bullying.* Retrieved from https://nces.ed.gov/fastfacts/display.asp?id=719

    Borowsky, I. W., Taliaferro, L. A., & McMorris, B. J. (2013). Suicidal thinking and behavior among youth involved in verbal social bullying: Risk and protective factors. *Journal of Adolescent Health, 53*(1), S4–12. https://doi.org/10.1016/j.jadohealth.2012.10.280

2. According to Gary and Ruth Namie in *The Bully at Work,* "Screaming Mimis" sound-blast their targets to humiliate them and gain compliance.

3. Gatekeepers are underhanded "weasels" who purposely keep information to themselves or who hide necessary tools for job completion to prevent their colleagues from advancing (from Namie, G., & Namie, R. [2009]. *The Bully at Work.* Naperville, IL: Sourcebooks).

—————

2

—————

Bullying Versus Misbehavior

Bullies are cowards and are driven by deep-seated insecurities and fears of inadequacy, they intentionally wage a covert war against an organization's best employees—those who are highly skilled, intelligent, creative, ethical, able to work well with others, and independent (who refuse to be subservient or controlled by others).[1]

—John E. Richardson and Linnea B. McCord

The Problem and Definition

Bullies exist in a variety of shapes and behavioral "sizes"—with the "out loud" types easily spotted. Less discernible (but no less insidious) are the ones who reveal themselves over time, who do their dirty work behind the scenes with a long-range plan that they keep under wraps. Some may even seem parental, trying to learn additional facts to draw their prey into an unbalanced power differential, from which it is later difficult to break free. The lesser tenured may appreciate a hand up and initially accept overtures that appear questionable, not realizing that they are part of an established bully's ploy to test the waters. Because there is confusion about the concept of bullying (and coworkers' poor choices often go unchallenged), nasty behavior may go unaddressed—uncomfortable, yet unclassified.

—————

Case in Point

Fred's boss (Abigail) berated him at work, saying **everything** was wrong with the report he'd so meticulously prepared. Afterward, Fred sat dumbfounded and silent, shell-shocked by the unexpected "carpet calling" that had embarrassed him in front of his peers and senior management.

That afternoon, Abigail popped into Fred's office—once again outraged (but for a different reason). She barked at Fred, one word at a time: "You don't <u>have</u> to look so **miserable**!"[2]

Not all abuse arises from malicious intent. Consider when a kind, otherwise considerate colleague does something unexpected that later makes them cringe. Everyone harbors regret about something they said or did, something they wish they had said, or something they did not do. Sometimes a slip of the tongue, a failure to think before speaking, a focus on our personal perceived failings instead of coworkers' well-deserved accomplishments, or a blue moon bad mood can result in hastily spoken words and possibly in irreparable relational damage. These gaffes may be inadvertent, but they can have just as much impact. Sometimes unawareness, personal style, or a penchant to offer unwanted advice may rub coworkers the wrong way. Problems can arise when incivility is misinterpreted as aggression, when managers and colleagues do not consider the bigger picture, or when they do not have all the information.

The Gallery

Intentional and unintentional abuse take many forms. These include:

Pet ownership: the result of low self-esteem or insecure bosses who encourage sycophancy from the lesser tenured and who play subordinates against one another;

Stealth bombing: a willingness to appear helpful that can backfire when gossip is the outcome;

Envy: covetousness that results in a desire to upstage someone else's achievements; and

Stalking: deliberate behavior from people who have a plan and a premeditated desire to dominate their prey.

Pets and Pet Ownership

Employees can fall into the pet category when they are dependent on their boss for their political survival. Sycophants arise when bosses reward people who praise them and stock their personal menagerie with employees who behave as lackeys, informants, servile flatterers, and toadies in continual "tail wagging" mode.[3] When supervisors fail to elicit feedback or let others know they're open for discussion (and by proxy suggest that disagreement equals disrespect), an *in-group* can result—an insular clique made up of members who reflect a powerholder's desired image.

Pets in a boss's protective pouch

Scene: Big Ed is talking to Albert, who has stopped by to secure some brownie points ahead of his next performance review.

"Say, boss man, what'd you think of Outlaw Bandit's play on the 50-yard line last week? I thought they were going to suffocate that Kikei Zunteel. I mean, they were running all around and then whoosh, everyone piled up on top of him like a Thanksgiving feast. It's the next best thing to watching gladiators go at it."

Big Ed stared at him, eyes narrowed, relishing the thought of getting his number two onstage.

"You know Al, I think we need to let all our new hires go at it one-on-one with the other newbies, like in that movie *Hunger Games*. We can split the top 15 or so that make it through the process among our three sister companies. That way, we know that all our employees have that killer spirit. You and I both know we need that to get ahead around here."

Albert lit up, toady-style, the way he did every time Ed flipped his switch.

"Yeah, boss, we can send them out with clubs and knives and put bets on who gets killed first. Use their personality profile to pick the winners and televise it to our clients."

The beady-eyed corporate marsupial nodded approvingly.

Few wish to experience either a bullying boss's wrath or pointed exclusion from the in-group. This can result in an unstated norm that suggests employees should be careful around boss surrogates, close-lipped about boss antics, and silent with unpopular viewpoints. Conniving pets may try to squash competition by pushing their colleagues from the corporate nest and by counterpunching any opposition to the zookeeper. "[Pets] are bequeathed unearned chips of organizational capital, which they use either for or against other people at work." [4]

Scene: Stan is talking about office politics to Blanche during her probationary period.

"If you want to see the mistress of the art, watch Korie. She sure as heck knows who's boss. Every time she turns around that's what she's calling Big Ed: 'Yes sir, yes sir, three bags full, sir.' Kirlian photography would show them as kindred spirits, intertwined even when they're apart.

"That woman has a direct line to Big Ed Almighty, which is why we need to make sure you don't make any mistakes. The thing to remember about Big Ed is if you take care of him, he'll take care of you."

Assessment

Indicate whether you've been affected by the following behaviors and explain how they made you feel:

1. Supervisors display favor and friendliness toward people who agree with them and who behave as sycophants.

   _____

   _____

   _____

   _____

2. The boss is quick to tell other employees to "stay out of their friends' way."

_____

_____

_____

_____

3. "Boss buddies" receive special attention, rule-bending, bounteous rewards, and perks of which outgroup members are deprived.

_____

_____

_____

_____

4. Pets' exaggerated stories are believed without investigation, although the person about whom they're complaining has a long work history of unquestioned achievement. The object of the smear attack is left defenseless.

_____

_____

_____

_____

5. Individuals with contrary viewpoints are prevented from offering their opinions on pets' work product, thus ensuring that the evaluation/promotion process is one-sided.

_____

_____

_____

_____

Employees who refuse to make a deal with the highest-ranking "pack animal" may be punished if they step on a favored pet's toes. Pets thus learn they can behave with impunity and enjoy protection gained at the expense of sidelined peers. Combine dysfunctional culture with the 80/20 rule (where only 20% want to step outside a bully's established boundaries), and employees will see more of the status quo.

Exercise:

The *HR FOCUS* magazine article "How to Manage Difficult 'Breeds' in the Workplace" describes several animal "types." These include the Great White—aggressive, in-your-face carnivores who prey on the less assertive; Scorpion—abusers who deliver explosive, unanticipated outbursts; Mule—stubborn sticks-in-the-mud who figure out how not to get things done; and Snake—subversive, bellyaching backstabbers.

Have you played any of these roles? Why? (To achieve a sense of power at the expense of someone else, or to be accepted?) Describe the best way to deal with any of the animal types you have encountered. Are there any positive ones? What do they look like? Draw these in the space below.

_____

_____

_____

_____

Drawing:

Exercise:

From your web research, what is the most effective way to deal with pets at work? How can you neutralize their behavior and succeed despite their attempts at sabotage? Which animal type do you routinely see sitting next to those in power?

_____

_____

_____

_____

Accidental Pets and Boss Unawareness

Although some employees wish to have an exclusive relationship with their boss (and some bosses wish to build a personal fiefdom), employees can achieve most-favored work status for other reasons, and bosses may unwittingly impact their interactions with subordinates at work. In the article "Sick of Sycophants," authors Deborah and Mark Parker emphasize that "intent matters."[5]

If you are a boss, you can avoid adopting your own personal menagerie by:[6]

- *Acting as a self-managed team "unleader,"* who behaves more like a conduit, facilitator, cheerleader, or expeditor. Let employees take the lead in managing their workflow so that they feel less of a need to check in.
- *Speaking to everyone on a periodic basis* (in groups and one-on-one). Insecurity, hubris, or a need to hear compliments can prevent managers from soliciting contrary opinions. Taking the initiative to ask questions of all workgroup members, listening before speaking, avoiding using employees as confidants, planning gatherings that include the entire department, and interviewing all involved parties when a problem arises can instigate honest conversations—and help the manager to improve their behavior. Employees won't share information unless they have a rapport with their manager or team leader.
- *Explaining to pet wannabes that gossip is unwelcome* and that they should concentrate on their work instead. "Managers who court juicy morsels undercut the connective fabric in which teams

thrive."[7] Advise employees that behaving as a supportive team member is expected office behavior. Correspondingly, "Problems arise when managers take [sycophants'] word at face value ... and fail to consult maligned parties."[8] If managers are receptive to tattletales, then "tattling" will become the office norm. Alternatively, employees can be encouraged to " mentor [their] colleagues, provide helpful examples, and [behave] as [departmental] role models."[9]

If you are an employee, to avoid becoming a pet:

- *Actively build relationships with your coworkers.* Senior employees and mentors have a plethora of advice, wisdom, and benefits to offer. Establishing a relationship is as simple as asking an admired coworker to share their time. Conversely, colleagues may choose to sabotage people who enjoy cloistered, most-favored pet status.
- *Approach the boss as a team* or with another colleague. Working through issues with peers builds camaraderie and departmental cohesion.
- As a corollary to the above, *make a habit of inviting colleagues to lunch.* Large gatherings are less likely to be mistaken for a singular case of favoritism or preferential treatment.
- *Avoid indiscriminate sharing.* Don't "run to the boss's office with the enthusiasm of [someone] who has just unearthed a rare gem."[10] Instead of following the boss's lead or instigating a slam session, change the subject or choose to share positive information.

To change your perspective, and to increase your visibility and workplace status:

- *Instead of blaming pets* (or the situation), examine how you contributed to your current status. Do you keep to yourself, avoid small talk, or hold grudges that later create friction? Have you tried to create a comfort zone between you and your boss by discussing how you can improve? Passive-aggressive people stonewall—a tactic that can escalate an already tense situation. Although management by wandering around should be modus operandi, widening spans of control (as a result of layoffs and cost-cutting measures) may spread managers thin. They might appreciate an unexpected, friendly initiative.
- *Showcase your personal achievements.* Have "pets" provided additional value for the department, the organization, and/or the profession

at large? Have they been able to create awareness of their unique capabilities in ways that you have not? Hidden talents are not helpful. Although people may have learned growing up that boasting is inappropriate, in an arena where people compete with peers and with people in their industry, the right kind of self-promotion is essential. Is your latest project something that could benefit the wider community? Have you contacted your internal public relations department, written an article for the company newsletter, offered to volunteer as an industry expert, or spoken to a local news organization? Exposure may attract followers who can provide introductions to powerful network players and lead to inclusion within important meetings. Top managers with limited time and attention are more likely to notice people who stand out from the crowd. Describing your positive contributions or emphasizing how your personal qualities would be beneficial for an in-house job can contribute to perceptions of person-job fit.

- *Network.* People who receive attention may know more well-connected colleagues. Network centrality, or the measure of connection to influential persons within an organization, increases promotional chances.[11]
- *Consider your persona.* The ability to discern facial cues and body language, to sense nuances in social situations, and to adjust responses based on feedback can help to bridge structural holes by brokering information between otherwise disconnected parties. Employees who can sense the emotional tenor of a room and regulate their behavior develop stronger relationships with their peers, find and capitalize on nonredundant information sources at work, and experience better job performance.[12] Tact, social savvy, and positive nonverbal expressions—like smiling and making eye contact—establish employees as approachable[13] and increase colleagues' comfort level.
- *Play enough office politics to stay out of trouble.* A colleague at the end of a 25-year career shared with me that she would have paid more attention to office politics—things like volunteering for the annual charity drive, learning to play golf and attending departmental tournaments, and joining colleagues for lunch instead of eating alone at her desk. Exceptional employees who believe they will be promoted solely on merit may advance to the top of their profession,[14] but for the remainder, learning what informal activities are expected and trying to be a part of the group are essential. Standoffishness only serves to keep others at arm's length.

Stealth Bombing

Stealth bombing can occur from bullies who appear to be your best friend—asking intrusive, increasingly personal questions after encouraging you to let down your guard. What you don't realize until it's too late is that they've been stashing choice bits of information—either doing the bidding of someone up the line or saving their bounty to advance their self-interest. Friendly abusers, or *stealth bombers*, at work may go unrecognized. Craftier bullies do their work behind the scenes—by first attempting to gain trust (e.g., think of Tess in the movie *Working Girl* where her boss planned all along to steal her business idea).

A stealth-bomber variant—an office "busybody"—is less calculating but can inflict just as much harm.

Scene: Newbie Blanche is accosted by her stealth-bombing coworker.

Hazel turned out to be my winning ticket. She had a broad, imposing, sumo wrestler-style body encased in a conservative business suit and propelled by short, stocky, support hose-covered legs. She moved fast, like a corgi trying to keep up. Hazel held a nondescript secretarial position, one that amounted to rearranging files in electronic folders. It was yeoman's work, in which she took pride. So the organization forgave her meddlesome peccadillos, and most people ran for cover when she neared close range. Because I was nonconfrontational and mostly passive, she homed in on fertile soil. As a probationary employee I found myself in an intrusive face-to-face.

"Hello," she said, peering at me, smiling inquisitively.

The strong scent of drugstore hair spray, sticky glue that cemented a multi-tiered, teased, cotton-candy hairdo, stung me. But as a child, I'd been conditioned to be polite.

"Hello. I don't believe we've met," I said.

She sensed an unspoken invitation, inching closer.

"I'm Hazel, the Electronic Records Manager. And you're Blanche. You're so pretty. I've heard all about you. Don't you worry, it takes our new hires a while to get with the program. But I've been here so long I know every nook and cranny of this company. I've been through the wars, learned things most people don't know anything about. If you have time, maybe we could get together for lunch? I'd love to be in the mentor program, but that's only open to 'professionals.' I know I'm classified as Secretary #2, but that never prevented me from coming to work every single day and doing my job. And let me tell you, in the 20 years I've worked here I've won the Administrative Associate of the Month award three separate times. Gold-plated plaques with my name engraved on the front—I can show them to you sometime. I feel like you're someone I can trust. And you're such a good listener! If you stick with me, I'll show you the ropes. Are you busy Friday?"

She stopped to mentally refuel. I didn't know this person, but she seemed friendly enough. And I was never one to refuse an outstretched offer of help. I decided to keep the lines of communication open.

"How about 1:00 at Starbucks?"

It sounded like a fair exchange—spending time with a lonely employee to obtain useful tidbits.

"Sure, Hazel. Sounds good."

She briskly nodded, offering a closed-lipped smile. She seemed pleased, in fact, delighted, that I'd returned her lob. She looked to the right and spotted something that intrigued her.

"Oh, there's Stan. I need to tell him something right this second. See you Friday! Toodles!" Quickly she took off in her corgi-style walk, as if the company was populated by flowers and Hazel was in the business of cross-pollination.

She winked in collusion, then whisked out the door.

* * *

For me, Friday was like hitting the lottery. I learned that Hazel had attended the mother of all beehives, the monthly secretaries' luncheon in which assistants did a conversational dance—one that indicated where and how much information they had gathered. The result of the confab had congealed into a gooey, gossipy nectar that was almost unrecognizable, indivisible from the original parts. Everyone's missteps, maladjustments, and mental gaffes somehow interrelated into a circular loop.

She arrived late, words practically overflowing from her lips. She grabbed my hand, squeezing hard.

"Blanche, have I got some news for you. I just got back from our monthly luncheon, you know, the potluck where all the secretaries get together to share food and exchange gossip. This time Mavis brought a salad with kiwis, but she hadn't shaved off all that furry skin that gives most people the willies, and Ethel almost gagged when she tried to swallow a piece. I don't have to tell you the commotion that caused."

She shuddered as if a kiwi could, via astral travel, inflict physical harm. After settling back into her chair, she dropped a bombshell. As best friend of Edwin's secretary (Mary), she was privy to copious hot poop regarding executive comings and goings. According to her, Mary had covered Big

Ed's behind so many times she had lost count.

"Friday morning Mary saw Ralph, Edwin, and Stan go into Big Ed's office in a closed-door session. And that got her to thinking, just what are those three knuckleheads up to? So, she did some investigating on the sly. Apparently, Ralph is too lazy to keep up with his own schedule, so he gives his secretary his iPhone password. And you won't believe what she found."

She looked straight at me, on the brink of birthing a whopper. She reminded me of the few vocal virtuosos who practice circular breathing, allowing them to hold a note for extended periods of time without pausing for air.

True friends on the job may be hard to find.[1] Having others jump through some hoops may be a prerequisite before anointing them as your BFF at work.

Envy

If you don't have anything good to say, silence is golden.

The feeling of inferiority or twinge when a colleague, friend, or acquaintance achieves something noteworthy can occur instantaneously. Despite a wish to act on our better angels, a snarky, knee-jerk remark may emerge,[2] and instead of congratulations, recipients may hear something that deflates their self-esteem. Acting on the very human emotion of envy or engaging in expressions of nonsupport (when saying nothing would be the best course) is a common occurrence. A failure to self-edit can lead to indiscretion even for bosses, who may envy their subordinates for their superior social, technical, or leadership skills and use their legitimate power to discredit or oust them from the organization.[15] Hastily spoken words (if unamended) create a chasm. Who can forget the infamous Fuzzy Zoeller "fried chicken" remarks when Tiger Woods won the 1997 Masters Tournament? Couching hurtful comments as "jokes" does not remove their sting.

Envious people perceive other people's success as a personal threat and desire to belittle them or torpedo their best efforts.[16]

Case in Point

After 3 long years, Frances had finally completed her law degree. Not only had she finished on time, but she'd graduated cum laude to boot.

Her "friend" Janine stared at her diploma. She then asked in a voice dripping with jealousy, "Was it worth it?"

Assessment: Are You Falling Into the Envy Trap?

Think about a person in your organization who is at a similar level and with whom you often compare yourself. Think about one of this person's recent accomplishments. Describe it. Then answer the questions below.

1. **Did you congratulate this person?** *Yes* (0), *No* (1)
2. **How did the news of his or her achievement make you feel?** *Happy* (0), *Neutral* (1), *Vaguely disturbed* (2)
3. **Did you worry that superiors might devalue your own achievements as a result?** *Yes* (1), *No* (0)
4. **When was the last time you gave public credit or kudos to this person?** *Last time he or she had a success* (0), *Don't remember* (1), *Never* (2)
5. **Do you sometimes catch yourself obsessing over how much status this person has?** *Yes* (1), *No* (0)
6. **Imagine that this person suffers an embarrassing public failure or professional loss. Does this make you feel sad, indifferent, or happy?** *Sad* (0), *Indifferent* (1), *Happy* (2)
7. **I'm always willing to admit it when I make a mistake.** *False* (0), *True* (1)
8. **I have never intensely disliked anyone.** *False* (0), *True* (1)
9. **I sometimes feel resentful when I don't get my way.** *True* (0), *False* (1)

What the Scores Reveal

First, tabulate your scores for Questions 1–6.

7–9 Congratulations on having the self-awareness to admit your envy!
4–6 You have moderate envy.
2–3 You have low envy.
0–1 You have reached *mudita* (joy for others' good fortune)! Or you are in denial.

To help differentiate *mudita* from denial, now tabulate your scores for Questions 7–9.

These questions come from the Crowne-Marlowe social desirability scale, which measures your tendency to convey a self-image that conforms to social expectations.

2–3 You might want to think deeply about whether your responses on this survey accurately reflect your behavior.
0–1 You're comfortable admitting to behaviors that don't conform to social ideals, and a low score on items 1–6 is likely to truly indicate that you are managing your envy effectively.

Source: Reprinted by permission of *Harvard Business Review.* (Self-assessment: Are you falling into the envy trap?). From "Envy at Work" by Tanya

Compliments from the envious may come across as: (a) "Thank you; you finally did it" sarcasm; (b) "Congratulations, and here's what I did" non-compliment; or (c) "Congratulations, [your name]" delivered in a mocking tone of voice. A true endorsement makes the recipient light up (as opposed to wince or look for the Delete button). Although compliments are free, ministry to others' spirits is hit-and-miss—unless it's nurtured through "other" focus.

In *Nonviolent Communication: A Language of Life,* Marshall Rosenberg suggests that compliments that are delivered as evaluative judgment are not kudos at all, but rather strong-armed attempts to make the speaker look superior. He explains that "other-directed" gratitude should consist of the following components:[17]

Explanation of what someone did that pleased you	How those actions made you feel	What need of yours was met?

Judgment: "That went well."

Gratitude: "When you engaged my husband in conversation, I felt included as a couple. It's important to both of us that he feels like a part of the group."

Rosenberg[18] further explains that reparation should occur when someone is injured, whether deliberately or accidentally. A meaningful apology consists of three parts:

Expression of remorse *I'm sorry.*	Declaration *I'll make sure this never happens again.*	Reparation *Is there anything I can do to make things better?*

Expression of remorse: I'm sorry I yelled at you in front of the group. I feel embarrassed at using you to make myself look important.

Declaration: I can only imagine how hurt you felt at being singled out like that. It will never happen again.

Reparation: What can I do to make it up to you? Our relationship means a lot to me.

A half-hearted, mealy-mouthed excuse like, "I didn't mean to" does little to help others heal.[3] Similarly, a "chew-out" session followed by a smile the next day is not an apology, nor is leaving a gift and expecting that to suffice for recompense. Humility is necessary to repair emotional hemorrhage. A recognition of having caused ill feelings is many times all an injured party wants, and then everyone can move forward on a more positive note.

A world of difference exists between having a bad day and intentional mean-spiritedness. The former we can forget, but the latter may fester if unaddressed. If you're not clear into which category you've fallen, apologize regardless. What is intended (even with the best intentions) may sometimes backfire.

Scene: Korie refuses to congratulate Blanche because she feels that praising someone else diminishes her self-worth.

Blanche: A landmark in my hometown was named after my uncle.
Korie: Well, sounds to me like it's a small town. Did I tell you about the award I think I'm going to receive? Only two other women in the company have ever gotten it. Big Ed nominated me, so I think I'm a shoo-in.

Exercise:

After reading "Restoring Ourselves and Others after Personal Injustices," [19] discuss what type of restorative justice is appropriate for the injured party. What can you say to the abuser? Restorative justice is an attempt to make targets whole and reinstate them to their pre-abuse place.

_____

_____

_____

_____

Singular envy can multiply when peers, who might be supportive individually, engage in gossip crowdsourcing—with group pressure swaying them to say things they might not articulate one-on-one. Backstabbing through the back door of trying to maintain team cohesion can result in coworkers parroting abusive peers' speech. To counter scuttlebutt with a positive tone, ask yourself the following questions:

- Would you be comfortable if the target learned what you said?
- Would you mind if your musings were published in a newspaper or shared with family members?

Mirroring a colleague who maintains the moral high ground produces a contagion effect that can spread throughout an office.[4] The ability to administer well-deserved compliments, even in the face of personal failures or perceived inadequacies, is an indication of good character. Battling envy is a challenge that can be undertaken in several ways: focusing on self-improvement/skill development/becoming more accomplished, and measuring improvement against the yardstick of past achievements, instead of the momentary shock and awe of someone else. Recognize and own personal accomplishments in an "I love me" file that contains notes and letters from colleagues, friends, or students. Concentrate on areas at work that are not in direct competition with a rival's expertise.[20] No one was ever intended to be a carbon copy of someone else, and comparisons with other people undermine personal talents and cause us to embellish the facts.[5] That can project an inauthentic and perhaps less likeable persona.

Stalking

"The term 'stalking' conjures chilling scenarios from movies like *Fatal Attraction* and *Enduring Love* [where enraged ex-lovers (or acquaintances) assaulted unsuspecting targets]. Intrusion into one's personal space can unfortunately be so much closer to home."[21] Stalking (which is illegal within the United States, the District of Columbia, and the U.S. territories[22]) consists of unwanted phone calls and gifts, and unsolicited appearances that escalate over time. Unlike previously mentioned forms of misconduct, stalking is not a one-off, a lapse in judgment, or an "oops" moment. It is planned, premeditated, and calculated behavior.

Stalking is a delusion that originates from psychosis, narcissism, lack of target empathy,[23] loneliness,[24] and a desire to "own" another person.[25] Stalkers interpret rejection as encouragement from their targets to continue.[26] Actions that grow to more than interest first incubate within our mind's eye. In *The Intuitive Way,* Penney Peirce[27] suggests there is little difference between obsession and what we know as possession. In each case, the mind is seemingly overtaken and controlled by an unseen force. "Stalkers also think *constantly* about the object of their pursuit. They telephone, fax, text, and e-mail. They physically chase. This is *obsession.*"[28] Sophisticated stalkers are careful not to leave a message trail; they may instead call a victim's home multiple times per day, hanging up (each time) until they force someone to pick up the telephone; "Phone calls were the most prevalent and frequent stalking behavior..."; "...He had to be in constant contact with me..."; "...almost like having a bell on me..."[29]

Stalker Traits
- Obsessive personality—the target is constantly on their mind.
- Inability to take a hint.
- Self-centeredness and a lack of concern for the target.
- Recent death of a parent and/or partner or a string of broken relationships.[30]

Stalker Behaviors[31]
- Asks intrusive, inappropriate questions (about the target's personal finances, love life, home ownership, and physical condition).
- Attempts to make targets feel like possessions, an entitlement of rank and privilege.
- Covers his or her tracks by trashing targets at work, at the same time throwing people off their scent (and narrowing targets' base of support).
- Directs targets not to speak to the supervisor if the stalker is having a problem with targets' behavior.
- Grows jealous when targets speak to someone they consider a rival and accuses targets of having a sexual relationship with that person.
- Incessantly talks about the target to peers, coworkers, and friends; talk turns malicious if stalkers feel ignored or cast aside.
- Learns targets' schedule so that the stalker can be in proximity. Phone calls can be a precursor to physical stalking and drive-bys, in which stalkers attempt to engage targets (or target family members) in conversation through neighborhood visits.
- Makes implicit threats, implying there will be trouble if anyone makes the stalker angry. Tells the target that the stalker is connected to powerful people in the company.
- Makes inappropriate remarks regarding targets' appearance. If stalking escalates, these remarks may progress into sexual innuendo and propositions.
- Makes unwarranted assumptions (e.g., assumes the target wants to sit next to them at organizational events).

■ Slanders targets who attempt to extricate themselves from the relationship. Verbal assault may be particularly damaging to someone less senior in rank, whose reputation is dependent upon others' perceptions of their performance. Lack of a formal power base leaves probationary workers reluctant to counter or make any effort to stop abuse. As Harvey Hornstein points out in *Brutal Bosses and Their Prey*, a female executive hesitated to say no (too forcefully) to a boss who desired after-dinner "entertainment." Instead of traveling to his home after a business trip, the executive showed up on her doorstep fully expecting to spend the night.

■ Tells targets that they find their pictures on the Internet.

■ Uses the telephone to say things they wouldn't dare say in front of other people.

Stalkers' lack of empathy can result in alarming contact.

Scene: Blanche's neighbor reports on Big Ed's stalking.

Blanche, there's someone who's been looking for you. He drives by real slow past the complex, like he's casing the joint—so I asked if he needed some help.

He told me, "I thought I might see Blanche around here. Who are you? Do you know anything about her?"

And then he started asking all kinds of things about how I knew you, what's our relationship, nosy things I wasn't expecting. And then I began thinking, maybe this guy's some kind of a psychopath. Before he drove off he asked me if any of these condos were for sale. Do you know this character?

They then can slither into a throb of incessant behavior, as in a stalker who uninvitedly appears—just so she can comfort herself with knowing that someone else is at home,[32] or one who decides to live underneath a target's crawl space so that she can tap her landline, track her telephone calls, and follow her each time that she leaves her house.[33] Stalkers are an ever-present watchful eye, one that seeks to be a permanent and pervasive feature of a target's life. Rejected stalkers trample all known boundaries. They are intent on punishing targets who refuse to play along.[34] Their prey experience a continual state of powerlessness and unease, especially if the stalking continues outside of work; for example, on the Internet, landline or cell phone, GPS tracking, or drive-bys in the target's neighborhood. Although stalkers are (in many cases) highly educated and intelligent, they feel that if they only try hard enough, the object of their obsession will come around.[35] Stalkers misconstrue workplace functions (and meetings) as dates.

Scene: Big Ed talks about his feelings for Blanche.

She's nice enough when I call her, so I think she's warming up to me. You know how women find powerful men like me attractive. What with all the new hires flashing their pretty smiles my way, I'd say it was true. I don't let any of this go to my head, of course, but a man has to know who he is. Sooner rather than later, they all come running straight to Big Daddy.

Unchallenged, this "testing the waters" phase can lead to something much worse. Suddenly targets are "conquests" to whom stalkers have first claim, unwilling participants in a lurid reality that exists only in a stalker's mind's eye. Toxic offices can engender breeding grounds for senior persons who leverage their power and "lean" on coworkers (who believe that complaining about well-connected, more tenured individuals is futile and potentially career-damaging).[36] They prey on the lower-ranking, the emotionally mishandled, and the individuals on the periphery of power networks.

Scene: Blanche talks about her fears.

I considered writing all of this in a journal, but that would have doubled the time I spent thinking about "Papa Bear." He'd dropped enough hints to make me unhinged.

One time he'd described a double-crossing former employee:

"I could really fix his wagon if I wanted to."

This was no idle threat. Big Ed was a sought-after speaker at financial conferences, a "talking head" on TV guest spots, and an expert witness in global antitrust lawsuits. More than that, his "fist-first" approach made him a formidable opponent.

The implications of being on his blacklist could be life-altering.

"A person who's been blackballed in this company would have a hell of a time finding work elsewhere. It's cold out there for people who don't have any prospects.[6] And you and I both know what happens to anyone who runs up against the wrong side of Big Daddy."

He pulled me toward him.

> "It's a good thing the two of us are so close. Just hearing me talk about your future with this company makes it seem like a damn certainty to me. Now you run on back to your office and think about what I said. And if you ever want to talk to me real friendly like, well, you know where to find me. And Blanche, honey, if you have an issue with Papa Bear, you be sure you run straight over to me. Don't be making a beeline up to those airheads in HR.
> "That'd be awful."

Stalkers suffering from *erotomania* (defined in DSM-IV, 4th ed) are infatuated with the target, mistakenly believing (despite evidence to the contrary) that their obsession is reciprocal. The problem is that things are never *okay* for targets—because predators are not happy when they no longer experience relational consistency. When their fix wears thin, they ramp up the abuse. Rejection can result in a smear campaign to discredit the victim through lies and malicious gossip.[37,38]

> **Scene: Korie is upset with Matthew, her assistant, after he rejected her advances.**
>
> He couldn't seem get with the program, so I had no other choice. I told all the managers that I thought he was shifty—that he fell apart under pressure and came apart at the seams. And then none of them would touch him with a ten-foot pole. He couldn't make it through required rotations as a management trainee. At Catug*n, if another department won't hire you, you end up screwed, blued, and tattooed. So he got RIF-ed right out of here—right back to where he came from—without any references to his name.

Although stalking is a dysfunction that cuts across social class, race, gender, and occupational status, most stalkers are men,[39,40] with studies indicating that 91% of male stalkers pursue women.[41] Reports of stalking from men may go unreported because they feel that law enforcement or human resource managers may not take them seriously.[42]

Stalking is more widespread than people think. In a study of 241 targets registered with the Dutch Anti-Stalking Foundation, 13% reported stalking that lasted more than 10 years, 65% suffered destruction and/or theft of their property, and 74% said they were followed.[43] Targets suffer fear, anxiety, depression,[44] and a nagging feeling that stalkers will show up unannounced and harm them or their belongings. Although stalking is a crime in the U.S. Territories, the District of Columbia, and in fifty states, the omnipotence that stalkers feel[45] propels them to continue.

A desire to think the best of people can undermine targets' initial instincts and their sense of discomfort. No one wishes to believe a seemingly "decent" person would have a slimy underbelly: They must have been kidding. They didn't think about what they were saying. They're just good ol' boys/good ol' girls in an off-color mood. You misinterpreted their intentions.

Indeed, U.S. courts as late as 1991 described a workplace stalking incident (in which a coworker repeatedly sent another employee unwanted love notes) as nothing more than "a modern-day Cyrano de Bergerac."[46] Unwillingness to act, combined with targets' failing to explicitly say "no," may signal acceptance to stalkers. Moreover, targets may not want to hurt a coworker's feelings, become a nuisance, experience retaliation,[47] or receive "threats of exposure, paycheck loss, and the dispatch of undercover, surreptitious goons who [are] supported by a cadre of well-connected attorneys."[48]

> If people behave as if abuse didn't happen, they reinforce an abuser's feelings of entitlement. Abuse unaddressed may continue and escalate over time.

Work can provide an entrée when managers or senior members expect lower-ranking employees to "compensate" by performing nonwork-related activities. These include "staying in the background"[49,50] and "flirting"[51] (or, conversely, displaying corporate nun syndrome[52]), combined with a steady stream of deference, capitulation, and obsequiousness. An established mentor can prevent this from happening. Although over 71% of surveyed Fortune 500 firms reported having a formal mentoring program,[53] surveyed women reported receiving dissimilar benefit in terms of top management interaction and advice.[54] The benefits of an experienced mentor are many. They provide a firewall, serving as "voucher" by removing obstacles, creating opportunity, making introductions to powerful players in their personal networks,[55] and providing a moat of protection against malicious employees. They might also provide a "shiny lacquer" for someone who might otherwise be perceived as ordinary or suspect.

**Blanche describes employee perks accrued
by an employee at Catug*n.**

Korie's rapid ascent could not have occurred without a higher-level mentor clearing the path, pulling the strings, saying "Do this, not that."

Attention-seeking crosses the line when it makes the object of attention feel uncomfortable. Repeated workplace education that explains what stalking is (and isn't), policies that describe explicit sanctions and expectations for behavior at work, along with procedures that guide managers in dealing with stalking incidents are necessary to prevent stalking from continuing—or from occurring in the first place. Managers must recognize that workplace stalking is an organizational issue and not an individual one. Companies should provide annual training on stalking so that people have a clear idea of what constitutes repeated, obsessive behavior. Training should also cover applicable stalking laws in the municipality, region, and state. If firms do receive a complaint about an internal stalker, they may consider the following responses:

- questioning potential witnesses and establishing the facts through investigation;
- refraining from forcing targets to meet face-to-face with their accuser. Intervention or arbitration may not be an option if it creates discomfort;
- asking for any documentation that the targets may have; and
- imposing sanctions, with possible suspension or termination of the employment contract if those actions are warranted.[56] If the company phone system provides a log, inform employees that this log is periodically audited. Stalkers are more likely to make suggestive remarks in a private forum or show up in places where they are less likely to be seen by other employees (like the target's neighborhood). Reiterate to office staff that employees' personal information should remain private.

How to Best Deal With Bully Types and Misbehavior? The Importance of Finding a Prosocial Advocate at Work

Social support is a potent antidote to bullies' poison arrows. Research has found a strong positive association between one's number of friends and one's personal happiness.[57] Camaraderie can provide benefits that bolster a target's esteem. These include:

- a sounding board for advice;
- a sense of normalcy in unsettling/unfamiliar circumstances;
- resources to plan campaigns, gain additional supporters, and turn the organizational tide in one's favor; and
- invitations so the label of "newbie" falls quickly by the wayside.

Organizational diplomats, or *anti-bullies*, create lasting connections. They may be especially important for people who are less aware of the impression they are making.

Case in Point

Those with Asperger syndrome, or "Aspies," have been described as bully targets and as people who may be perceived as aggressive.[58] Their mannerisms include brusque demeanor; talking at (instead of with) another person; and trouble interpreting nonverbal cues, subtle hints, and facial expressions—a result of their tendency to interpret events literally. This inability to process emotions can result in meltdowns,[59] and they displace anger onto unsuspecting persons who happen into the crossfire. Targets may be treated with harsh upbraiding and disrespectful name-calling.

Miscommunication between neurotypicals and those with Asperger's occurs when the people with Asperger's think others should overlook their misconduct because they had no intention to harm—not realizing that emotional outbursts can hurt others deeply.[60]

Finding insiders who will act as friends, allies, and advocates can be invaluable.

Assessment

Indicate whether you have done the following in the past month:

- ■ _____ Made friends with a newcomer at work and/or school.
- ■ _____ Sat with a "newbie" at lunch who was alone.
- ■ _____ Approached someone who is a service provider (e.g., fast-food worker, bank teller, restaurant server) to make small talk and to inquire about their day.
- ■ _____ Looked someone in the eye when greeting them.
- ■ _____ Called a friend you have not heard from in a while.
- ■ _____ Sincerely thanked someone who helped you, in person or over the phone.
- ■ _____ Included a "newbie" in a project.
- ■ _____ Offered to mentor someone at work.
- ■ _____ Explained office politics to someone who could benefit from support.

Exercise:

If you have not done any of the above, what could you do differently? How can you build a firewall to protect potential targets?

_____

_____

_____

_____

Online Resources

- ■ Gilbert, J. A. (2012, April 25). Everyday sociopathy [Blog post]. Retrieved from https://organizedforefficiency.com/everyday-sociopathy/
- ■ Gilbert, J. A. (2012, July 29). The perfect patsy [Blog post]. Retrieved from https://organizedforefficiency.com/the-role-of-the-patsy/
- ■ Gilbert, J. A. (2012, October 15). [MTSUBullyAwareness]. *Take a stand stop the bully/The face of a new resistance* [Video file]. Retrieved from https://www.youtube.com/watch?v=J9XzvyUQIwE

- Gilbert, J. A. (2014, November 13). Asperger's unwrapped [Blog post]. Retrieved from https://organizedforefficiency.com/aspergers-unwrapped/
- Gilbert, J. A. (2015, July 19). The highs and lows of histrionic personality disorder [Blog post]. Retrieved from https://organized forefficiency.com/the-highs-and-lows-of-histrionic-personality-disorder/
- Gilbert, J. A. (2015, October 16). The inner workings of a stalker [Blog post]. Retrieved from https://organizedforefficiency.com/the-inner-workings-of-a-stalker/
- Gilbert, J. A. (2016, October 15). Pets on parade [Blog post]. Retrieved from https://organizedforefficiency.com/pets-on-parade/
- Gilbert, J. A. (2017, November 22). Peering inside the mind of a predator [Blog post]. Retrieved from https://organizedfor efficiency.com/peering-inside-the-mind-of-a-predator/
- Gilbert, J. A. (2017, December 6). The leadup to lewd commentary [Blog post]. Retrieved from https://organizedforefficiency .com/the-lead-up-to-lewd-commentary/

Web Quests

1. After reading "How to Stop a Jealous Thought in its Tracks"[61] and "Dealing With Envy: What Envy Teaches You,"[62] explain how you can positively handle your own inclinations toward schoolmates or fellow workers.

   _____

   _____

   _____

   _____

2. Describe components of an onboarding program that is designed to acclimate employees to corporate culture. What benefits do they provide, and how do companies use them?

_____

_____

_____

_____

3. After reading "Bullying and the Boss's Buddy" [63] and "Being the Boss's Favorite is Great, Until it's Not," [64] describe repercussions to the "pet," to those who do not receive special treatment at work, and to the organization where favorites abound.

_____

_____

_____

_____

What Would You Do?

1. Fastidious Frank saunters into your office with the latest gossip about his coworker. After reading "The Case for Reverse Snitching," [65] enlist a game plan for how you (as the boss) should behave.

_____

_____

_____

_____

2. Janine is the new kid on the block. She's having a difficult time fitting in, with not a single teammate willing to lend a hand. What can you do to make her feel welcome?

_____

_____

_____

_____

3. Charlene receives the lion's share of perks, far more than any of her peers. This special treatment, in her case, is not performance-based. How can you create a fair mentoring program, one where high-potential performers are chosen regardless of unrelated attributes? See "The Development of a Diversity Mentoring Program for Faculty and Trainees: A Program at the Brown Clinical Psychology Training Consortium"[66] web article.

_____

_____

_____

_____

Notes

1. Management researchers Julianna Pillemer and Nancy Rothbard hypothesize that workplace friends can be distractions, because coworkers may feel obligated to listen to friends' problems, provide suggestions, and offer socio-emotional support. See Pillemer, J., & Rothbard, N. P. (2018). Friends without benefits: Understanding the dark sides of workplace friendship. *Academy of Management Review, 43*(4), 635-660. https://doi.org/10.5465/amr.2016.0309
2. Susan Cain explains that extroverts are less likely to consider the potential ramifications of their behavior and are more likely to act impulsively. See Cain, S. (2012). *Quiet.* New York, NY: Crown.
3. The "I didn't mean to" mea culpa is another way of saying that you let other people know your true feelings, according to Cloud, H., & Townsend, J. (1992). *Boundaries: When to Say Yes, How to Say No.* Grand Rapids, MI: Zondervan.
4. Attempting to be a target hero in unsupportive or toxic climates (especially if one is lesser-tenured, lower in rank, or new to the organization) can be tenuous. If top leaders who set the tone, corresponding expectations, and com-

pany policy look the other way (or in the worst-case scenario, participate), bad behavior will result. In toxic environments, abuse is recycled. Slam sessions occur more frequently in offices where oversight is absent.

5. Brian Williams was removed from his position as anchor of NBC news for reporting that his helicopter was shot down in Iraq and surrounded by enemy forces. He and his crew actually were in a Chinook that arrived on the scene an hour later.

6. In a lawsuit settled for $1.25M against Columbia University, Enrichetta Ravina claimed that her reputation and her academic standing were tarnished when a senior colleague e-mailed disparaging messages that impugned her job competence, questioned her integrity, and maligned her stability to influential colleagues. See Maki, S. (2018, July 27). Columbia bias case ends in $1.3M payout to professor. *Bloomberg*. Retrieved from https://www.bloomberg.com/news/articles/2018-07-27/columbia-bias-lawsuit-ends-in-1-3-million-payout-to-professor

3

Childhood Background

The tinderbox for incivility tolerance is set early.

The Problem and Definition

What determines who becomes "bully bait" and who evades an abuser's line of fire? Factors beyond children's control, such as early life experience, personality, and upbringing, influence their attitudes. Interactions at a young age can follow people for a lifetime—with exclusion, rumors, taunting, mocking, name-calling, blackmailing, shunning, and insults creating problems that plague children well into adulthood.[1] If abuse begins early, targets may develop low self-esteem, learned helplessness, a belief that they are deserving of punishment, and a receptivity to continued maltreatment. In a longitudinal study of almost 4,000 participants, researchers found that emotional abuse experienced at age 13 was associated with depression in approximately 29% of persons age 18.[2]

Children may internalize "bully talk" they hear from other children. In "My Worst Nightmare – What If I Accidentally Raise The Bully?"[3] blogger Leslie Blanchard describes lessons she relayed to her own daughter:

How to Transform Workplace Bullies Into Allies, pages 55–73
Copyright © 2020 by Information Age Publishing
All rights of reproduction in any form reserved.

She learned that, while I may not be overly-interested in what she gets on her Science Fair project, couldn't care less if she's Lactose Intolerant or whether her long blonde hair is snarled, she's going to damn well treat people right.

Exercise

Think back to your childhood. Did you feel bullied, or were you "one of the gang?" Did anyone accuse you of being a bully? How can you instruct your own children and people at work and/or school to be more accepting, particularly of people who seem reluctant to speak?

_____

_____

_____

_____

Formative Experience and Its Impact

The theory of nature/nurture suggests that environment accounts for approximately half of our personality. People are products of either good or bad situations, with terrorizing, threat-based schools and households creating compulsive children[4] through caregiving that was administered in an unpredictable, frightening, or explosive fashion. Screaming and yelling, quiet freeze-outs, put-downs, refusal to praise, continual nitpicking, or purposely ignoring children's needs can result in their impaired brain development and their belief they are unworthy/lack good judgment/live in a cruel world of ubiquitous abuse and are at the mercy of other people.[5] Caretakers who use a punitive, hostile, authoritarian disciplinary style may oversensitize the electrical activity that occurs in the brain, the error-related negativity (or ERN) that alerts people when they have made a mistake. Research has found that harsh parenting was associated with increased ERN, which in turn was associated with greater anxiety within children 3 years later. Persistent and frequent overcorrection can influence whether messages that occur when children make a mistake are interpreted as cautionary warnings, or whether they appear as a potential recipe for disaster and/or result in neuroticism, OCD, abnormal worry about committing an error, and inhibited behavioral effect. Internalized shame can produce a hypersensitive danger-sensing mechanism.[6]

Scene: A child describes an abusive babysitter's behavior.

We took an alternate route through Jersey, a road marked by right-angle turns downhill, almost vertically, like a snake. At each turn our babysitter floored the pedal before she slammed on the brakes—so our car lunged forward in jerky, erratic movements. My big sister tried reasoning with her. "Slow down, we're going too fast!" she pleaded softly, almost like a prayer.

The babysitter glared, shaking her fist at us and hurling razor-sharp words. Her utter and complete lack of control terrified me. In my dreams, I saw an oversized rotund mass, sound-blasting a miniature round speck.

Bullying among young adults can occur from what Lisa Damour, author of *Untangled: Guiding Teenage Girls Into the Seven Transitions Into Adulthood*, calls "social glue"—a need for teens to bond through scapegoating one of their classmates. She argues that "singling out" escalates when a child feels isolated. Peer isolation can be a by-product of the caretaking that children experience.

Parental, as opposed to peer abuse, can be especially damaging. Imagine how menacing an out-of-control, bellicose adult might seem to a small child. Narcissists raise children who are overly sensitive to critique, inflexible, pessimistic, insecure, hypervigilant, and deeply afraid to express their own opinions.[7] Hidden danger makes for fearful adults and emboldens playmates who test the waters. Systematic emotional, mental, and psychological bullying sets a baseline for exploitation and a reluctance to establish boundaries. Research with young adults who experienced "scolding, yelling, swearing, blaming, insulting, threatening, demeaning, ridiculing, criticizing [and] belittling" as children indicated that they were later subject to anger-hostility, depression, limbic irritability, and dissociation—a sensation where people suddenly feel alienated from their past.[8]

Insensitive adults may be loath to apologize. They might feel humbling themselves diminishes their authority and damages their power. Apologies, however, demonstrate that children are worthy of respect.[9] Conversely, a pattern of abuse (followed by a self-righteous assertion for why it occurred) sends a message that recipients are dumping grounds for maltreatment. "Magnets for abuse" are made, not born. Adults either erode or reinforce the moorings of self-worth that help fend off an attack. Threats of physical punishment and/or abandonment, combined with a barrage of insults, do lasting harm, develop children who set ineffectual boundaries, diminish trust between children and adults, and create unpredictability that puts caretakers center stage. Maladaptive behaviors to deal with the lack of a role model can cripple a child's relationships. Adults who normalize abuse develop a willingness in children to accept it.

Shouting has been deemed "the new spanking." Examples that leave lasting scars include phrases like:

1. "You make me sick."
2. "I wish you'd never been born."
3. "You can't do anything right."
4. "I'm going to give you a beating."

Research on corporal punishment is mixed. Some analyses indicate that spanking is less effective than nonphysical techniques;[10] others argue that spanking, when used as a "backup" by "in-control" parents, can reinforce milder punishment methods. Only when severe disciplinary tactics were used, or when physical punishment was the primary method, did research find that corporal punishment was less effective than nonphysical discipline. *Severe* punishment was defined as face-slapping, striking a child with a fist, and cutting and/or bruising.[11] David Seamands, author of *Healing for Damaged Emotions*, argues that a slap across the face can destroy a recipient's spirit, dehumanize them,[12] and lead them to believe that power differentials between children and adults permit savagery.[13] Slapping a child's head (or face), according to the Supreme Court of Canada, is a form of assault, as is slapping a child in anger.[14] Sixty countries have outlawed any type of physical discipline.[15] More recent advice from the American Academy of Pediatrics expresses disapproval for spanking, citing research that it increases child aggression, decreases a developing brain's cortical mass, and increases cortisol levels in children, which may, in turn, alter their brain architecture.[16]

Barbara Coloroso, the author of *The Bully, the Bullied, and the Bystander*, [17] argues that in "brick wall," or rigid, authoritarian families:

- love is conditional on obeying parents or custodians without question, pleasing them, and conforming consistently to their expectations;
- caretakers behave disrespectfully toward one another, their children, and other people they encounter;
- children's feelings, opinions, and needs are dismissed as unimportant; and
- physical punishment, threats of punishment, parental shame, ridicule, and sarcasm are used to control children.

The result will be children who behave in one or more of the following ways:

- seething with pent-up aggression and bullying other people;
- feeling consumed with self-hatred, passively withstanding abuse, or begging abusers' forgiveness because they feel that they caused the misbehavior; or
- following the dominant person as either a passive or an active bystander.

What shame may be teaching children to think about:	What parenting without shame can teach children to think about:
• "I am worthless." • "I'm incapable of solving problems." • "I can't trust anyone." • "I am bad, and I do bad things." • "Power always wins out."	• "I belong." • "Problems can be solved." • "I can trust my parents to guide me." • "I made a mistake. I can make amends." • "Everyone deserves respect."

Information used with permission of Brill, A. (2013, May 21). Shame does not teach children to do better. *Positive Parenting Connection*. Retrieved from http://www.positiveparentingconnection.net/shame-does-not-teach-children-to-do-better/

Reflection:

At work, do you feel that people take advantage of you? Are you typically the target of poor treatment? If so, what are some ways you can set boundaries for yourself? The book *Boundaries: When to Say Yes, How to Say No to Take Control of Your Life*, [18] by Henry Cloud and John Townsend, suggests that adults who were victimized as children through physical, sexual, and emotional/verbal abuse may outwardly manifest their history through inadequate boundary development—and through an inability to say "no," which leads to accommodating other people by default.

Children who self-blame experience low self-esteem long before they appear on the job. At work, stalkers (and other employees) may see easy pickings, little pushback, and a clinging neediness that reinforces unbalanced power dynamics.[1] Internalizing negative feedback,[19] perpetuating their abuse via bruising self-talk, and behaving in a one-down position during conflict lowers the opinion they place on themselves. The blog post "The Legacy of Power Imbalance and Emotional Abuse" by Jacqueline A. Gilbert describes some of the long-lasting impacts of emotional, verbal, and mental abuse:

> The reaction to emotional debasement can be as devastating, if not more so, than physical abuse. Even when children grow to adulthood, abusers at work or at home may seem like abusive caretakers, ones whose tirades immobilized them. Targets may reenact the only response they could express as children [*Silence*].[20] [Adults (bullied as children) may later be more susceptible to corporate bullies and to supervisory abusers]. Alternatively, children should be treated with dignity and respect, "as if the child were a friend of the family."[21]

When parents exploit their children and expect them to remain silent, they suggest their children's feelings are unimportant. Bari-Ellen Roberts, author of *Roberts vs. Texaco*, describes her role as decoy sitting in the backseat of the family station wagon, with her father and another woman romantically engaged in the front. "It suddenly dawned on me why Mom had been so insistent about me accompanying him: to keep him from being alone with another woman."[22] Ironically, Roberts' father had asked her to tag along to avert suspicion from his wife.

Scene: A child's aunt discovers that her nephew has told his uncle about her rendezvous.

Every Saturday morning, we drove to the gym. I tagged along as a cover so that my aunt could swim with another man.

In between putting on her makeup and driving, my aunt gave me instructions.

"Now Jimmy—you know not to say anything about what's going on to your uncle. That would only upset him, and more importantly it would mean I could never take you back to the pool."

She gave me a serious look.

"Your uncle Dave's so fragile, he just might have a heart attack. But don't you worry. As long as you stay quiet, I'll buy you an ice cream on the way home. And you can tell your uncle what a nice time we had at the pool."

Even a child knows that keeping secrets from someone is wrong. One day while my aunt shopped for groceries, I told my uncle everything. Then I hid when she came home.

Hushed, excited words, then the sound of her footsteps racing toward my end of the hall.

I locked the bathroom door. It was the only barrier between us.

She screamed, rattled the lock, and banged with her hand as hard as she could.

"You let the cat out of the bag, you let the cat out of the bag, I'm never going to trust you again."

Heavy-handed correction and permissive, overly indulgent caretaking lie at opposite ends of the parenting spectrum. Kevin Leman, author of *The Birth Order Book*, explains that parents may become laxer and more permissive after the birth of each child. Laissez-faire rule (more typical for last-borns) may engender self-centeredness and adults who treat others with disdain.[23]

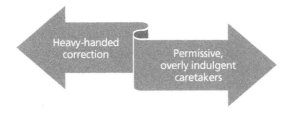

Consider the following outcry:

"Billy broke my favorite toy on purpose!"

Does this sound familiar? Some of us grew up in messy clans where siblings wrangled for attention, while others were the apples of their parents' eyes. Family trees influence the way people live, work, and communicate, with aftereffects that surface years later—within marriages, relationships, and even within careers.[24] Although Leman's advice spans each family tree position—only, oldest, middle, and last-born—he argues that firstborns (and onlies) may be more susceptible to anxiety, low self-esteem, perception of personal failure, and bully exploitation.

> And let's face it—poor Billy is probably the one with a roomful of broken toys.

Parents expect their onlies/firstborns to be "the smartest, the best-behaved, the best-looking."[25] They may be pushed harder by caregivers (and teachers) to exceptionally high levels of academic and career achievement.[26] They are overrepresented within the ranks of Nobel laureates, U.S. presidents, astronauts, and CEOs—a fact that may have a lot to do with their upbringing.

> *Firstborn Characteristics:* Some include perfectionism, organization, list-making, and a willingness to lead. Firstborns' "special" relationship with parents causes adult-like behavior early on and can result in children who shoulder a disproportionate share of responsibility.[27]
>
> *Only Characteristics:* For every adjective that applies to firstborns, onlies get a sticker of "super" preceding it.[28] They are super-dependable, super-organized, super-careful, and super-reliable. As super perfectionists, they seldom feel pleased with their efforts—a reason why so many of them bemoan their "inferior" work product.[29]

Exploitative managers may find perfectionists appealing.[30] The combination of last-born boss (and firstborn/only employee) can be problematic—with the former taking advantage and the latter cringing in the face of supervisory criticism. *Accommodators* may be more susceptible to uninhibited types, and to aggressors who won't take no for an answer. Acquiescence may temporarily appease bullies, but it does little to reinforce a feeling of fair play and empowerment at work. People conditioned to be "nice" regardless of circumstance may fold; their learned dynamics equate anger in other people with peer or parental explosion.

> This sends a silent message of surrender . . . to bullies at large who stand ready to oblige.

Author and school counselor Signe Whitson[31] explains that children should protect their "personal boundaries," which is advice that could apply just as well at work. In firstborns'/onlies' efforts to get other people to like them, they may inadvertently attract the wrong behavior. A middle-of-the-road response that calls bullies on their manipulative ploys, while simultaneously pivoting to how they can improve, may be the most productive thing to do.

Example:

Abusive coworker:	I noticed you submitted your report to the marketing department. You're wrong. I'm fed up with constantly telling you new people what to do.
You:	Albert, instead of complaining, why don't you send an e-mail that explains where departments should send their month-end summaries?

It may be easier to understand the source of dysfunctional behavior if we can view its antecedents and consequences. Conceptual mapping enables people to see the impact of their family history in their lives today and how they repeat historical patterns. Were your family members overly distant or close, were they volatile (emotionally abusive, controlling, cut off/estranged)? Conversely, were they nurturing, warm, supportive, and encouraging?[32] Author Sylvia Lafair suggests that we can transform into bolder, confident persons by becoming aware of and breaking free from past dysfunction.

After completing the following charts, ask yourself if the feelings and experiences you recall from childhood could be reexamined from a more grown-up and accurate perspective, one that encompasses your caretaker and family circumstance. In *Unlocking the Secrets of Your Childhood Memories*,[33] authors Kevin Leman and Randy Carlson suggest that parents had their own life challenges and difficult childhood experiences—ones that made them less-than-perfect caretakers. The exercise of reframing them as people who did the best they could with what they had may lessen grown children's feelings of victimhood. Mature adults let others off the hook, move forward, forgive, and make peace. Rather than a parent or sibling poking fun at you, can you instead see someone who was trying to have fun themselves (albeit in an awkward, seemingly mean-spirited manner)? If you were in the role of counselor, what would you say to yourself to reconcile and move forward? Subpar parenting can be inherited and inflicted unknowingly. It may therefore be more an issue of poor programming than of deliberate intent. Consider that other people want the same things you do (love and affection). Like struggling parents and siblings, though, they sometimes seek them in ways that are injurious to themselves and to other people.

Illustrations by Middle Tennessee State University

Family Tree Chart
PAGE ONE

Information about you and your siblings

If any of your **brothers, sisters, or step-siblings** influenced your life
in a strong way (positive *or* negative),
please list them below and describe their impact.

NT = **Non-toxic** (**Positive influence:** beneficial, helpful, nurturing, loving, supportive)

T = **Toxic** (**Negative influence:** volatile, emotionally abusive, controlling, rejecting)

---

1 BORN 1st ☐ ME ☐ SISTER ☐ BROTHER

FIRST NAME ONLY _____
IF THIS IS YOU, STOP AND GO TO NEXT BOX.
IF THIS IS A SIBLING, <u>CHECK ONLY ONE BOX</u> THAT BEST
DESCRIBES THEM: ☐ NT ☐ T

_____
_____
_____
_____
_____

---

2 BORN 2nd ☐ ME ☐ SISTER ☐ BROTHER

FIRST NAME ONLY _____
IF THIS IS YOU, STOP AND GO TO NEXT BOX.
IF THIS IS A SIBLING, <u>CHECK ONLY ONE BOX</u> THAT BEST
DESCRIBES THEM: ☐ NT ☐ T

_____
_____
_____
_____
_____

---

3 BORN 3rd ☐ ME ☐ SISTER ☐ BROTHER

FIRST NAME ONLY _____
IF THIS IS YOU, STOP AND GO TO NEXT BOX.
IF THIS IS A SIBLING, <u>CHECK ONLY ONE BOX</u> THAT BEST
DESCRIBES THEM: ☐ NT ☐ T

_____
_____
_____
_____
_____

---

4 BORN 4th ☐ ME ☐ SISTER ☐ BROTHER

FIRST NAME ONLY _____
IF THIS IS YOU, STOP AND GO TO NEXT BOX.
IF THIS IS A SIBLING, <u>CHECK ONLY ONE BOX</u> THAT BEST
DESCRIBES THEM: ☐ NT ☐ T

_____
_____
_____
_____
_____

Family Tree Chart
PAGE TWO

If any of your **brothers, sisters, or step-siblings** influenced your life
in a strong way (positive *or* negative),
please list them below and describe their impact.

NT = **Non-toxic (Positive influence:** beneficial, helpful, nurturing, loving, supportive)

T = **Toxic (Negative influence:** volatile, emotionally abusive, controlling, rejecting)

---

5 BORN 5th ☐ME ☐SISTER ☐BROTHER

FIRST NAME ONLY _____
IF THIS IS YOU, STOP AND GO TO NEXT BOX.
IF THIS IS A SIBLING, CHECK ONLY ONE BOX THAT BEST
DESCRIBES THEM: ☐NT ☐T

_____
_____
_____
_____

---

6 BORN 6th ☐ME ☐SISTER ☐BROTHER

FIRST NAME ONLY _____
IF THIS IS YOU, STOP AND GO TO NEXT BOX.
IF THIS IS A SIBLING, CHECK ONLY ONE BOX THAT BEST
DESCRIBES THEM: ☐NT ☐T

_____
_____
_____
_____

---

7 BORN 7th ☐ME ☐SISTER ☐BROTHER

FIRST NAME ONLY _____
IF THIS IS YOU, STOP AND GO TO NEXT BOX.
IF THIS IS A SIBLING, CHECK ONLY ONE BOX THAT BEST
DESCRIBES THEM: ☐NT ☐T

_____
_____
_____
_____

---

8 BORN 8th ☐ME ☐SISTER ☐BROTHER

FIRST NAME ONLY _____
IF THIS IS YOU, STOP AND GO TO NEXT BOX.
IF THIS IS A SIBLING, CHECK ONLY ONE BOX THAT BEST
DESCRIBES THEM: ☐NT ☐T

_____
_____
_____
_____

Family Tree Chart
PAGE THREE

Information about your parents and/or caregivers when you were growing up

If any of your **parents or step-parents** influenced your life in a strong way (positive *or* negative), please list them below and describe their impact.

If you have more than one "other relative" or caregiver in your life, please fill in the information for the person who influenced you the most (positive *or* negative).

NT = **Non-toxic (Positive influence:** beneficial, helpful, nurturing, loving, supportive)

T = **Toxic (Negative influence:** volatile, emotionally abusive, controlling, rejecting)

9 ☐ FATHER

FIRST NAME ONLY _____
CHECK ONLY ONE BOX THAT BEST
DESCRIBES THEM: ☐ NT   ☐ T

_____
_____
_____
_____
_____

11 ☐ MOTHER

FIRST NAME ONLY _____
CHECK ONLY ONE BOX THAT BEST
DESCRIBES THEM: ☐ NT   ☐ T

_____
_____
_____
_____
_____

10 ☐ STEP-FATHER
　　 ☐ OTHER CAREGIVER or RELATIVE
　　　 (e.g., aunt / uncle)

FIRST NAME ONLY _____
CHECK ONLY ONE BOX THAT BEST
DESCRIBES THEM: ☐ NT   ☐ T

_____
_____
_____
_____

12 ☐ STEP-MOTHER
　　 ☐ OTHER CAREGIVER or RELATIVE
　　　 (e.g., aunt / uncle)

FIRST NAME ONLY _____
CHECK ONLY ONE BOX THAT BEST
DESCRIBES THEM: ☐ NT   ☐ T

_____
_____
_____
_____

Family Tree Chart
PAGE FOUR

If any of your **grandparents** influenced your life
in a strong way (positive *or* negative),
please list them below and describe their impact.

NT = **Non-toxic** (**Positive influence:** beneficial, helpful, nurturing, loving, supportive)

T = **Toxic** (**Negative influence:** volatile, emotionally abusive, controlling, rejecting)

---

13 ☐ PATERNAL GRANDMOTHER

FIRST NAME ONLY _____
CHECK ONLY ONE BOX THAT BEST
DESCRIBES THEM: ☐ NT   ☐ T

_____
_____
_____
_____
_____

---

15 ☐ MATERNAL GRANDMOTHER

FIRST NAME ONLY _____
CHECK ONLY ONE BOX THAT BEST
DESCRIBES THEM: ☐ NT   ☐ T

_____
_____
_____
_____
_____

---

14 ☐ PATERNAL GRANDFATHER

FIRST NAME ONLY _____
CHECK ONLY ONE BOX THAT BEST
DESCRIBES THEM: ☐ NT   ☐ T

_____
_____
_____
_____
_____

---

16 ☐ MATERNAL GRANDFATHER

FIRST NAME ONLY _____
CHECK ONLY ONE BOX THAT BEST
DESCRIBES THEM: ☐ NT   ☐ T

_____
_____
_____
_____
_____

Online Resources

- Babbel, S. (2011, March 15). Child bullying's consequence: Adult PTSD [Blog post]. Retrieved from https://www.psychologytoday.com/blog/somatic-psychology/201103/child-bullyings-consequence-adult-ptsd
- Brill, A. (2013, May 21). Shame does not teach children to do better [Blog post]. Retrieved from http://www.positiveparentingconnection.net/shame-does-not-teach-children-to-do-better/
- Emotional abuse signs (n.d.). [Blog post]. Retrieved from http://www.teach-through-love.com/emotional-abuse-signs.html
- Caprino, K. (2016, July 9). How being raised by a narcissist damages your life and self-esteem [Blog post]. Retrieved from https://www.forbes.com/sites/kathycaprino/2016/07/09/how-being-raised-by-a-narcissist-damages-your-life-and-self-esteem/#21a00ef42c67
- Gilbert, J. A. (2013, September 13). The delight of doing one's own thing [Blog post]. Retrieved from https://organizedforefficiency.com/the-delight-of-doing-ones-own-thing/
- Gilbert, J. A. (2013, September 23). Shouting and shame at work [Blog post]. Retrieved from https://organizedforefficiency.com/shouting-and-shame-at-work/
- Gilbert, J. A. (2014, February 28). Dishonor and disgrace at work [Blog post]. Retrieved from https://organizedforefficiency.com/dishonor-and-disgrace-at-work/
- Gilbert, J. A. (2015, June 8). The legacy of power imbalance and emotional abuse [Blog post]. Retrieved from https://organizedforefficiency.com/the-legacy-of-power-imbalance-and-emotional-abuse/
- Gilbert, J. A. (2015, July 11). How to hire a million-dollar baby [Blog post]. Retrieved from https://organizedforefficiency.com/how-to-hire-a-million-dollar-baby/
- Gilbert, J. A. (2018, August 13). Inappropriate office parenting [Blog post]. Retrieved from https://organizedforefficiency.com/inappropriate-office-parenting/
- Gross, G. (2014, October 14). What causes your child to become a bully? [Blog post]. Retrieved from http://www.huffingtonpost.com/dr-gail-gross/what-causes-your-child-to_b_5980002.html
- Marche, S. (2018, September 5). Why you should stop yelling at your kids. *New York Times*. Retrieved from https://www.nytimes

.com/2018/09/05/well/family/why-you-should-stop-yelling-at
-your-kids.html

- McCollom, R. (2019, September 9). How bullying may shape adolescent brains. *UNDARK*. Retrieved from https://undark.org/article/can-bullying-change-brain/?utm_source=pocket-newtab
- McGregor, J. (2017, May 11). Your mean boss is secretly miserable. *The Washington Post*. Retrieved from https://www.washingtonpost.com/news/on-leadership/wp/2017/05/11/your-mean-boss-is-secretly-miserable/?utm_term=.b45e958d07bb
- Spencer, P. (2011, July 12). 9 things you shouldn't say to your child. *CNN*. Retrieved from http://www.cnn.com/2011/LIVING/07/12/dont.say.to.child.p/
- Whitbourne, S. K. (2016, October 4). Six of the more subtle signs of narcissism [Blog post]. Retrieved from https://www.psychologytoday.com/blog/fulfillment-any-age/201610/6-the-subtler-signs-someone-may-be-narcissist

Web Quests

1. After reading "7 Crippling Parenting Behaviors that Keep Children From Growing Into Leaders"[34] "8 Guaranteed Ways to Emotionally F*ck up Your Kids"[35] and "5 Glaring Signs that Your Childhood has Negatively Impacted Your Career"[36] write a synopsis of parenting behaviors that people should avoid and those that contribute to healthy esteem. What happens to children when caretakers engage in negative child-rearing techniques? Sam Vaknin, the author of *Malignant Self-love: Narcissism Revisited*, explains that narcissistic parents believe they do their children a favor when they use harsh parenting methods.

_____

_____

_____

_____

2. People in the United States who are viewed as meek, quiet, and reserved may also be perceived as weak. The web article "8 Advantages Highly Sensitive Persons Bring to Business"[37] suggests that "still waters run deep," and that introverts' unseen processing can produce valuable workplace insights. Describe ways firms can capi-

talize on introverts' strengths and how they can successfully mine "deep thinker" perspectives.

_____

_____

_____

_____

3. After reading "Birth Order in the Workplace" [38] and "Is Your Workplace Personality out of (Birth) Order?" [39] web articles, describe work roles that may be especially suited to last-borns, onlies, middle-borns, and firstborns. In supervisor/subordinate relationships and in team settings, what are some ways that birth orders may clash?

_____

_____

_____

_____

4. Barbara Coloroso, author of *The Bully, the Bullied, and the Bystander*, argues that children in "backbone families" model the respect parents give, learn to make their own decisions, help to solve the problems they create, behave compassionately toward other children, and feel their opinions at home matter. This is because their parents provide unconditional love, reasonable expectations, second chances, validation ("You may have a point. Let's talk about how you came to that conclusion."), positive role modeling, and encouragement for their children to stick up for themselves and other people. From your research, what other parenting behaviors create confident, well-adjusted children who can fend off a bully, and, thus, who are less likely to attract bullies?

_____

_____

_____

_____

What Would You Do?

1. While standing in line at the grocery store, you see a customer berating the grocery store clerk, using foul language in an accusatory tone of voice. How can you behave as "peacemaker" to defuse this situation? (See the ABC News video "Woman Berates Clerk with Down syndrome."[40])

    _____

    _____

    _____

    _____

2. Your quiet, shy coworker (Amabile), is sometimes "caught in a slow roast"[41] before her colleagues at work:

    "The bully pounces on the quiet, non-expressive person, assuming that he or she will not fight back when attacked."[42]

    How might she misinterpret "good-natured" roughhousing like teasing, play complaints, and practical joking?

    _____

    _____

    _____

    _____

3. Sometimes companies must be creative to foster inclusion. One example is Exxon Baytown, where engineers had trouble communicating with their Asian colleague who remained silent during meetings. Her coworkers discovered that she "rolled words" on her tongue seven times before she spoke, so that she would not offend anyone. Her customs made rapid-fire give and take with teammates difficult. When her group gave her time at the end of each meeting to speak, she was able to contribute and provide a reflective viewpoint on the proceedings.[43]

How can you as a leader follow Exxon's example to prevent "shy-shaming" at work?

---

4. At work, home, school, and within families, people compliment the talkers—those effervescent social butterflies who are the life of the party. To mine the hidden gems of quiet people takes work. "I's," or introverts, have strengths that might not be as obvious. Their preparation, research, and execution tend to be more meticulous than those of their extrovert counterparts because they are unable to rely on off-the-cuff, extemporaneous speech. What they lack in hard-knuckle presentation is replaced with "quiet persistence," willingness to listen, and insight that escapes their more "ready fire aim" peers. [44]

Meetings in which managers expect introverts to participate in back-and-forth with continuous talkers fail to showcase the introverts' talents. Introverts' "reflected best self" [45] is not evident within bullpen battles, and people are left with the impression that they have little to say. "You didn't say much" is a criticism of people who are compared with their more gregarious colleagues.

"Fish out of water are immobilized. [Susan Cain, author of *Quiet: The Power of Introverts in a World that Can't Stop Talking,*] explains that [introverts] are more reactive to novel situations, and may temporarily 'freeze' until their nervous systems have time to [adjust]." [46]

As a manager, how can you solicit contributions from less chatty colleagues, create a safe space for everyone to contribute, and encourage introverts to speak freely in meetings?

Notes

1. The U.K. Office for National Statistics reports that abused girls are four times more likely to experience sexual abuse as adults, and more than half of abused children experience domestic assault later in life. It defines *domestic abuse* as sexual abuse, non-sexual abuse, and stalking experienced from a partner or family member, and child abuse as both physical and psychological.

Office for National Statistics. (2017, September 27). *People who were abused as children are more likely to be abused as an adult.* Retrieved from https://www.ons.gov.uk/peoplepopulationandcommunity/crimeandjustice/articles/peoplewhowereabusedaschildrenaremorelikelytobeabusedasanadult/2017-09-27

4

Toxic Workplaces

Toxicity seeps into companies, coating its recipients with shame.

The Problem and Definition

To someone who's never been targeted for workplace abuse or imagined what may happen when good people feign ignorance, destructive office politics may seem unbelievable—something like a Grimm fairy tale with a 21st-century spin.

When we think of "work" we conjure images of racing toward deadlines, productive project discussions, and collegial office conversations. Most people don't give bullying much thought; they consider it childish antics in the realm of preschool children, and thus a trifling matter not worthy of managerial attention.

That could not be further from the truth.

Some workplaces are remnants of the Wild West, frontiers of incivility overrun by outlaws who figuratively impale their coworkers, attacking them from behind closed doors and with high-tech means.[1]

On-the-job attacks are widespread. A 2017 Workplace Bullying Institute U.S. survey found that 19% of adults had experienced workplace abuse, 15% had witnessed it, and 3/10 of a percent had instigated an attack.[2] The WBI estimates that 60.3 million people are affected by workplace bullying, a number equal to "the combined populations of six Western states." Malcontents, despots, sociopaths, narcissists, and Machiavellians, along with an almost impenetrable glass ceiling, may be a reality in many companies.[3]

Toxic behavior occurs when managers tolerate it and when misbehavior becomes institutionalized as a standard practice. Bosses encourage wrongdoing when they are afraid to confront bullies, and thus remain silent,[4] or when they ignore, rationalize, and excuse bad behavior—saying things like "We do that to everyone." Employees engage in survival-of-the-fittest battles in companies where toxicity manifests as fear, exclusion, backstabbing, and disempowerment. Daily infighting leaves employees drained of energy that they could otherwise channel into productive pursuits. "[The] meta variable that permits untoward acts is culture[—]the collection of policies, practices, people, systems, and standard operating procedures that run like invisible scaffolding throughout [organizations]."[5]

Assessment

Rate Your Culture

To rate your workplace culture, work along each of the components in Figure 4.1 and tick the statement that most closely reflects your situation. For every tick in the Toxic Zone, score a −2, for every tick in the Unaccountable Zone, score a −1, and so on; then add up the total score (it should be between −8 and +8).

If your total score is less than zero your culture is sucking energy from your organizational system, reducing your competitive advantage and needs to be improved urgently.

If your total score is greater than zero your culture is pumping energy into your organizational system and adding to your competitive advantage.

The impact of the scores is not a straight line. Energy is sucked out of the system exponentially faster as the score becomes more negative and energy is pumped into the system exponentially faster as the score becomes more positive.

COMPONENTS OF CULTURE	Toxic Zone (score −2)	Unaccountable Zone (score −1)	Compliance Zone (score 0)	Sustainable Zone (score +1)	More Conscious Zone (score +2)
ATTITUDES	I will defeat you	I will use you	You scratch my back and I'll scratch yours	We are partners	We are for each other and for the whole
PHILOSOPHY	Do others in before they do you in	Do it to others because everyone else is	Do unto others in a way that is fair	Do unto others as you would have them do unto you	Do for all in a way that best serves all
BELIEFS	Might makes right	It's a hard cruel world	Ideal organisation is a well-oiled machine	Organisations are living systems	Organisations are consciously evolving living systems
RELATIONSHIPS	Attaching and blaming	Disrespect, discounting, dishonest, denial, defensive	Non-judgmental, purposeful, honest	Caring, appreciative, high-integrity	Co-creative, evoking Genius in each other

Score _____

Figure 4.1 How toxic is your culture? *Source:* Used with permission of Holland, B. (n.d.). How Toxic is Your Culture? Retrieved from http://www.virtual.co.nz/index.php?n=StrategicSnippets.HowToxicIsYourCulture (from Bruce Holland—CrackingGreatLeaders.com).

Culture Can Be Deeply Embedded and Highly Contagious

The endoderm, or cultural skin, of companies exists below the surface. Values, attitudes, moods, words, policies, and meetings define an organization to its membership. Although outward appearances may suggest that everything is okay at work, the unseen lifeblood[6] may be contaminated. Ex-employee Greg Smith (in his farewell letter to Goldman Sachs) complained of a toxic climate. He suggested that Sachs pivoted from being a client-centric company to one that bypassed its customers' best interests. Bad practice can solidify within cultures that train people to be Machiavellian—ruthless in pursuit of profits—and through ringleaders who advocate duplicitous management techniques. In *Winning Through Intimidation: How To Be the Victor Instead of the Victim in all Areas of Life*, author Robert J. Ringer explains that plowing through coworkers and clawing to obtain perks are the two primary ways to succeed.[7]

Few employees have the luxury of quitting. Because they have personal and family obligations, or because they feel constrained by golden handcuffs, unhappy workers may not feel they have the capacity to pick up and go. As a result, toxic employers can write their own playbooks in companies where jungle law rules.

Telltale signs of a toxic culture:

- Employees almost always sit with their doors closed.
- Management issues memos stating that workers should keep their doors open.
- Bosses discuss employees behind their backs. They select favorites who are sycophantic.
- Cabals choose scapegoats who excel at their jobs, who belong to an "objectionable" demographic class, and who refuse to kowtow to cabal members.
- Meetings are open forums where employees are humiliated and gang bullied.
- Bosses talk to employees only about issues they consider important. They behave angrily, defensively, or aggressively when workers attempt to discuss problems.
- People in work units don't socialize with one another.
- Employees exploit those of lesser rank by using pressure tactics to obtain perks for themselves.
- Workers don't celebrate one another's achievements. They are instead envious, and in the worst-case scenario they devise ways to undermine their peers' success.
- Performance criteria are subjective and non-quantifiable. If multiple people are responsible for individual ratings, subgroups

vote as a block to send someone a message. Nonquantifiable criteria may include sycophancy and accomplishments that do not upstage more-senior employees.

- Cabal members use their collective influence to extract work and nonwork-related benefits from lesser-tenured employees. They feel they can say and do anything they want because "it's all good."
- Stalking occurs behind the scenes.
- Minorities who hold a rank equal to their majority peers are perceived as lower ranking.
- Smear campaigns and negative gossip occur in hallways, and often within earshot of those who are affected. Powerful network members who feel invincible lead the charge.
- Minorities take sides against people of their own race and sex to demonstrate their solidarity with majority employees.[8]
- Organizational politics produce an inverse correlation between rank and emotional intelligence.[9]
- Managers and senior members attack employees in front of other people.
- Managers and senior members attack employees, period.

Toxic firms provide an entrée for the emergence of evil—planned, calculating, systematic disregard that manifests in "political power,"[10] where bosses behave more like shame-inducing parents than professionals at work.[11,12] Continuation of abuse (or worse, a regression of psychologically healthy workers) can occur. Toxic ethical culture at Toshiba allegedly incited accounting fraud, which occurred when subordinates accepted their superiors' orders at face value,[13] not realizing or wanting to consider that they had the options of questioning or quitting.

Character-disordered caregivers (either through ignorance or ill intent), abuse their offspring.[14] Similarly, character-disordered bosses:

- hold employees accountable for not doing others' work;
- hold employees accountable for things they should have done themselves;
- take second-hand reports at face value instead of investigating the source of a problem;
- explain that a subordinate's behavior is deficient but fail to provide suggestions for improvement;
- fail to acknowledge exemplary work; and
- blame employees for managerial mistakes and throw workers under the bus.

Maltreatment occurs through trickle-down management, when workers observe bosses gaining power at their coworkers' expense and when bullied targets repeatedly experience vindictive workplace conduct.[15]

Rude People Spawn Noxious Acts

Workplace bullying (interpersonal mudslinging, rudeness, yelling, and aggression) and counterproductive workplace behaviors (wasting materials/time, damaging the workplace, and refusing to follow instructions) are positively correlated. Management researcher Clive Boddy found a positive association between psychopathy and workplace conflict. Managers who lack a conscience, who look for scapegoats, and who exploit their coworkers are managers who instigate and maintain fear-based work cultures. Although psychopaths in the general population number about 1%, the correlation rises with the hierarchical level in companies; surveys indicate that psychopaths were 3½ times more prevalent in a sample of high-potential executives.[16] Targeting, bullying, and blaming employees are tactics that psychopaths use to accomplish their agenda, minimize complaints, and bulldoze opposition.

Scene: Edwin, senior vice president at Catug*n, is in a meeting with IT manager Stan and HR manager Ralph. The scene demonstrates the toxic workplace culture.

"Stan, I think you need to get down here. We need to have a meeting with Ralph to iron out the kinks in this new RFID system. I want you to explain the technical side. What do you say, boy?"

Ralph was one of those smiley, rotund HR types who administered benefits and threw employee birthday parties—basically, a fluff job for sorting out employee paperwork. He struck me a lot like a frosted cardboard wedding cake: scratch the surface and there's nothing there. But the important thing is that he doesn't give me any guff. He told me he's got some questions about how this Network Resource Planning System's going to work. The way Martha S.—Chipp*n Ch*m's computer gal explained it to me, time and attendance data are transmitted to our cloud-based server when employees arrive at work. On the sly, I had readers installed in the break rooms and in the bathrooms as well, just to make sure people were sitting at their desks doing their jobs. In my opinion, there's entirely too much tomfoolery going on around here.

Just as I expected, Stan shows up late dragging his "Hey, you don't jerk my chain" attitude. If I didn't need him so much, I'd tell the cleaning staff to use that shaggy head of his to mop my floor. But all things considered, he knows his job better than my proctologist knows Papa Bear's backside. At 10 minutes past time he finally shuffled in and flopped himself in my chair.

I tried to be friendly.

"Well, looky here. If it isn't our esteemed senior systems analyst. What do you know good? We were just sitting around here chewing the fat. We've added a few fine-looking things to this company of late, wouldn't you agree?"

Didn't take the bait, got right down to business. Typical.

"Ed, I think you wanted me to explain how this RFID system works."

Heaving a boatload of worry, Stan started in.

"Here's the way it works, Ralph. Employee data is transmitted by over-head readers—array antennae systems—to our back-end server. At the push of a button, you can locate anyone, anywhere, anytime; it's known as Reality Time-Based Solution and Tracking, or RTBST for short. RFID chips are continually talking to one another, so if an employee gets too close to a secure area, it locks them out. The electronic log that comes from each lanyard chip allows you to see who interacted with whom or what, and when. That data's displayed on your HR dashboard in real time. Plus, you can request log information on any employee whenever you please. This function's limited to top management personnel who have special access and an app. The exec level—like you—already has read/write privileges, which is why I think we need some training in supervisory due diligence."

Well, every time I turned around Stan was preaching this ethics crap. What most people at Catug*n don't know is that Mr. High and Mighty here worked as an exotic dancer to put himself through school. I can't be-lieve people paid money to see that flabby gut gyrating around on stage.

It's ammunition I keep in my back pocket just in case.

Ralphie sat there with his mouth flapping wide open as if knowledge was somehow going to be sucked up into his brain. Stan attempted to spackle the holes.

"HR staff has a special password[1] that permits only them to have data access; it's to help cut down on résumé fraud. For all the pre-hire false leads we get around here, I could just as well use them as fodder. Anyway, the Electronic Enhancement Act allows you to store data to the cloud, things like performance reviews, commendations, reprimands, hiring, and terminations, which of course you can do remotely. Where this gets inter-esting is that in the future, artificial intelligence will accumulate historical data from all the companies they've worked for, then perform predictive analytics. Instead of sitting down with someone to map out their career, the software using big data does that for you. And it ranks people by value.

What this means is that your 'survival of the fittest' performance appraisal system has never been easier. If you do this pre-recruitment, the program automatically flags things like employment gaps and potential job-hoppers—anything that doesn't look kosher."[2]

Well, that sounded good to me. The last thing we needed is someone sucking up months of our training and then getting into bed with somebody else. But the more Stan talked, the more pissed off he looked—like one of us had just stolen his lunch money. The problem was that once he mounted his high horse it was hard to knock him off.

"I'll say it again. We need training on how to conduct performance reviews and what to write about employees, because this record will stay with them for a lifetime."

Stan should have known me well enough by now to know what I was up to. Ralphie, on the other hand, sat there looking bumfuzzled. He was nice enough in a roly-poly sort of way, but he was a little slow on the uptake. I tried to sand off the rough edges.

"So, Stan, are you telling me that with one push of a button I can rewrite history for somebody else, change their future entirely—not just in this company, but the industry?"

Just then Ralphie's eyes registered "tilt" as he contemplated the possibilities. After some more explaining he came to his senses and saw the practical side.

"Ed, what I think this boils down to is that people here better start doing some boot licking! Basically, this means I'm the lockmaster—I decide who gets ahead and who gets held back."

Right then I could see Ralph spinning out of control, so I decided to pull back on the reins.

"Ralphie, my man, you need to use the information managers give you. But if somebody pisses you off, you can always find some trumped-up reason to write 'em up. I'll tell you what, I'll put out a memo tomorrow morning to let people know just what kind of power you have."

Well, with all of this good news dropped on us like Santa Claus, Stan stood up, about ready to tear off my face. I had to defuse the big hairy grenade.

"Stan, looks to me like you got a stick up your butt. What the hell you so steamed about?"

He stood there scowling, all prissy and self-righteous-like.

"Ed, what you're doing here is 10 times shadier than anything I've ever seen. You're using this chip business to make Catug*n employees your possessions—why not just buy some high-functioning bots? It'd be so much easier. People at work here aren't slaves."

I had to squash this bug before it grew wings and multiplied.

"Boy, you didn't seem to mind that chip and everything that went with it when I doubled your paycheck. Just between you, me, and that confidentiality agreement you signed, I'd say I was paying you to have my opinion. If you want to let off some steam, I suggest you go to open mic night at O'Chanahan's. But don't be bringing your piss-poor sourpuss attitude up into this office. Catug*n's not the place for independent thinkers; it's the place for people who follow the program. Now you, more than anybody else in this company, should know what I mean. How many heads you seen me roll? Now you best run on back to your office before you do something I'll regret."

Well, that ole boy shoved his swivel chair, leaped up, and slammed the office door behind him. Good riddance. I'm giving these people a salary, and if they don't like it they can leave. Stan is, of course, a special case, but that don't mean I can't occasionally smack him upside the head.[3]

The Gallery—How Culture Affects Employees

Characters in Ray Bradbury's *The Martian Chronicles* knew they had gone native when their irises, like those of the original inhabitants, turned golden.

Culture can shift employee perspectives and modify their behavior. As in Stockholm Syndrome, where prisoners develop an attachment to their captors, employees within toxic firms may eventually take management's side. Corporate retreats, employee boot camps, and after-hours socializing are methods to inculcate new recruits with company dogma and to integrate them[17] into established culture.

Astra Pharmaceutical

The "Astra Way" provides a telling example of corporate reeducation. [18] The one trip that Astra allowed home for new hires during its 9-week institute discouraged contact with friends and family and physically and psychologically isolated recruits. Astra's militaristic, rigid, and controlling culture, established by former CEO Lars Bildman, resulted in a strict management style that required employees to eat lunch at the same time, to dress according to a precise code, and to socialize after work to receive positive evaluations. Even slight deviations from policy, including forgetting to wear the Astra pin, could result in reprimand. Sales recruits reported rampant sexual harassment, leering, grabbing, inappropriate remarks, touching, retaliation, quid pro quo, and an Astra Glamour Girls calendar that featured pictures of female employees.

Enron

Once the darling of Wall Street, Enron culture imploded through internal abuse, misconduct, misappropriation of resources, boss enhancement, and a winner-take-all mentality—one that manifested in slipshod and aggressively creative accounting practices. The Enron scandal erupted from outdated disclosure and questionable oversight, and from investors themselves who chose not to voice their concerns.[19] Ironically, the regular paycheck that kept workers tight-lipped evaporated—because they'd remained quiet.

Enron reinforced toxic culture through its forced-ranking appraisal method, in which managers numerically ordered employees. One problem with the forced ranking—labeling workers with numbers one through five—is that it deprives recipients of a descriptive indicator of their performance.

Employees may not know what criteria discriminates a 1 from a 2, or a 3 from a 4, or know what specific information any of the numbers represents. Nondescript appraisal criteria, decoupled from objective performance indicators, can result in skewed perceptions of employee achievement[20] and leave subordinates guessing what behaviors they should change. In *Roberts vs. Texaco*, Bari-Ellen Roberts described how unnerving she found the Texaco system, in which subjective evaluations and the presence of an overall ranking provided a portal for supervisory abuse. Problems escalate when multiple employees provide ratings on a single person. Workers who excel may thus be condemned by shelf-sitters, the less-gifted, and people embittered by their own encounters with lethal company politics.[21] Performance appraisal can be misused as a method of "guerrilla warfare" to oust unfavored workers.[22] At Facebook, the use of *stack ranking* compels employees to concentrate on short-term results to achieve the best rating.[23]

Similarly, rank-and-yank performance appraisals at Amazon have been criticized for promoting employee sacrifice that results in exhaustion. [24,25] Workers, who refer to themselves as "amabots," traded free time to "up the ante" in their next performance appraisal so they could outdo peers. Employees and managers admitted to a survival-of-the-fittest culture, in which the hardiest and hardest-working were both rewarded and retained. Management professor Dave Arnott explains that insular cultures create cult-like atmospheres in which workers are expected to sacrifice their personal lives for their corporate family.[26]

Exercise

Review the performance appraisal system at your current job. What changes would you make to create transparency and to make it more objective, useful, and employee-friendly? Would you use an appraisal system at all? Patty McCord, former Netflix Chief Talent Officer, argues that traditional once-a-year appraisals could be replaced with a more dynamic alternative,[27] like ongoing, mutual interaction between leaders and employees. If your company does use appraisal criteria, how could these be reworked to emphasize developing other people and mentoring peers?

_____

_____

_____

_____

Why It's Important

When people-centered appraisal criteria are absent, employees may:

- game the system;
- use an "end justifies the means" method to accomplish their work;
- stack the deck in their favor[28] by exploiting coworkers or lying to bosses;
- refuse to acknowledge support staff's contributions or share managerial bonuses;
- hoard resources and information;
- act supportive only when it suits their purposes; or
- display an arrogant demeanor and risky behavior that contribute to toxic workplace culture.[29]

The Stanford Prison Experiment

Role reversal and power dynamics were explored in a classroom "prison" setting, where students played the roles of guards and prisoners. After only 6 days, the experiment was discontinued due to unexpected realism and over-the-top brutality that student guards exhibited and to psychological issues that student prisoners who grappled with the after-effects of abuse experienced. A takeaway from the Stanford experiment is that people easily adapt to their roles, in that employees who work in a toxic culture are reinforced by people who were socialized in the same way. Over time, they may lose their initial misgivings, acclimate to their surroundings, and rationalize what they formerly considered to be poor behavior. Correspondingly, employees "have similar perceptions of what constitutes acceptable behavior and tend to behave in a fairly homogeneous manner."[30] By the time MBAs ascend the ranks, their ethical/moral reasoning has (in some cases) disappeared, resulting in an inability to lead effectively.[31] In the blog post "Machiavelli Meets Civility," Jacqueline A. Gilbert describes the negative consequences for employees who stand their ground in a toxic culture:

> In combative situations, individuals fight, crumble, or flee. In toxic companies, survival chances are weighted in favor of the craftier, more guileful, more shameless corporate game players. Organizational death occurs through exit, corporate divorce (euphemistically known as delayering, downsizing, housecleaning, or regrouping), or through a psychological hijacking in which employees subsume the dominant culture. While the former are career-related deaths, the latter is a much more insidious type of passing. It is the replacement of people's moral compass with company mandates.[32]

What happens when workers protest[33] may be why whistle-blowers remain scarce. Examples include:

- Roger Mark Boisjoly—a former Morton Thiokol booster rocket engineer who was shunned after he handed over documents to a presidential investigatory committee after the Challenger disaster. Shortly thereafter, he experienced double vision, chest pains, and chronic anxiety that resulted in a diagnosis of post-traumatic stress disorder.[34]
- Sgt. Greg Ford—who, 36 hours after complaining about prisoner abuse in Iraq, was involuntarily strapped into a gurney and flown to Landstuhl Army Regional Medical Center. Commanding officer Capt. Victor Artiga allegedly insisted that Ford was delusional, despite his evaluation results of normal by an army psychiatrist. Another army whistle-blower reported being locked in a psychiatric ward for complaining about abuse within rank.[35]
- Gustavo German—a Harvard doctoral student, underwent a forced mental health exam at the request of his laboratory advisor, who was purported to have fabricated data that was later published.[36] An affidavit reported that Rubin (the advisor) suspected that German was the one who filed the complaint of impropriety against him.

Theranos

Theranos, whose founder and president/CEO has been criminally charged, is an example of unabashed greed and cultural implosion. Top management's misrepresentation of core blood analyzing technology resulted in massive investor losses, charges of fraud, and the public's being deprived of potentially fast, cheap, life-saving technology that was intended to revolutionize the future of blood testing. There also were employee departures and lawsuits that alleged lies and an elaborate cover-up to deceive the public. Holmes claimed that Theranos was more like a religion, where employees were expected to unwaveringly agree with management even though practices like cutting corners, overpromising with a rushed release timeline, and dilution of blood samples happened behind the scenes. Micromanagement and excessive checking occurred to ensure control.[37] Cover-up cultures such as that of Theranos attempt to make employees fearful of expressing alternative viewpoints or questioning dubious practices.

Exercise

Answer the following questions to determine if poor working conditions at your company are systemic or are just rogue employee behavior:[38]

1. Does your manager discuss improving the work climate? _____
2. Is training to improve civility and to reduce workplace abuse taken seriously? _____
3. Are managers held accountable for ignoring or permitting bullying? _____
4. Does anyone model civil behavior at work? _____

If your response to any of these questions is no, your workplace situation may be unsalvageable.

Employees within toxic firms:

- regularly ask their manager's opinion even on minor issues, instead of making independent decisions;
- keep misgivings to themselves;
- smile and nod even when they disagree with their bosses;
- weather mercurial and unpredictable boss moods and outbursts but receive no apology;
- arrive at their boss's office holding an invisible sign that reads, "I want to be part of it"; and
- devise ways to perform favors, stay within their boss's good graces, and above all, support management.

Scene: Blanche discusses her future at Catug*n with senior coworker Stan—who educates her on "hidden" workplace culture.

"Job postings at Catug*n are a sham—most times filled from whomever management talks to on the fairway. Don't get me wrong, I'm not saying skills don't matter, but by themselves they can be a career-killer. One time I hired this guy—Frank—a real Cro-Magnon with gnats in his beard and the personality of a brick. I moved his office to the basement because no one could stand to be around him.

"Listen up, Blanche. Catug*n can get anyone to do a job—any contractor, freelancer, part-timer, or free agent. But it can't get just anyone to 'fit' within this company. That's an art form, and I've got my work cut out for me if I'm going to make you into a keeper."

His eyes flicked toward my corduroys, casual shoes, and coordinating paisley cardigan.

"And one other thing," he said.

"Dress for the job you want, not for the one you've got. With some tweaking, you could look like a million bucks. You'll need that advantage because it's way harder for women. The ugly truth, Blanche, is that each year Catug*n cuts thirty percent of its workforce. Top management calls it 'rank and yank.' I'm telling you this because if you don't figure it out, you'll fail. Nothing's off the table. The horse-trading that occurs inside these walls could put the equestrian industry to shame. Speaking of which, I heard you rubbed up against the wrong side of Big Ed. Everyone here's figured out that a single blow from Big Daddy can be disastrous. I'd lick the ground he walked on if I were you."

I gulped.

"Book learning won't teach you survival skills. Here's an example: New people can't go around making their own rules, like you—trying to leave at 4:30 instead of 5:00. Lay low and watch what the higher-ups do. Being a rabble-rouser won't get you anywhere; in fact, you might end up in the same place as Frank. We started our mentor program because new people couldn't figure out how to play politics the 'Catug*n way,' and we were spending way too much time on cleanup. The feeling is if you want to make a statement, run for Congress. Catug*n's not the place to fly your freak flag."

He handed me a cup of coffee.

"If that's what you want to do, order a designer cup of joe. Cheers," he said, lifting his cup.

Exercise:

What type of politics do you see within your own company? What impact do these practices have on employees? What policy or training changes would you make so that currying "boss favor" does not occur?

_____

_____

_____

_____

> **Scene: Blanche finds herself in the throes of toxic corporate politics, "blame the victim" mentality, and "circling the wagons" posturing. Office busybody Hazel gives her some advice about sidestepping corporate traps.**
>
> She buttonholed me, grabbing my jacket as we ran down the stairs.
>
> "Blanche, I need to talk to you, it's urgent."
>
> I'd never seen Hazel in a panic. Sunny, chirpy, and radiating smiles, she was Catug*n's unofficial happiness-dispensing ice cream truck. But today was so different. At O'Chanahan's she fidgeted, her brow furled in a gridlock. She rocked back and forth, pursing her lips like she afraid of what was inside.
>
> All at once, the unexpected truth hit me.
>
> "Blanche," she said. "I've been hearing some things. I don't know if I should tell you this, but I like you. And I feel if I don't, you don't have a chance in Hades of sticking around. So here goes."
>
> She paused after taking a deep breath.
>
> "Word on the street's that you're squirrelly. I heard it from Mary, Ralph's secretary, that you fall apart at the seams. At first I didn't believe it, but when there's smoke, there's fire. And I thought, they couldn't be talking about my Blanchie! So I went to my usual sources, rooting around the water cooler, you know, dropping a few hints. I called in some favors, all in the name of helping a friend. And do you know what I found?"
>
> My stomach cartwheeled.
>
> "Big Ed thinks you're frigid. A client asked you out for drinks, and you

said no, drinks were not in your budget. And when he invited you to his hot tub, you refused to join in.

"Blanche, I've seen friends get trampled in this company before. Sometimes, you just have to play the game and get with the program—let loose and be one of the clan. That way, people know they can trust you. As things stand, everyone [she grabbed my hand]—present company excluded—thinks you're a cold fish. So I think we need to hatch a plan."

* * *

I could see lips move but I couldn't hear words. Ironically, not one of my coworkers knew anything about the big-game hunt that occurred behind the scenes. Office talk insinuated that I kept to myself, overshadowing the real story of Edwin's prurient interest *in me*. He was an overbearing, love-starved stalker who didn't take no for an answer. I was left with one of two options: quit without references and torpedo my chance for future employment, or bear indentured servitude and the incognito status of corporate whore. I grasped at a long shot, a tribunal of last resort—the "impartial" corporate ombudsperson.

* * *

Angie seemed affable enough. She was a longtime Catug*n employee who appeared every so often in our quarterly magazine.

She rose from her seat.

"Ms. G, what can I do you for?" she said, with a with a toothy, paste-on, customer service smile.

I made some chitchat, fingered my hair, and looked down at my shoes. But her barrage of friendly questions, one after the another, encouraged me to let down my guard.

If I jumped, just maybe she would catch me. I grabbed my chair arms just in case.

"Has anyone ever complained about Edwin?"

My words fell into a ravine as they plummeted to the floor.

She leaned forward.

"Do you mean about his workaholism? Big Ed's been known for setting high standards, which is the reason, young lady, this company is number five in the Fortune rankings."

I shifted to the side.

"No, that's not what I mean. Has he ever crossed the line? Has anyone complained about him going too far?

Her smile vanished. She slapped her palms on top of her desk.

"Everybody knows Big Daddy's a 'tell it like it is' kind of person. In all the years I've been here, we've never had one single complaint about our senior vice president—because most people know where he's coming from. If I were you, Blanche, I wouldn't take things so personally. We here at Catug*n don't punish friendly people."

I didn't know what to say. Was I the one with the problem? Could I have mangled Big Ed's intention that badly? I thanked her for her trouble and turned to leave.

"And another thing, young lady . . ."

Her unstated demand ricocheted me back to my seat. The way she peered over her wire-rimmed glasses implied she'd caught me by the short hairs. The wooden arms of my chair became slippery, almost too wet to touch.

"I did hear through the grapevine that you're having problems. I see this in a lot in new hires, especially during their probationary period. I'm referring you to the EAP. It's worked wonders for new people who feel overwhelmed. Here's a name and number."

*　*　*

Catug*n doublespeak. Why hadn't anyone explained this to me before?

Character assassination, venomous words, and cutthroat interactions fail to nurture independent thinking or positive self-concept. Emotional and psychic damage within toxic firms include:[39]

- a feeling of invisibility,
- nervous system on high alert or hyper-vigilance,
- expectation of future abuse,
- playing a dysfunctional role at work, and
- post-traumatic stress disorder.

The Flip Side of Toxicity

A spirit of respect can permeate organizational culture and transform company norms into community—a place where employees are "(a) surrounded by mutually supportive persons, (b) in an environment comprised of policies that are egalitarian and fair, and (c) supported by colleagues who are engaged in the process of self-development."[40] When mutual assistance is the organizational expectation, employees and leaders look for common ground because everyone feels like they are working toward the same goal. Likewise, policies that impede relations and blame employees are replaced by ones that stress managerial accountability. In community-centric companies, executive-level decisions and actions are examined, disassembled, and redesigned by group consensus; rank-and-file employees make decisions previously made by managers, and they are given a stake in the company's success.[41] *Unleaders*, unlike dictatorial bosses, are responsible for clearing roadblocks and for obtaining needed resources for employees. As coaches they offer insider advice, employee support, mentoring, and suggestions on career development to encourage employees' latent capabilities and strengths.

Table 4.1 explains how conflict resolution, culture, interaction, managerial behavior, selection and promotion, appraisal, and change efforts benefit from community-centric practice, and conversely, how toxicity can ruin organizational relationships. Table 4.2 describes the impact of community-centered firms on employees.

Virtues like trustworthiness and genuine humility[51] are trademarks of community-centered firms.

> *Vulnerability*, or intentional peacemaking (through which we see each other with the "soft eyes" of respect),[52] is the choice not to respond in kind to another person's toxic conduct.

Ricardo Semler, ex-CEO and president of Semco and author of *Maverick: The Success Story Behind the World's Most Unusual Workplace* explains that an employee described his company as "a paradise to work in [where] Nobody wants to leave."[53] Employees at Semco had the latitude to express disgruntlement with any part of their employer—even if that meant a bad report on a boss. Managers did not behave as taskmasters but rather as teammates, ones that steered clear of micromanagement, excessive rules, write-ups, spying on employees, and monitoring by proxy. Semler explained that employees should have a stake in the company through setting their own dress codes, working hours, and personal touches within their workspace. Employment was based on a self-determination model, one where workers were free to assemble, strike, question management, disagree, make suggestions, and formulate rules for their own areas. Open pay, where salaries of all employees were transparent, forced the salaries of employees and managers closer together. Top managers were paid about 10 times the salary of the lowest-level worker. Semler created an organization of "cathedral builders"—visionaries who took pride in their work because they had become a part of the process.

TABLE 4.1 Differences Between Toxic and Community-Centered Organizations

	Toxic	Community-Centered
Conflict Resolution	Winners and losers; conflict is squelched; a model of conversation as a point-scoring coup.[42]	Differences are openly discussed; all employees feel equally comfortable in openly challenging company policy; dialogue is the norm.
Organizational Culture	In-group/out-group; forced acceptance of the dominant viewpoint; groupthink is prevalent.[43]	Community and a sense of company ownership; a sense of safety, recognition, and empowerment.
Interaction	Patronizing, arrogant condescension; managers give orders instead of asking for feedback; tattling, scapegoating; feedback occurs only in a top-down direction.[44]	Respectful discourse among independent professionals; frequent solicitation of viewpoints and opinions; horizontal as opposed to hierarchical.
Managers	Suspicious truant officers and omnipresent watchdogs; micromanagement; a plethora of rigid rules and restrictions.[45]	Servant leadership; humility; coaches and unleaders who direct others with circumspection; solicitation of others' opinions.
Selection and Promotion	Organizational citizenship to achieve self-promotion; cronyism, bias, and an undue emphasis on sycophancy.[46]	The result of other-enhancement and self-development, and a track record of relational and job mastery.
Appraisal	Reprimands without investigation or two-way communication; fearful, degrading episodes of abuse; only administered at annual intervals; subjective criteria that give managers room for political maneuvering.	Collegial, ongoing discussions that focus on enhancing employee strengths; performance based on pre-specified contracts and explicit job criteria.[47]
Organizational Change	Individuals conform themselves to a fixed unyielding set of policies; inflexible and unresponsive attitudes toward change; preserve the status quo and vested interests.	Modeled after processes in nature that continually regenerate themselves in response to environmental conditions and external threat; impetus for change is the voice of dissent from employees who have access to free expression.[48]

Source: Gilbert, J. A., Carr-Ruffino, N., Ivancevich, J. M., & Konopaske, R. (2012). Toxic versus cooperative behaviors at work: The role of organizational culture and leadership in creating community-centered organizations. *International Journal of Leadership Studies, 7*(1), 29–47. Tables 4.1 and 4.2 reprinted with permission.

TABLE 4.2 Descriptors of a Connective Community-Centered Organization
Members in Community-Centered Organizations:
1. Feel safe
2. Feel accepted
3. Feel included
4. Experience recognition for their efforts
5. Celebrate differences
6. Work with clear and noncontradictory rules
7. Receive rewards for success that are far greater than the penalties for failure[49]
8. Experience tranquility
9. Feel relaxed
10. Feel empowered—participate fully in decisions affecting them[50]
11. Have options
12. Feel that heaven and earth have somehow met
13. Have relationships that go deeper than their masks of self-composure; and
14. Willingly extend themselves on behalf of others

Source: Adapted from Peck, M. S. *The different drum: Community-making and peace.* New York, NY: Simon & Schuster, 1987. Used by permission.

In community:

- Employees and leaders share reciprocal trust;
- People work with their bosses to resolve problems;
- Management solicits employee opinions, and employees feel free to express their true feelings;
- Leadership holds a town hall before it enacts major policy;
- Employees are supportive and complimentary of one another; and
- Differences are settled when all parties who could be impacted by a decision have voiced their concerns. The outcomes reflect an amalgam of viewpoints and a "win-win" for everyone involved.

Online Resources

- Gilbert, J. A. (2012, March 25). Five ways to avoid a toxic workplace culture [Blog post]. Retrieved from https://organizedfor efficiency.com/five-ways-to-avoid-a-toxic-workplace-culture/

- Gilbert, J. A. (2015, September 13). RFID up close and personal [Blog post]. Retrieved from https://organizedforefficiency.com/rfid-up-close-and-personal/
- Gilbert, J. A. (2018, January 31). Highlight culture to harness abusers [Blog post]. Retrieved from https://organizedforefficiency.com/highlight-culture-to-harness-abusers/
- Glazer, R. (2016, April 13). Do nice businesses finish first? The perils of a toxic culture [Blog post]. Retrieved from https://www.business.com/articles/do-nice-businesses-finish-first-the-perils-of-a-toxic-culture/
- Hansen, D. (2016, March 8). Is leaderless management a fad or the future of business? [Blog post]. Retrieved from https://www.forbes.com/sites/drewhansen/2016/03/08/leaderless-management/#194c7a0f207f/
- Kakkar, H., & Tangirala, S. (2018, November 6). If your employees aren't speaking up, blame company culture [Blog post]. Retrieved from https://hbr.org/2018/11/if-your-employees-arent-speaking-up-blame-company-culture
- Lipman, V. (2013, May 30). The surprising managerial power of common decency [Blog post]. Retrieved from https://www.forbes.com/sites/victorlipman/2013/05/30/the-surprising-managerial-power-of-common-decency/#5b50356f9fe5
- Lipman, V. (2015, August 4). People leave managers, not companies [Blog post]. Retrieved from https://www.forbes.com/sites/victorlipman/2015/08/04/people-leave-managers-not-companies/#39e149e847a9
- Morgan, B. (2015, April 27). Why a corporate culture of "kindness" is great for your brand [Blog post]. Retrieved from https://www.forbes.com/sites/blakemorgan/2015/04/27/why-a-corporate-culture-of-kindness-is-great-for-your-brand/#5193cfbe681d
- Ovide, S., & Feintzeig, R. (2013, November 12). Microsoft abandons "stack ranking" of employees. *The Wall Street Journal.* Retrieved from https://www.wsj.com/articles/SB10001424052702303460004579193951987616572/
- Post Staff Report. (2018, May 3). Nike CEO apologizes for toxic workplace culture. *New York Post.* Retrieved from https://nypost.com/2018/05/03/nike-ceo-apologizes-for-toxic-workplace-culture/
- Schwantes, M. (2016, February 18). Five signs that you work in a toxic office. *Inc.* Retrieved from http://www.inc.com/marcel-schwantes/5-sure-signs-that-you-work-in-a-toxic-office.html/

Web Quests

1. After reading the "Dish Network: The Meanest Company in America" [54] web article, describe practices that earned this company its poor reputation and what you as leader can do to create a more civil, cooperative culture.

   _____

   _____

   _____

   _____

2. *The No Asshole Rule: Building a Civilized Workplace and Surviving One that Isn't* [55] book explains the damaging impact that bullies have when they obliterate relationships at work. Summarize the reasons why Robert Sutton considers his work important after reading the "Why I Wrote the No Asshole Rule" web article. [56]

   _____

   _____

   _____

   _____

3. Treating people with respect provides dividends to stockholders. Describe at least two of these after reading "The Strong Business Case for Civility in Management" [57] web article.

   _____

   _____

   _____

   _____

4. From the following list, select two behaviors that you think most contribute to dysfunctional work culture. Provide a rationale for your choices, citing web research.
   - Favoritism
   - Shouting
   - Unclear performance-appraisal criteria
   - Gossip
   - Backstabbing
   - Sycophancy
   - Ostracism

_____

_____

_____

_____

TAKE THE SELF-ASSESSMENT SOCIAL INTELLIGENCE QUIZ: TOXIC VS. NOURISHING SCALE[58]

What Would You Do?

1. You are the leader of a X*YZ Company, a new start-up that just instituted an anonymous rating system where anyone can send comments about coworkers to the director of human resource management. You notice that Tam (a quiet, shy, noncombative new hire) has received several scathing reviews, despite exemplary objective performance indicators. How would you as the leader handle this situation? Would you continue to use information gathered from an anonymous rating system, would you lobby for its discontinuance, or at the very least would you do some investigatory work yourself on potential problem areas? What underlying dynamic could influence coworkers who select

a scapegoat for dismissal? (See the web article "Inside Amazon: Wrestling Ideas in a Bruising Workplace"[59].)

_____

_____

_____

_____

2. At X*YZ Company, employee meetings quickly devolve into shouting matches. After an especially brutal tongue-lashing, a recipient of harsh criticism burst into tears.

   In the above situation, who do you think should receive a reprimand? What type of discipline would you administer? Which policies and practices would you institute to avoid a repeat performance?

_____

_____

_____

_____

Notes

1. Cloud data set software can recognize thresholds, and issue alerts based on pre-programmed criteria. Visual dashboards with drop-down menus can be shared, configured on the fly, and incorporate outside data sources. See Handley, R. (2018, August 2). Soracom adds provisioning service for IOT devices in field, serverless visual dashboard for IOT application services. *RFID Journal.* Retrieved from http://www.rfidjournal.com/articles/view?17724/4

2. Social ranking is a reality in some places. See Ma, A. (2018, October 29). China has started ranking citizens with a creepy "social credit" system—here's what you can do wrong, and the embarrassing, demeaning ways they can punish you. Retrieved from https://www.businessinsider.com/china-social-credit-system-punishments-and-rewards-explained-2018-4, along with Botsman, R. (2017, October 21). Big data meets big brother as China moves to rate its citizens. *Business Insider.* Retrieved from https://www.wired.co.uk/article/chinese-government-social-credit-score-privacy-invasion. Low scores can result

in being banned from luxury hotels, higher education, and train or air travel. Participation in the rating system will be mandatory by 2020.

3. Some information contained in the above scenario was modified and adapted from the blog post "RFID up close and personal." See Gilbert, J. A. (2015, September 13). RFID up close and personal [Blog post]. Retrieved from https://organizedforefficiency.com/rfid-up-close-and-personal/

5

The Bystander Effect and Mobbing at Work

The Problem and Definition

You may have witnessed or experienced the following behaviors more than once:

> It's Monday and an unexpected horror scene unfolds. Unprovoked and on a roll, an employee erupts during a meeting and shouts at a fellow coworker. Following the assault (and in a feeding frenzy), bully minions run to the abuser's side. In the following weeks, people who were previously supportive feign ignorance. They pretend like the attack didn't happen, and they treat targets like pariahs.

> If you witness bullying at work, what should you do?

Because saying nothing is easier, some people lapse into the "silent and unsupportive" category more times than they would like to admit. Although staying in the background is self-protective, it can result in

How to Transform Workplace Bullies Into Allies, pages 101–117
101

groupthink where people choose to self-censor and hide their feelings instead of speaking their minds. When NASA management pushed for the Challenger shuttle launch despite the evidence that O-rings could malfunction in cold weather, Morton Thiokol employees, under duress, supported their decision.

Discomfort with the status quo, a desire to challenge authority, and a deep sense of conviction are characteristics of organizational change agents. Sherron Watkins (who alerted former Enron CEO Kenneth Lay of potential accounting fraud), recalls the inspiration she received from a quote incorrectly attributed to Martin Luther King Jr., which—ironically— was printed on her Enron notepads: "Our lives begin to end the day we become silent about things that matter."[1] Watkins did not fall into the category of troublemaker. She was loyal, genuinely concerned, and terrified about the damage that could occur if conditions at her company did not change. She demonstrated courage in a situation where free expression could result in profound discomfort. Respect is what Robert Solomon and Kathleen Higgins in their book *A Short History of Philosophy* call "the essential virtue."[2] A respect for justice incites a willingness to withstand hostility and promote ethics at work.

Bystanding occurs when people let the situation take the lead,[3] and when they are silent, assenting crowd members. "I want to be part of it," "I don't want to make waves," "I want to be the 'good' employee," "I want bosses to like me," "I don't want to get in trouble/stir the pot/create a stir" mentality predominates within toxic firms, and thus witnesses are reluctant to step forth and share their unique accounts of abuse.[4] The silence of surrounding onlookers can amplify the voices of people who abuse their colleagues or who actively support the abusers. Professor of Psychology Dan Olweus, a leader in school bullying prevention (and creator of the Olweus® Bullying Prevention Program) describes a continuum of bystander support, one that ranges from people who act as spectators to those who proactively support targets. Workers may be reluctant to challenge their aggressive peers because doing so may place them in the same predicament as targeted coworkers. In *Christ in the Margins*, authors Robert Lentz and Edwina Gateley describe "crusaders" as courageous souls whose willingness to "sacrifice for other people [and for a larger cause] make them extraordinary."[5] One supportive voice can triumph if it gathers enough champions. The "Bystander Continuum" depicts the positive impact of people who are supportive of targets and, conversely, the fallout from those who stand to the side or who actively participate in the abuse.

The Bystander Continuum

Less supportive   More supportive

Bully Minions...	Fallout	Timid Onlookers...	Fallout	Target Heroes*...	Outcome
support bullies they regard as heroes by contributing "with their own [slanderous] variation of ... assault" [6] or silent approval.	People act as spectators while bullies clobber a hapless target, saying nothing because they don't wish to be associated with a "marked" individual. Bullies and their minions become more powerful.	disapprove of the abuse but say nothing to avoid being "steamrolled" [7] by bullies and their minions.	Bullies and their backup interpret inaction as a nod of approval. Bullying becomes commonplace, because there is no countervailing force.	proactively behave as peacemakers to address the situation, effective in setting an example even though they may act alone.	They set a positive standard and diminish the occurrence of bullying at work. They attract like-minded people who feel emboldened to speak.

* Information from Olweus, D. (2001). Peer harassment: A critical analysis and some important issues. In J. Juvonen, & S. Graham (Eds.), *Peer harassment in school: The plight of the vulnerable and victimized.* New York, NY: The Guilford Press.

Culture plays a large role in determining whether managers cut mobbing, or gang bullying, off at the pass or whether they allow it to metastasize across departmental boundaries.[8] Singular focus on the "bully," "bad apple," "asshole," or abuser misses the role of top management (and human resources) in creating conditions where employees behave solely in their self-interest.[9] Top leadership sets the tone, and a zero-tolerance policy, or its converse, creates an environment where abuse can occur.

Subordinates who are reluctant to question authoritarian bosses,[10] deference to corporate bullies, and an obsessive need for rule conformance[11] result in exploitation and maltreatment that destroy reciprocal dialogue.[12] The type of bystander that appears at work depends largely upon organizational culture. Toxic, abusive companies encourage an "ends justify the means" mentality within their workers. Some people choose bystanding to avoid suffering backlash or incurring the label of bully. The most productive behavior occurs in people-centered organizations, where members are supportive and where sniping is discouraged. Leaders set the tone that determines which organizational type will emerge.

Organization Type		
Toxic (abusive)	**Laissez-Faire (no rules)**	**People-Centered (proactive)**
Mobbers: Attack targets in meetings because they see management engage in similar actions and because they see no consequences for behaving poorly. They try to court favor with their bosses and senior employees by attacking disliked coworkers.	**Cliques:** Exclude employees who refuse to play by their rules. They enjoy making a spectacle of "outsiders" by ostracizing them and by trying to make them feel uncomfortable.	**Community:** Members are part of an inclusive, supportive network that proactively helps employees. If workers are targeted by an occasional wrongdoer, target heroes engage the bully head on to effectively defuse the conflict.[13]
Bully minions: Gang up on targets to support the bully and the abuser's position. They rationalize the abuse as punishment that targets deserve.	**Onlookers:** Do not support the target purely out of self-interested concern. They feel an overwhelming sense of relief when they are bypassed for abuse. These people are concerned first and foremost with avoiding punishment.	**Supporters:** Affirm the "target hero" in both chastising bullies and in eliminating abusive claims.* Hero behavior happens in the target's presence (during face-to-face attacks) and behind the scenes when targets are the brunt of gossip or online libel.
Targets: Roll with the punches, keep their mouths shut, and accept blame without protest. They suffer psychological and physical symptoms from the abuse.	**Survivors:** Sit by themselves. They feel isolated because they are the target of repeated sniper attacks at work.	**Affiliates:** Feel part of an organization that embraces them and quickly handles unfairness.

* Information from Olweus, D. (2001). Peer harassment: A critical analysis and some important issues. In J. Juvonen, & S. Graham (Eds.), *Peer harassment in school: The plight of the vulnerable and victimized.* New York, NY: The Guilford Press.

Bullies gain momentum in toxic companies when they're granted accolades and acceptance.[14]

Hear No Evil, See No Evil, Speak No Evil Bystanders

Illustration by Middle Tennessee State University

> Witnesses to abuse are not innocent; they are vicariously guilty of coworker dismemberment and are an integral component of a seedier agenda.[15]

Bystanders can behave as part of a larger network, or mob, that acts in tandem and coalesces into a powerful force.

Mobbers, or active bystanders, reap secondhand rewards[16] of:

- social prestige, from supporting a popular or perceived "strong" bully;
- approval from peers who mock "weaklings" unable to fend for themselves;
- enjoyment from seeing someone else suffer, or schadenfreude.[1] The thrill of seeing pain inflicted on sentient beings occurs in cockfights, dogfights, hazing, sadistic porn, cruelty to animals, violent/slasher movies and/or cinema/TV/lyrics that glorify violence, and in sporting matches with fans spinning out of control. Even children experience vicarious pleasure when they see people kicked, shoved, humiliated, and/or embarrassed[17]— which may explain why high school students at Richmond High School in October 2009 gathered to witness the rape of a fifteen-year-old classmate. Investigators concluded that as word spread, more came to witness, with some joining in.[18]

▪ camaraderie from being part of an "insider" group. The feeling of strength in numbers discourages people from stepping outside a protective clique's net of support and emboldens them to bully targets.

> Coworkers perpetrate mobbing against talented, creative, conscientious employees, those who by contrast make mobbers look bad. A litany of voices compounded by a rank differential may lead other people to believe there is a problem[19] where none exists.

"At work [mobbers appear] as 'cliques,' close-knit groups bound together by a mission to drive out undesirables—[individuals] who threaten their dominance, challenge their agenda, or who violate [mob-accepted] norms."[20]

Reflection

Have you ever watched silently as a colleague was tormented, either at work or at school? Why, in your opinion, do most people do nothing?

_____

_____

_____

_____

Telltale Signs of Mobbing at Work: [22]

▪ A small group speaks first—pulverizing opposition.
▪ Junior workers go out of their way to stay in the good graces of the dominant group, seek agreement, and side against anyone the cabal deems unworthy. In the best-case scenario, they remain silent when these same people are attacked.
▪ Cabal membership demands compliance from lower-ranking employees and from those who are on the periphery of power networks. Members have a history of bullying coworkers out of the company.

- Gang members spend time spreading negative gossip, exposing colleagues who do not support their positions, and plotting coups against coworkers they consider deviant.
- Everyone remains silent while cabal members or their ringleader overpower meetings.

Stakes at work are high. Paychecks, most-favored employee status, and a range of perks and rewards hang in the balance. "See no evil, hear no evil" bystanders work to be politically correct when they marginalize the people that cabal membership shuns, when they look over their shoulders for cues (that sometimes result in "speaking evil" to impress bosses), and when they act in ways they think cabal membership will reward. One aim of Texaco's top management was to drive some people out of the company[23]—a scheme that can occur when abuse is ignored and encouraged or when employees despise or envy their coworkers.[24] Bari-Ellen Roberts in *Roberts vs. Texaco* describes what she considered a common scenario of black employees who were hired, deprived of opportunities like high-potential assignments and specialized training, then shuttled elsewhere in the company or off premises.

[Mobbers] prey on individuals who outshine peers, with an emphasis on . . . illegitimate climbers. Their approach is systematic, cruel, and unrelenting—[one] designed to break the will of anyone [who is forgetful of] their place.[25]

Scene: Blanche is sideswiped by office sidewinder Albert— Edwin's number one apple-polisher and a member of his inner clique. He has jumped on the bandwagon against Blanche.

Unannounced, Albert showed up at my office.

"I have an idea for a project . . ."

What he wanted was a white paper explaining the differences between U.S. and Malaysian culture—something we'd call "CliffsNotes" for Catug*n expatriates. I'd spent hundreds of hours interviewing off-shore employees and even more time transcribing tape-recorded notes.

I shot Albert an e-copy.

When I walked into his office, he leaned backward—a smirk spreading thin lips like a can opener, out of which crawled small, diabolical, horn-rimmed words.

He eyeballed me.

"I put your name in the footnotes," he said, pausing to savor the moment.

The floor shook.

As if he could toss this big flipper lie in front of me, without creating either stink or ill feeling. It was a slap across the face, corporate-style. But as new kid on the block, what was I going to say? And he knew it.

* * *

Later that afternoon Hazel cornered me in the breakroom.

"Blanche, what's wrong? You don't look so good. What's going on? Did somebody hurt my little Blanchie?"

Her eyes grew wide and her mouth grew small as I told her how Albert had double-crossed me. She put her hands on her hips, lecture-style.

"That Albert, what a bonehead. When he's not following Big Ed around the office, he's looking for new workers to notch his Catug*n belt. Blanche, there's something you need to know. Albert's nobody's friend. He's a user and an opportunist, a greedy self-promoter is what I call him. And I'm not sure what value either he or Korie adds to this company other than smooching Big Ed's heinie."

She grimaced and grabbed my hand.

"Blanche, now you know to keep this under your hat. Nincompoops like Albert are nothing but trouble, watchdogs and lapdogs for top management. The problem is, he's now barking at you. If I were you, I'd put more effort into that plan we talked about."

Insidious office politics result from poor supervisory choices.

Reflection:

If you witness mobbing at work and/or school, how can you be an "upstander," or a positive bystander? How can you behave in the target's best interests?

Bystanding can even extend to small matters. Do you say anything if you're pleased with someone else's performance? Do you extol the virtue of a front-desk clerk, call a manager to the table when you are the recipient of exemplary service, or complete an online review for someone who just made your day? Do you stay on the telephone the half-minute it would take to note a service provider's performance, or do you remain anonymous after they satisfy your needs? It is easy to ignore people if no one else is the wiser. Praise can generate gratitude and positivity[26] in the recipients, and in people who administer the compliments.

Reflection:
How can you incorporate lessons of gratitude into your everyday routine by going against "grab and go" culture?

_____

_____

_____

_____

How Bystanders Can Make a Difference

Proactive bystanding occurs when people know that something is wrong, and when they choose to solve problems. Potential champions and target heroes have an opportunity to change their situation because:[27]

- Emotions generate a contagion effect. People sense either a positive or negative mood and act accordingly. Bystanders can set the tone by affirming positive statements or by challenging aggressive behavior.
- They outnumber bosses and bullies. They have a greater opportunity to support their peers and to recognize them with micro-affirmations. At some companies (like Zappos and Cisco), employees can nominate one another for special recognition and/or cash awards.[28]
- They may hear information from the organizational grapevine that bypasses supervisors, and they can alert management (or the authorities) if a situation has a potential to be explosive. If bystanders think bully grandstanding may occur, they can rally supporters and leaders in the workplace who will address contentious situations. Active bystanders can be reframed as allies who assist colleagues and who pivot negative comments even in the

target's absence. Because of their proximity, bystanders can react immediately, confront the bullies, behave as target heroes, and improve organizational climate. Training on the role of proactive bystanding creates a sense of responsibility and a willingness to intervene.

The Equal Employment Opportunity Commission (EEOC) argues for empowering bystanders as part of a comprehensive strategy to recognize and respond to workplace harassment. At its Select Task Force on the Study of Harassment in the Workplace (STF) meeting, Green Dot etc. Inc. emphasized that businesses can become enmeshed within communities by recognizing that consumers and vendors, along with third parties, are potential bystanders and stakeholders who can benefit from understanding their connection, their ability to effect change, and their responsibility to mitigate abusive conduct by instituting a coordinated change effort.[29]

Bystanders can demonstrate their support for other people through:[30]

■ *Extending friendship.* Striking up a conversation, acting as a sounding board, providing encouragement, introducing employees to powerful network players (a tactic which may discourage future attacks), affirming others' character, and making others aware of company resources. Providing a context for an aggressive colleague's behavior can promote understanding.

Scene: Korie tells Blanche about Edwin's past.

Truth be told, there's a backstory to our boy most people don't know anything about. He was raised by his maternal aunt. I think the reason Edwin became such a Catug*n "yes boy" was that it offered him the security he craved. So that's a reason he defends his company with such a passion— coworkers were the relatives he'd never had, kinspeople he now considers part of his clan.

■ *Looking for ways to be proactive.* Lack of effort is the reason that only 20% of people represent Lawrence Kohlberg's top tier moral category. If bullies don't receive pushback, they may assume that it is okay to continue. Mobbing happens when no one confronts the bully and when people are reluctant to challenge their coworkers. If managers (or the people in charge of meetings) address disrespect, they send an unmistakable message about what behavior is tolerated and about expectations of how to behave. Be the first person to come to a target's aid or to affirm them when they present an idea. Heroes can build positive momentum by taking the high road. They can convert coworkers who behave as holdouts, gawkers, or bully minions. If blaming the victim is a common reaction, try looking at the bigger picture. What circumstances contributed to the incident, and how could they have been prevented? Could you spearhead change by chairing a committee to enact anti-bullying/civility policy? Could you create an internal public service announcement or a respectful interaction campaign? A codetermination council comprised of a cross-section of employees that meets regularly with human resource managers could suggest ideas for improvement. Employee councils provide a venue to express concerns, voice objections to policy, lobby for change, suggest training, and garner support from top management.[31] A large-enough grassroots effort could even affect toxic management, especially if social media broadcasts its efforts in a Twitter #bystander campaign.

▪ *Supporting a targeted coworker.* Incivility is not a spectator sport. *Silent* is another name for *complicit.* In the blog post "Leadership is not About Getting Things Done," David Foote describes the introspection in which leaders should engage: "Think back to one of those moments in your life when someone asked a 'why' question—a question about your own behavior—that exposed a conflict between that behavior and the values you say you believe in. Or, maybe it was a question about the values we all supposedly believe in. In the intervening seconds before anything else happened, perhaps you began to really think about the question and you took a good, hard, honest look in the mirror. Maybe you liked what you saw and decided that particular [moment] was no conflict after all. On the other hand, maybe when you looked in the mirror you saw something you didn't like . . . and you realized that things had to change."[32] Choosing to do the right thing (regardless of what other people do) is empowering. Try putting your colleagues in a position where they can shine.

▪ *Providing affirmations.* Writing an "attaboy" or "attagirl" is a terrific way to reiterate someone's job competence—especially if companies provide a formal portal for recognition. If not, consider penning a letter to the target's boss and sending them a copy. The uplift may be just what they need.

■ *Positively impacting meetings.* One of the ultimate onlooker activities occurs within organizational walls. Meetings can rapidly disintegrate into alpha and subservient roles when the majority remains silent or participates in the charade. Bystanders can:

– *Piggyback on the comments of less-talkative members.* Corroboration increases their confidence and alerts other people that they made valuable contributions. Introverts may contribute more often to meetings that reflect a balance of employee viewpoints. Leaders do not encourage participation by calling on people. They create inclusion by creating an atmosphere in which no one is called out.

– *Refrain from becoming part of the pack.* Some abusers can denigrate lower-ranking employees in a way that makes them look culpable and that seems more like correction than abuse.[33] Scapegoating creates an atmosphere of "haves" and "have nots" within meetings. When bullies choose a public forum to humiliate targets, a pack mentality may result—especially if abusers are in powerful, more-senior positions. A brother or sisterhood of bullies reduces the risk of getting caught and mitigates the possibility of prosecution. Some workers practice "contingent civility," or good manners only to people who pose a threat.

– *Be a change agent.* It only takes one person to set a positive example. Be the change you want to see instead of observing the drama unfold.

Online Resources

■ Active bystander strategies. (n.d.). *Active Bystanders.* Retrieved from http://web.mit.edu/bystanders/strategies/

■ Anonymous Academic. (2015, June 5). "My professor demands to be listed as an author on many of my papers" [Blog post]. Retrieved from https://www.theguardian.com/higher-education-network/2015/jun/05/my-professor-demand-to-be-listed-author-on-research-paper

■ Bryner, J. (2011, December 9). Schadenfreude explained: Why we secretly smile when others fail. [Blog post]. Retrieved from http://www.livescience.com/17398-schadenfreude-affirmation.html

■ Gilbert, J. A. (2011, February 7). Bullying is bad for business [Blog post]. Retrieved from https://organizedforefficiency.com/bullying-is-bad-for-business/

- Gilbert, J. A. (2011, June 16). Preventing the cold war at work [Blog post]. Retrieved from https://organizedforefficiency.com/preventing-the-cold-war-at-work/
- Gilbert, J. A. (2011, August 5). The emperor has no clothes [Blog post]. Retrieved from https://organizedforefficiency.com/the-emperor-has-no-clothes/
- Gilbert, J. A. (2012, August 2). Taking the workplace bully by the horns [Blog post]. Retrieved from https://organizedforefficiency.com/taking-the-workplacebully-by-the-horns/
- Gilbert, J. A. (2015, June 2). The ebb and flow of emotional abuse [Blog post]. Retrieved from https://organizedforefficiency.com/the-ebb-and-flow-of-emotional-abuse/
- Gilbert, J. A. (2015, November 30). Modern day nobility [Blog post]. Retrieved from https://organizedforefficiency.com/modern-day-nobility/
- Riggio, R. E. (2011, January 26). Why workplace bullies thrive: The bystander effect [Blog post]. Retrieved from https://www.psychologytoday.com/blog/cutting-edge-leadership/201101/why-workplace-bullies-thrive-the-bystander-effect
- What is the bystander effect? [Blog post]. (n.d.). Retrieved from https://www.psychologytoday.com/basics/bystander-effect
- What you can do to stop bullies—Be a supportive bystander: Violence, harassment, and bullying fact sheet. (2012, December 14). *Australian Human Rights Commission*. Retrieved from https://www.humanrights.gov.au/what-you-can-do-stop-bullies-be-supportive-bystander-violence-harassment-and-bullying-fact-sheet
- Whitbourne, S. K. (2010, September 28). How and why do we help? From one-ness to we-ness: The courage to be a hero [Blog post]. Retrieved from https://www.psychologytoday.com/blog/fulfillment-any-age/201009/why-and-how-do-we-help
- Workplace bullying: The bully's spell over the bystander (n.d.) [Blog post]. Retrieved from http://www.bullyfreeatwork.com/workplace-bullying-the-bullys-spell-over-the-bystander/

Web Quests

1. After reading "How and Why Do We Help? From One-ness to We-ness: The Courage Needed to be a Hero,"[34] paraphrase tips on how to behave as a proactive bystander.

_____

_____

_____

_____

2. According to your web research, what are some long-term effects of bullying, and what are some intervening variables? What type of situations and conditions might lessen a bully's impact and mitigate the outcomes of mobbing: irritable bowel syndrome, hypervigilance/ PTSD, trouble sleeping/concentrating, withdrawing from work (mentally, and/or physically), organizational departure, and energy diverted from creative pursuits?[35] A "pull yourself up by your own bootstraps" expectation puts the onus of fighting insults on targets, who (because of smear campaigns) may feel debilitated. Toxic companies, the penultimate mobs, spend time gathering evidence against targeted employees—a task that is made easier by anxiety disorders that targets exhibit.[36] "To the extent that managers ignore mobbers or consider their story, overall productivity [may] suffer from psychological withdrawal/physical exit...and from the reluctance of onlookers to challenge [an angry, powerful group]."[37]

_____

_____

_____

_____

3. After watching "Would You Help a Child Being Bullied?"[38] list personality traits of people who come to a target's aid. Also see "What Makes First Responders Run Toward Danger?"[39] web article.

_____

_____

_____

_____

What Would You Do?

1. In a workplace meeting, you notice that Angie (the office bully), enjoys looking big and powerful at her coworkers' expense. She habitually calls out quieter, conscientious employees, ones who are unable to craft an on-the-spot retort. You are a manager at this company. What do you say to Angie and to the bullied employee? Should there be consequences for people who emotionally abuse their colleagues? If so, what should they be?

_____

_____

_____

_____

2. Even though X*YZ Company hasn't provided raises in the past 5 years, employees are afraid to upset the apple cart—unsure of how their bosses might perceive a request for a salary increase. Would you ask for a raise? If so, how would you approach your supervisor? Explore "Bystander Effect: If You Need Help, You'd Better Ask for It"[40] and "How to Ask for a Raise—and Get It"[41] web articles.

_____

_____

_____

_____

3. Frangeline refuses to intervene when she sees coworkers targeted because she is secretly pleased when they suffer. What steps can she take to develop greater empathy and to discontinue watching from afar? See "Six Habits of Highly Empathic People"[42] web article.

---

4. In your clique, the ringleader often shares negative statements about people when they are absent. You know that Buster, the one leading the charge, behaves mercilessly to anyone who takes the smeared party's side. As a bystander, what should you do? If the target hears secondhand about the group smear, what should he/she do? See "The Witness: 6 Steps to Take if You See Workplace Bullying."[43] From your research, what is the best way for employees/students to handle office/classroom gossip?

Assessment

Bully, Bystander, or Intervener?

Respond either "yes" or "no," depending on whether you engaged in the behaviors (below) in the past 12 months:

1. Sat silently while coworkers or colleagues were verbally harassed or emotionally abused in a meeting forum.
2. Voiced an oppositional viewpoint to undermine a colleague.
3. Told someone they appeared passive or fearful after they had been mobbed.
4. Pretended like nothing happened after you saw a person mocked in a public forum.

5. Publicly supported targets during office savagery.
6. Ostracized someone at work or at school.
7. Befriended a new employee/student or office transfer.
8. Failed to acknowledge targets' feelings after a "mobbing" incident.
9. Shouted at and humiliated a colleague in front of other people.
10. Pretended you did not know what targets were talking about when they described a bullying event that you'd witnessed.
11. Refused to apologize after you had hurt someone else.
12. Sat with someone who typically eats alone.
13. Gotten up and moved when a certain person sat at your lunch table.
14. Made sure you were on the "right" side of management—even if their rendering was hurtful or inaccurate.
15. Offered to mentor a "newbie" at work and/or school.
16. Provided helpful advice to a lower-ranking employee.
17. Refused to help to someone in need, when doing so was clearly within your capability.
18. Included an "outcast," one whom people avoided or ignored, within your work/school project.

Give yourself one point for each of the following statements to which you answered "Yes," then total the columns:

Bystander	Bully	Intervener
#1	#2	#5
#4	#3	#7
#8	#6	#12
#10	#9	#15
#14	#11	#16
#17	#13	#18

Inaction (in situations where individuals are targets) occurs often. Your highest column score is an indication of your predominant behavior.

Note

1. In an experiment where subjects were presented with four different tasks (e.g., grinding live bugs, helping the experimenter to grind the live bugs, cleaning filthy toilets, or tolerating ice-cold water) those who chose the "bug killing" task indicated the highest sadism scores of all (see "Everyday sadists."[21]).

6

The Importance of Effective Dialogue

When it occurs seamlessly communication is a social lubricant, a means to inform, enlighten, persuade, uplift, and embrace.[1]

The Problem and Definition

Mutual give and take creates rapport and a platform on which to build relationship, dialogue, and fellowship at work. The average person speaks approximately 16,000 words a day,[1] but they sometimes do not select them with care. Sometimes "conversations can be a form of stealth weaponry...and a very real way" for bullying to occur.[2] If words are cruel, cutting, thoughtless, curt, or shared deliberately to undermine another person, they may create a lasting negative impression.

Irresponsible word choice and an off-putting[3] communication style can sever relationships and contribute to a perception of a hostile work environment. Gruff tone can be more than a bad mood.[4] Words can ruin people's lives, torpedo their careers, and destroy a feeling of mutual safety at work—particularly if targets experience PTSD or other mental health issues as a result.

How to Transform Workplace Bullies Into Allies, pages 119–140
Copyright © 2020 by Information Age Publishing
119

Scene: "Throwing in the kitchen sink."

Partner: You left the air on 70! Our air conditioning bill last month was a whopping $859.00. If you do that again, I'm going to cut off the electric.

You: You think that's bad? At our yard party last Sunday, you "cooked" Pastor Fred's pork chop to a crisp. He almost gagged when he finished his meal.

Partner: Well, that's nothing. Whenever I use the bathroom, I see your nasty clump of hair in the sink. Next time I'm going to throw it on the floor.

Poor word choice can leave lasting scars.[5]

Unilateral directives, criticism, judgment, blame, evasiveness, and mockery are verbal techniques that can intimidate, hatch disgruntlement, and divide a company. But fighting fire with fire will incinerate both parties. People may forget who initiated the fray, but they will always remember who continued a fight.

Examples of aggressive speech include:

- *Speaking incessantly* in a boisterous, loud-mouthed manner
- *"Butting in"* to other people's conversations
- *Finger wagging*
- *Mocking*—embarrassing someone by imitating their speech[6]
- *Objectification*—speaking about someone in the third person when they are within earshot. "He's not coming with us, is he?"
- *Interrupting*—knocking someone off the conversational stage when they are in mid-sentence
- *Funneling*—relaying messages through a third party

Example: Instead of asking you herself, your coworker instructs her assistant to ask if you can cover her shift.

- *Unloading*—asking under a false pretense to obtain favors

   Example: a coworker enters your office under the guise of a friendly visit.

   Coworker: Do you have plans for lunch?

   You: No, what did you have in mind?

> **Coworker:** Well, I wanted to see the new museum exhibit, so can you pick up our copies?

- *Cold prickly*—conveying irritation, annoyance, and offense when someone asks a question, then officiously stating your position instead of respectfully addressing their concern

  > **Coworker:** Could you explain our client's perspective? I want to make sure that I understand this project's history before I begin the report.
  >
  > **You:** I thought I made myself clear.

Exercise:

Which barriers to communication have you experienced, and how did they make you feel? How do you think recipients felt when you communicated aggressively with them?

_____

_____

_____

_____

Where Do Barriers Begin?

Mind clutter can be disseminated by open mouths.[7] In the heat of the moment, people may lack circumspection and talk about events that have nothing to do with the conversation at hand. Throwing in the kitchen sink may score someone points, but it does little to solve a problem. Words solidify thought into form. Cleaning up a mess before it leaves our mouths can prevent future conversational regret.

thoughts ⇒ words ⇒ actions ⇒ habits ⇒ character ⇒ destiny

Information from Frank Outlaw, late president of the BI-LO stores.

Misguided words can represent malicious intent. Gossip is an attempt to self-aggrandize through deriding its subjects in absentia and by depriving them of an opportunity to defend themselves.

Example:

Coworker: Did you hear what Hazel did at the office party? A picture's worth a thousand words. I'll show you some on my cell phone.

Reflection:

If you overhead a colleague deriding another person, what could you say to bolster the target and to turn the conversational tide in their favor? See "Gossip Kills Possibility"[8] web article.

_____

_____

_____

_____

Lucy Leu, the author of *Nonviolent Communication Companion Workbook*[9] explains that we can uncover hidden issues and empathically connect with other people by asking them a series of questions. Explosive speech and an immature approach to problem-solving may be anger in disguise.[10] People who respond with a short fuse, and those who run for cover, can allow conflict to fester.

Assessment

1. Someone cuts you off in traffic. Do you
   a. speed up to the other car and make menacing gestures while yelling epithets out the window?
   b. let drivers go their way, realizing that life is short and not everything is a battle worth fighting?
   c. feel ashamed that you drove in a way that evoked someone's ire?
2. After badgering you for several weeks, a colleague arrives at your office. She tells you to place her name on your applications for organizational awards. You handle the situation by
   a. calmly explaining that mutuality assumes equal work on behalf of both parties.
   b. conceding her point and agreeing to include her on future applications—even when you know they contributed little or nothing to your work.

    c. angrily explaining that you have already put them as project co-author when they didn't deserve it, and that you do not intend to give them any more freebies.

3. A colleague lashes out at you in a meeting. To resolve the conflict, you
    a. ask to meet them at a mutually agreeable time and try to reestablish a cordial working relationship.
    b. give them the cold shoulder and eliminate them from future dealings.
    c. go out of your way to appease them to prevent future outbursts.

4. A "friend" explains that you need to smile more and appear less rigid. Do you
    a. tell her that you can recount any number of negative things about her?
    b. ask for clarification and more information so that you can improve?
    c. explain that we are all works in progress and then change the topic?

5. A team member announces in front of other coworkers that you need to bring doughnuts to the next project meeting. You
    a. bring a dozen assorted types the following week, just to be nice.
    b. explain that you've done that for two meetings and now it's their turn.
    c. suggest that you would like to give someone else the opportunity to bring doughnuts. You then continue with the meeting.

6. Your friend asks if you can give her a ride to an upcoming party. You respond by
    a. explaining that you don't like to carpool and that you'll see her later that evening.
    b. giving her a ride, but later feeling resentful.
    c. telling her that you will make your own arrangements.

7. A colleague tells you how his boss made inappropriate advances toward him. You
    a. explain that it's people like him who allow things like that to happen in the first place.
    b. listen to his story, then offer solutions based on what you think would be the most beneficial course of action.
    c. secretly wonder if you contributed to the problem.

8. A coworker is on the phone when you walk into his office. Do you
    a. excuse yourself, then visit later?
    b. stomp your feet and gesture that he should hang up the phone?
    c. apologize profusely when you see him in the hallway and explain that it will never happen again?

9. A friend who refuses to acknowledge your greeting scowls at you instead. Your future responses entail
   a. ignoring this person and returning the favor.
   b. asking her if you have done something wrong.
   c. continuing to courteously greet her because you realize that you are not responsible for her feelings.
10. Your teammate chews you out in front of your peers. In your response to her, do you
    a. ask if there's anything you can do to help?
    b. up the ante and return volley with your own storehouse of homespun profanity?
    c. explain that the behavior is unacceptable and that you wish to be treated in a professional, respectful manner at work?

Scoring:		
Column A	**Column B**	**Column C**
#1a	#1b	#1c
#2c	#2a	#2b
#3b	#3a	#3c
#4a	#4c	#4b
#5b	#5c	#5a
#6c	#6a	#6b
#7a	#7b	#7c
#8b	#8a	#8c
#9a	#9c	#9b
#10b	#10c	#10a

Column A indicates an aggressive approach to problem-solving that may make you feel better in the moment, but it wins you few friends.

Column B indicates an emotionally mature person who handles work issues respectfully, head-on, and on-point.

Column C indicates people who give away the store. Emotional abuse survivors internalize a sense of inferiority and previous disempowerment,[11] and they may act fearful.

Emotionally mature people:

■ Respectfully ask for what they need instead of assuming they will be a bother.
■ Safeguard their personal boundaries from encroachment.
■ Strive to be a part of the group without taking center stage.

▪ Behave kindly toward themselves through positive self-talk and realistic expectations. They do not overextend themselves trying to keep other people happy.
▪ They use communication that excludes innuendo, sarcasm, and bashful pseudo-solicitation.[12]

Communication Styles		
Emotionally Immature: Aggressive	**Emotionally Mature: Assertive**	**Emotionally Abused: Acquiescent**
Threaten other people to get their own way.	Acknowledge when they're wrong and move forward.	Accept unsolicited advice. They assume they are the ones at fault.
Desire to be the center of attention.	Realize that sometimes other people like to shine and look for ways to help them do so.	Feel undeserving of awards and recognition and most times feel too embarrassed to accept them.
Use humor at someone else's expense.	Laugh with people, not at them; act lightheartedly to relieve the tension.	Say nothing if another person makes mean-spirited jokes. They fear retribution.
Regard the feelings of other people as unimportant.	Politely ask how colleagues feel when they sense a shift in mood.	Accept what other people say as gospel and place more credence on outside opinions.
Feel like they have won when they disrespect other people.	Wisely choose and calibrate their words.	Suffer from low self-esteem and behave self-effacingly.
Find giving compliments uncomfortable.	Actively look for ways to express appreciation through "lavish … praise" and "hearty … approbation."[13]	Shrink from the spotlight even if stepping forth could highlight an issue or a moral cause.
Ensure that personal connections are one-down, didactic, and authoritarian.	Express viewpoints in a forthright manner using "I" statements.	Readily accommodate the feelings and desires of other people at the expense of their own.
Mentally torture other people to feel powerful and in control.	Mentor people who are learning the ropes.	Feel like they have little to offer and easily give up.
Always put themselves first.	Remain flexible in the face of disagreement.	Possess an overwhelming need to please other people.
Engage in revenge and retaliation to even the scales.	Ensure that other people are not the recipients of any foul moods or angry outbursts; rarely hold grudges and often attempt to repair poor relationships.	Avoid confronting people who hurt or disrespect them. Their reluctance perpetuates a cycle of abuse.

Source: Information adapted from Gibson, L. C. (2015). *Adult children of emotionally immature parents: How to heal from distant, rejecting, or self-involved parents.* Oakland, CA: New Harbinger; and Brown, N. W. (2008). *Children of the self-absorbed: A grown-up's guide to getting over narcissistic parents.* Oakland, CA: New Harbinger.

Exercise:

You end up doing Myra's share of work projects, along with your own. How can you address her lack of contribution and preserve your friendship?

_____

_____

_____

_____

Scenarios

Whom do you consider the leader and why?

- Frank never apologizes. He feels that once things blow over, everyone should move on and forget about his misbehavior.
- Marj assumes that she's the one at fault without hearing the facts. Sticking to her guns and presenting her viewpoint don't come easily.
- Marv rarely loses his temper. But when he does, he is quick to apologize and make amends. His teammates cut him some slack because they realize he has a stressful position.
- Sheryl has a short fuse. She repents only if people she hurts are well-connected to powerful network players, and only if she thinks they might cause her a problem. With everyone else, she says nothing and goes about her business.

_____

_____

_____

_____

_____

_____

_____

Scene: New hire Blanche is blindsided by someone she considered both a mentor and friend.

I had to talk to someone. My workplace mentor and Catug*n soul mate Korie would know what to do. She had agreed to meet me at O'Chanahan's at 6 o'clock sharp. I rehearsed what to say by preparing out loud and trying to stay calm—but my voice was quivering so hard I almost choked on my words. I arrived at the restaurant ahead of time.

*   *   *

Crackling leather signaled the arrival of Catug*n's crown princess. She was, as usual, decorated from head to toe. Fiñera del Gado peau de soie, translucent light grey silk stockings with dark back seams, a two-piece tweed gabardine suit accentuated with a sky-blue cashmere sweater. She wore jewelry, rings, bracelets, and a matching semi-precious headband that completed her look. "Fierce" was I think Ed's typical assessment. Her Catug*n lapel pin flickered in the candlelight.

"Penny for your thoughts," she said, absentmindedly adjusting her skirt and looking past me to the next booth.

At this point I should have been able to spot a wolf in sheep's clothing. But some office politicos are so skilled and so subtle that their double en-tendre slips beneath the radar.

I practically whispered.

"Can I tell you something?"

"Of course!" she reassuringly cooed. "You're one of my BFFs; you're my sister."

I dropped my shoulders and took a deep breath.

"Can you remember anyone, any person in the history of this company who's ever felt harassed by Edwin?"

Her back jerked up ramrod straight, and she began reading me my rights regarding the proper attitude at work. She scanned my face like a border patrol agent.

"Big Daddy's just a good ol' boy. I don't think anything about it when he puts his arm around me or anybody else. He's one of most successful vice presidents we've ever had. Just last year he was named Catug*n's most promising new executive."

This reasoning caught me off guard—but in a way it almost made sense. Ed's words echoed in my mind: "We here at Catug*n keep things in our family..." The problem is that he'd ceased to be familial, unless you con-sider the incestuous uncle a part of the family tree. She sat me down.

"This company took a chance on you—Ed more than anyone—and if you think he's putting the moves on you, missy, then I think you're the one who needs to have her head examined."

She pierced me with a dagger stare. Her loyalty to Papa Bear apparently ran deeper than our sisterly ties.

"If you intend to stay here, I suggest you get with the program and keep that goody-two-shoes little mouth of yours shut."

Korie was determined to keep the status quo. With Big Ed's long-established tenure, filing complaints was almost impossible. Rumor had it he'd either bought off or silenced any woman who'd cried foul. And my new sister/girlfriend had just informed me that any sharing of my "crazy inner rumblings" would be career suicide.[2]

She changed the topic.

"Blanche, tell me about your new project. You know, that one where Albert made you first author? From what I hear, the client just loved it. If I were you young lady I'd count my blessings and be grateful."

Exercise

What communication style did Korie demonstrate (e.g., aggressiveness, assertiveness, or acquiescence)? What style did Blanche demonstrate? Rewrite the above dialogue so that both individuals communicate in a more respectful, emotionally intelligent manner. When you are done, see page 139 for the key.

When EQ Meets What's Inside our Mouths!

A world of difference exists between *relatedness,* or a purely transactional form of exchange, and *relationship*—where people experience and understand one another.[14] Mutuality takes effort and an assessment of what to say and how to say it. Bullies may be unaware of how other people perceive them.[15] Education on how to provide feedback, listen with respect, solve problems, express disagreement, and apologize when they hurt someone's feelings[16] may result in more effective communication—and in an understanding of how they affect their colleagues at work. People can improve their conversations through an objective analysis of their tone, communication tactics, and personal style.[17]

If someone is itching for a showdown, use a soft answer as an emotional fire extinguisher. In *Adult Children of Emotionally Immature Parents: How to Heal from Distant, Rejecting, or Self-Involved Parents,*[18] author Lindsay Gibson describes emotional maturity as a desire to:

- *Accept reality*—railing against what is does little to reverse the undesirable circumstance.
- *Address people without flying off the handle*—behaving hysterically, or shouting. What you see is what you get, and what you see is consistent across situation, place, and time.
- *Temper speech*—or at the very least, recognize discomfort in their conversational partners.
- *Let others off the hook* and realize that all of us are prone to occasional judgment gaffes. When individuals feel heard, they become less guarded, ready to explore alternatives, and increasingly receptive to problem-solving. Although author Marshall Rosenberg eschews outright aggression,[19] he indicates that "protective force" may be necessary to counteract ignorance. He defines ignorance as a desire to punish someone who caused us harm and/or to vindicate a trampled ego. In his opinion, blame and judgment prompt retaliation instead of contrition. Nonviolent communication (NVC) techniques of vulnerability, mutual sharing, openness, and equality provide an alternative to verbal fistfights. Organizations can create a baseline for civil conduct by benchmarking companies known for their civil cultures, and by "establishing an industry roundtable to share [anti-bullying] information."[20]
- *Anticipate the needs of other people* through calibrating words and adjusting responses. Empathic communicators encourage their

coworkers by making entrées to powerful employees and by defending them when they are attacked. In toxic companies, a free-for-all (with unwritten rules, unfortunate losers, and emboldened winners who convert ill-gotten currency into relational affluence) can occur. Companies where people are responsible and accountable for their word choice[21] promote civil culture.

▪ *Give a little to get a little,* and when they get a little they give back! Relationships are satisfying, mutual, and reciprocal. People high in emotional quotient, or EQ are quick to give other people the benefit of the doubt.

▪ *Appear open to change and feedback* because they realize that learning is a continual process and that every situation offers the possibility for a reboot.

▪ *Tell the truth,* apologize without prodding, and in the words of Mary Kay Ash, "make [others] feel important" by emphasizing their best traits. Emotionally mature people engage their brains in rational processing before their tongues have a chance to intervene. Taking offense is easy,[22] but responding (and not reacting) takes work.

Reflection

On the Communication Styles Assessment, indicate your behaviors that fall into either Columns A or C. Using information on pages 129–130, what behaviors can you change? How can you change them?

_____

_____

_____

_____

_____

_____

Exemplary Communication at Work

A key to effective communication is a trained, informed, and well-equipped workforce.[23] Willis Towers Watson Communication ROI Studies found that the most effective communicators (those in the top third of survey responses):[24,25,26]

- *Engaged* employees as partners, shareholders, and co-owners. Shared governance was characteristic of high performers, ones that solicited employee opinions. Effective companies "demonstrat[e] the courage to hear and share tough feedback," and let employees know where they stand so that performance issues can be addressed honestly.[27] Sugarcoating and/or glossing over potential problems, avoiding performance meetings altogether, or providing false information to avoid having an uncomfortable conversation can enable employee failure. New employees were integrated through onboarding programs that socialized them through a step-by-step introduction to company values, operating systems, and employees in disparate parts of the firm. Onboarding programs provide a springboard for conversations about a company's mode of conduct and the image it wishes to project.
- *Focused* on the customer. At exemplary companies, internal customers understand how their work affects end users. This understanding enhances employee engagement and financial performance. Intrinsic motivation increases when workers are fully trained, when they understand the intersection of their tasks with similar job functions, and when they appreciate their effect on people who use the company's product or service.
- *Worked to manage change*, instead of dictating what would occur. Modifications among top communicators were planned, tweaked, and adjusted before they were unleashed onto even a single employee. Productivity increases when employees support the company vision, when they know what's expected, and when they have a say in the process. The most effective companies solicited their employees' change readiness through two-way communication and prepared them by providing a change rationale. The least effective "charged ahead"[28] without obtaining employee input or a genuine commitment to a planned change effort.
- *Measured* communication effectiveness on strategic business goals, employee retention, and overall workforce productivity.

High performing firms frequently adjust control/feedback loops in response to survey analysis.

- ▪ *Trained* leaders to be impactful communicators. Exemplary companies address issues with a multitude of constituencies before they have an opportunity to morph into problems.

- ▪ *Used* employee satisfaction to brand the company as an employer of choice. Firms that solicit opinions and relay this practice across their communication platforms send a message about what it means to be a "Company X" employee. Transparent two-way techniques, like ones used at GE, include communicating change to external and internal customers; using LinkedIn, a platform where employees congregate, to share news; allowing employees to serve as spokespeople by sharing their stories on internal company media; and disseminating as much information as possible[29] in ways that promote cooperation, mutual support, and synergy among participants. Effective communicators shared good (and not so good) news in a variety of formats, including the Internet. Company status wasn't dispensed on an exclusively need-to-know basis.[30]

Willis Towers Watson Communication ROI Study Report Key Findings			
2007/2008	**2009/2010**	**2011/2012**	**2013/2014**
From 2002 to 2006, effective communicators' shareholder return was 47% higher than lower-performing companies.[31]	From mid-2004 to mid-2009, effective communicators' shareholder return was 47% higher than lower-performing companies.[32]	Effective communicators were 1.7 times more likely to outperform peer companies in metrics of shareholder return, market premium, and RPE (revenue per employee).[33]	Top performers in change management and effective communication were 3.5 times more likely to outperform peer companies in metrics of shareholder return, market premium, and RPE (revenue per employee).[34]

Reflection:

How would you describe the way people communicate with one another at your school or company? Is it toxic or cooperative? What happens to winners, and to losers? Provide a rationale for your description. See "Toxic versus Cooperative Behaviors at Work: The Role of Culture and Leadership in Creating Community-Centered Organizations."[35]

_____

_____

_____

_____

_____

_____

_____

Reflection:

If you are leading a meeting, do you encourage everyone in the group to participate? Some methods to create inclusion within meetings consist of:[36]

- *Nominal Group Technique,* which prevents discussion until everyone has presented an idea or expressed an opinion.
- *Sending an agenda before the meeting.* If meeting participants have an itemized agenda, they may be less likely to interject an irrelevant comment. Covering items one at a time and scheduling a variety of individuals to speak leaves little room for the unexpected. If conversational bullies insist on having their say (along with someone else's), curtail their outbursts by refocusing on the business at hand.
- *Stopping immediately when you witness disrepect.* Reiterate the behavioral expectations and ask to speak with the offending party after the meeting. The person in charge has a mandate to ensure that:
  - All employees who wish to speak are heard, and people who are reluctant to speak are encouraged, supported, and appreciated for their contributions.
  - People do not experience humiliation from bullying or mobbing, either individually or in a group setting.
  - Disrespectful behavior receives (at the very least) verbal sanction. If you are chairing a meeting but you are not the bully's manager, describe the incident to their boss.
- *Letting people know you will be calling on them.* Other ways to generate participation (without putting people on the spot) include suggestion boxes, electronic meetings, surveys, and electronic

polling. Introverts may be fearful of making a mistake, and they may appreciate some time to rehearse. Preparation is key for people who are unaccustomed to speaking in public and for those who feel uncomfortable presenting in front of a group.

Reflection:

If you are a boss, how can you expand the lines of communication between you and your employees? Have you tried:

- *Reinforcing and affirming their importance.* Mary Kay Cosmetics makes employees feel special, loved, admired, and respected by catching employees doing something right, celebrating their achievements, encouraging their progress, and using the sandwich technique to administer feedback. Instead of criticizing, Mary Kay Ash placed a developmental opportunity between two thick layers of praise.

Scene: A boss tactfully makes her employee aware of a skill deficiency.

Boss: I wanted you to know what a great job I think you're doing with our customers. I've received some stellar reviews on how much they appreciate your friendliness, your personal greeting, and your willingness to go the extra mile. Great job! I'm so proud of you.

I think the next step in your development might be to shore up your data-entry skills. For example, if you rush through your end-of-week report, it creates issues for our comptroller, who has to recheck the numbers. Her analysis depends on the accuracy of each person on the team. Your balance was either over or short 4 times last week.

I'm certain that with more instruction, you can be an expert in crafting reports. I've scheduled a general training session for next week; does that work for you? Do you have any questions, and is there anything I can do to help you?

[following the discussion] . . .

I'm so glad I hired you, and that you're a part of our team! Please remember that my door is always open.

- *Building rapport.* Jack Canfield, coauthor of *The Success Principles: How to Get From Where You are to Where You Want to Be,* asks his employees to rate their relationship on a scale of 1–10. If any rating is less than a 10, he asks what he should do to improve. Although it's difficult to hear no-holds-barred input, he acknowledges that the improvement it sparks in the relationship (and ultimately, in productivity) is worth the effort. If leaders fail to listen or disregard workers' feelings, employees may find an alternative means of expressing their dissatisfaction.[3]

▪ *Practicing vulnerability.* In the movie *Dances With Wolves,* Kevin Costner rides with his arms outstretched into enemy territory—where surprisingly, the enemy doesn't fire at him. As a boss, have you asked your subordinates the following questions: "How do I come across?"; "What would you change?"; and "What can I do to keep you?" Do you know if your workers are happy? Are they disgruntled with how you transact your business or with how you treat them? If you sense that something is amiss (or if someone is avoiding you), talk to that person or be proactive and schedule a meeting.

Online Resources

▪ Adams, S. (2014, November 18). How to communicate effectively at work [Blog post]. Retrieved from https://www.forbes.com/sites/susanadams/2014/11/18/how-to-communicate-effectively-at-work-4/#3928e65700c7

▪ Ashkenas, R. (2011, February 15). Your communications may not be communicating [Blog post]. Retrieved from https://hbr.org/2011/02/your-communications-may-not-be.html

▪ Gilbert, J. A. (2014, April 22). Bullying can wreak your personal brand [Blog post]. Retrieved from https://organizedforefficiency.com/bullying-can-wreak-your-personal-brand/

▪ Gilbert, J. A. (2014, September 7). Populate your thoughts with the positive [Blog post]. Retrieved from https://organizedforefficiency.com/populate-your-thoughts-with-the-positive/

▪ Gilbert, J. A. (2014, October 14). Compliments vs. recompense [Blog post]. Retrieved from https://organizedforefficiency.com/compliments-vs-recompense/

▪ Gilbert, J. A. (2015, January 6). The slick surface of organizational politics [Blog post]. Retrieved from https://organizedforefficiency.com/the-slick-surface-of-organizational-politics/

▪ Gilbert, J. A. (2015, April 12). Communication is not a one-size-fits-all [Blog post]. Retrieved from https://organizedforefficiency.com/communication-is-not-a-one-size-fits-all/

- Gilbert, J. A. (2015, December 30). The inconvenience of being nice [Blog post]. Retrieved from https://organizedforefficiency .com/7349-2/
- Gilbert, J. A. (2016, April 5). Honoring others with humility [Blog post]. Retrieved from https://organizedforefficiency.com/ honoring-others-with-humility/
- Giles, S. (2016, March 15). The most important leadership competencies, according to leaders around the world [Blog post]. Retrieved from https://hbr.org/2016/03/the-most-important -leadership-competencies-according-to-leaders-around-the-world
- Item 10: I have a best friend at work. (1999, May 26). *Gallup.* Retrieved from http://www.gallup.com/businessjournal/511/ item-10-best-friend-work.aspx
- Kerpen, C. (2016, June 6). The secret to effective communication in 2016 [Blog post]. Retrieved from https://www.forbes.com/sites/ carriekerpen/2016/06/06/the-secret-to-effective-communication -in-2016/#15533aa27e73
- Myatt, M. (2012, April 4). 10 communication secrets of great leaders [Blog post]. Retrieved from https://www.forbes.com/sites/ mikemyatt/2012/04/04/10-communication-secrets-of-great -leaders/#376444b922fe
- Satell, G. (2015, February 6). Why communication is today's most important skill [Blog post]. Retrieved from https://www.forbes .com/sites/gregsatell/2015/02/06/why-communication-is-todays -most-important-skill/#33a3d84e1100

Web Quests

1. On the *Forbes* website, search for articles about career-damaging communication techniques. Which do you consider the top three (and why), and how would you as a leader make your employees aware of these? What type of consequences would you like to see for people who intentionally violate workplace norms? See "A Failure to Communicate"[37] web article.

   _____

   _____

   _____

   _____

2. Search for ways to interact with people that make them feel engaged. From your web research, what are some of these?

   _____

   _____

   _____

   _____

3. Conduct a search for companies that use innovative ways to recognize workers and ones that use praise as a motivator. List ways that coworkers can communicate appreciation to one another. See "Thriving Cultures are Built With Recognition and Praise"[38] web article.

   _____

   _____

   _____

   _____

What Would You Do?

1. Sally has everything going for her; the "correct" educational pedigree, a sophisticated, high-class wardrobe, and a keen knowledge of industry trends. Unfortunately, when she opens her mouth all people can do is cringe and hope the onslaught will end soon. The problem is that Sally doesn't have a filter—or a clue. What advice would you give her? See "13 Things You Should Never Say at Work,"[39] and "10 Etiquette Rules for Meetings That Every Professional Should Know"[40] web articles.

_____

_____

_____

_____

2. Whenever coworkers speak to Marla about prickly office issues, she clams up, looks the other way, and refuses to speak. They know that something is wrong, but her uncommunicative style precludes them from quickly resolving an issue. How would you as a leader create a welcoming culture, one where employees feel comfortable speaking their minds? See "See 6 Ways to Get People to Open up,"[41] and "5 Simple Things You Can Do to Get People to Speak up in Meetings"[42] web articles.

_____

_____

_____

_____

3. Dale is the behavioral opposite of Marla. He speaks nonstop, interrupts his colleagues, and brags incessantly about his most recent achievement. What advice would you give Dale to become more of a team player? See "Study Reveals a Conversation Trick That

Motivates People to Change Their Behavior"[43] and "5 Steps for Dealing With People Who Talk Too Much"[44] web articles.

"Raise your words, not your voice. It is rain that grows flowers, not thunder." —Rumi

Key: *Scene in which new hire Blanche is blindsided by someone she considered both a mentor and friend*

In your rewrite, consider the following points:

- Blanche is about to approach her coworker with a sensitive workplace issue and include her in a problem that does not involve her. Before scheduling the meeting, Blanche should have shared more specifics about what she wanted to discuss and given Korie the option to show up—instead of implying, "I need to see you, but I can't tell you what it's about" over the phone.
- Korie behaves aggressively toward Blanche. The purpose of a fact-finding mission is to uncover the root of a problem and to offer potential solutions. Nonviolent communication techniques and emotional intelligence suggest that no matter how a situation is presented, the receiver's job is to peel back the layers of fear, incivility, and obfuscation to unearth the issues at hand.
- Wallowing in misery prolongs our agony. Active strategies, such as reaching out to former employees, contacting coworkers who behave as "resistance" behind the scenes, researching the best way to deal with a stalker, talking to an attorney, and contacting the EEOC are likely to yield problem resolutions. Similarly, in *Roberts vs. Texaco*, Bari-Ellen Roberts reached out to activist groups and civic organizations, met with colleagues who experienced similar difficulties, and ultimately initiated a class-action lawsuit against an oil and gas behemoth.

Notes

1. Dr. Matthias Mehl found that women spoke on average 16,215 words per day, while men spoke 15,669 words. Huynh, J. (2014, June 19). Study finds no difference in the amount men and women talk. *University of Arizona Undergraduate Research Program.* Retrieved from https://ubrp.arizona.edu/study-finds-no-difference-in-the-amount-men-and-women-talk/

2. According to a U.S. Equal Employment Opportunity Commission report, 4/5 of harassed employees choose not to file a formal complaint, and 3/4 at work remain silent (regarding the incident) with managers or human resource officers. EEOC files seven suits against harassment. (2018, June 14). U.S. Equal Employment Opportunity Commission. Retrieved from https://www.eeoc .gov/eeoc/newsroom/release 6-14-18.cfm

3. One response to pay inequity at work is employee theft. A *Journal of Applied Psychology* article reported when groups were not told the reason for their pay reduction, employee theft increased. Greenberg, J. (1990). Employee theft as a reaction to underpayment inequity: The hidden cost of pay cuts. *Journal of Applied Psychology, 75*(5), 561–568. https://doi.org/10.1037/0021-9010.75.5.561

How to Fix It? Communication

7

Bullying and Electronic Communication

E-comm: Impersonality solidified in the matrix of instant sending.

The Problem and Definition

Electronic communication (e-comm) happens at the click of a mouse, with off-the-cuff electronic commentary made in fluid, rapidly changing mediums. The Internet allows for 24/7 broadcasting from a superhighway that reaches billions. Instantly. Although the speed at which e-comm occurs and the potential for worldwide circulation should make users think carefully before they post, sometimes the opposite occurs: posting without thinking and without any thought to repercussions. Websites, blog posts, Tweets, uploaded Instagram photos, YouTube videos, livestreams to Facebook, wikis, and the gamut of social media[1] are places where people can become public spectacles without their knowledge or consent. Given that approximately four billion people have Internet connections, the potential for hostile online interaction is immense.[1]

Internet trolls, haters, and anonymous posters broadcast pejorative messages that leave recipients covered with indelible digital smear and

How to Transform Workplace Bullies Into Allies, pages 143–161
Copyright © 2020 by Information Age Publishing
143

that destroy reputations without the possibility of recourse or remedial justice. Afterward, the original poster may quickly forget what happened, even as the message sent around the world gathers steam and is transmitted into forums where it can be repurposed, shared, edited, cropped, taken out of context, and circulated in places the original poster had never imagined—all without any vetting of the truth of its content. Digital discourse enables anyone to say anything about anyone at any time. Instant dissemination may incite arrogance or a sense of entitlement[2] in which posters minimize the impact of their disparaging remarks and fail to consider their impact upon targets. The immediacy at which Internet communication occurs has spawned web impertinence, or cyberbullying, which is comprised of false or defamatory communication within: "(i) text messaging; (ii) pictures, photographs or video clips; ... (iv) e-mail; (v) chat rooms; (vi) instant messaging; (vii) websites; and (viii) social networking websites,"[3] intended to shame, harass, manipulate or debase[4] through exclusion, humiliation, or impersonation.[5]

E-comm removes people from looking someone in the eye and from carefully choosing their words. Targets may feel even more crushed when negative comments about them continue past work and school hours. People can implode others' lives from behind an LCD screen.

Cases in Point:

- *Tyler Clementi,* a Rutgers student, jumped off the George Washington bridge after he discovered his roommate had been secretly filming him and using Twitter to report on encounters he had with another man.
- *Phoebe Prince,* a 15-year-old Irish immigrant, hanged herself after months of relentless gang taunting.

Celebrities' looks, and even their personal lives and families, have become fodder for Twitter trolls who (in some cases) issued death threats and shared jokes about their appearance.[6] Research has found that individuals troll for *lulz* (sadistic pleasure[7]) and that measures of sadism are positively correlated with trolling activity. There is a distinction between Internet trolling, which consists of deliberately inciting controversy where none existed or posting "shocking" commentary on other people's e-comm, and cyberbullying, in which a barrage of pejorative, accusatory messages that are intended to create fear or psychological distress are posted about someone else's media activity[8] or about them personally. Newer social media (like Formspring) allow for open-ended questions to which anonymous, and sometimes cruel or rancorous, responses[9] are posted.

Types of cyberbullying include:

- *Anonymous posting/Cyberbullying by proxy:* secretive smear that occurs when people:
  - hide their persona through an online pseudonym, posting defamatory comments to ruin someone else's reputation[10] —"masquerading" either to defame a target or to lure someone into a fraudulent relationship.[11] Nafeesa Onque, a New Jersey cheerleader, was impersonated by a 15-year-old classmate who constructed a fake Facebook page, amassed followers, and sent them threatening and sexually explicit messages. Nafeesa was physically attacked when the impersonator challenged one of her classmates to a fight;[12]

  and when they

  - post comments via apps and websites that do not require ID. [13]
- *Outing:* sharing, forwarding, or posting online confidential information/correspondence without the original poster's permission, or posting online "revenge porn." Anon-IB (short for Anonymous Information Board) is a site where individuals from all 50 states and from 22 countries can post pornographic pictures and request them from cities or specific schools and colleges. The site boasts 170,000 hits per day, and its users trade pictures like baseball cards.[14]
- *E-stalking:* "sending repeats of the same e-mail or sending an inordinate number of e-mails within a short period of time" to the same person. Targets can experience chronic symptoms of stress, headaches, anxiety, depression, stomachaches, anorexia, mental strain, anger, and inability to successfully complete work or schoolwork, along with decreased self-esteem and job satisfaction[15, 16, 17, 18, 19] if their situation continues.

Exercise

If you find defamatory comments about yourself online, what steps can you take to remove them? Search for articles that suggest the best way to handle "haters," and outline what you can do if someone mars your electronic persona. Charlie Harary, in the *Entrepreneur* article "5 Ways to Cope with Online Haters"[20] suggests that targets of e-smear should graciously acknowledge the commentary that is posted about them before they respond.

_____

_____

_____

_____

> "[People] reside in self-made isolation chambers, adjacent to but unable to reach the vast array of riches at their disposal."[21]
>
> —Jacqueline A. Gilbert

Assessment

Indicate how often you experienced cyberbullying at work using the following descriptions: 1 (*never/infrequently*); 2 (*at least two to three times in the past 6 months*); 3 (*at least once a month*); 4 (*more than once a month*); and 5 (*weekly*).

_____ You received reminder e-mails from a colleague after failing to respond to them the same day.

_____ You discovered that you were the target of a mob that wanted to oust you from the organization. They were collaborating via e-mail to lower your next performance rating.

_____ Coworkers sent you suggestive and/or inappropriate e-information.

_____ Your boss sent you an e-reprimand for a minor infraction. Their behavior escalated the issue to a "code red" status.

_____ Your supervisor used e-mail to avoid face-to-face interaction.

_____ A meeting chair "forgot" to copy you on correspondence, an action that tipped the meeting outcome in their favor. You subsequently felt blindsided and ostracized.*

_____ A coworker sent a barrage of "harmless" but non-work-related e-mails to your office e-mail address.

_____ A colleague electronically scolded you before researching the facts or speaking to you in person.

_____ A coworker sent you an angry e-mail and copied your boss.

_____ Your supervisor discussed personnel or disciplinary issues via e-mail.

_____ You received an electronic job announcement from a colleague who thought you needed to apply.

_____ Your colleague suggested via e-mail that you should use their guidelines, or working papers, because in their opinion they were superior to yours.

_____ Instead of discussing issues face-to-face, a coworker (just steps away from your office) used e-mail. They use this medium to make demands they would not otherwise make in person.

_____ A supervisor and/or senior coworker used e-mail to dump work on you that they should have been doing themselves.*

_____ An infatuated colleague sent unnecessary e-mails to keep the lines of communication open.

_____ Total

Higher scores indicate a greater level of work-related cyberbullying and indicate a tainted, toxic workplace culture.

* Items adapted from the seventeen-item Workplace Cyberbullying Measure. Farley, S., Coyne, I., Axtell, C., & Sprigg, C. (2016). Design, development and validation of a workplace cyberbullying measure, the WCM. *Work & Stress, 30*(4), 293–317. https://doi.org/10.1080/02678373.2016.1255998

BT (Before Texting) and before e-mail, writers spent more time choosing their words and carefully considering their tone and tenor. The permanence of letters and the length of time it took to compose them inspired people to exercise greater care, civility, restraint,[22] and diligence in their construction. Although e-mail was originally intended to automate routine correspondence, it is also now used for less benign purposes.

E-Comm at Work

Managers who substitute e-mail for face-to-face contact may discover much later they have created conflict. E-writeups take less time to compose but have the same impact as a written reprimand because they become part of an employee's permanent work record. If correspondence is constructed in a slapdash, unceremonious manner, it can leave recipients feeling more like part of a drive-by than a respectful exchange.[23] E-blame creates embarrassed, one-down position workers who are unable either to respond or to provide explanation.[24] As a first-strike response, e-reprimands negate an employee's importance and undermine a spirit of mutual respect. "Technology [provides a way to send write-ups] quickly, easily, and without the messiness of emotions inherent in speaking with another [person]."[25]

"Electronic reprimands... [occur at a manager's] prerogative, [but] without the employee's [input or] defense."[26]

Before you press the Send button, consider the potential impact on your audience.[27]

- *Always give your fellow professionals the respect and the response that they deserve.* Ask yourself not: "What did they do wrong?" but "What did they do right?" Start there. How do you reply with a focus on what they did right and build from there and guide them to the next step so that they learn something, do something, and fulfill your request. Remember that people have different gifts and different talents. *Respect that.*

- *Inject your message with the missing tone and color—give your message a "human face."* The easiest way to do this has a parallel in a typical business call. In this setting, you rarely start out, point-blank, with the purpose for your call. More than likely, you begin with "How are you?" or "How was your trip to France?" Begin your e-mail by showing an interest in the e-mail recipient as a human being, not just someone who can do something for you. Inject a little humor whenever appropriate—there is only a two-letter difference between "humor" and "human"!

- *Learn the difference between a reaction and a response—and refuse to be reactionary.* A *reaction* is thoughtless and hasty, while a *response* is thoughtful and careful. Be sure to respond rather than react. One of the best things about e-mails is that they can be composed and then revised. If you react emotionally to an e-mail, close it, mark it as "unread," and give yourself some time to cool down before you reply. When you draft your response, stick to the facts.

- *Accept responsibility.* Another two polite words that have enormous power are "I'm sorry." Be quick to acknowledge your mistakes, to apologize, and to correct your errors. Many e-mail exchanges flare up because senders want to place blame rather than accept responsibility. The truth is, that even when you are not literally responsible for the error, accepting responsibility for it can gain you more standing in your organization. Someone who deflects responsibility soon appears irresponsible; someone who absorbs responsibility—and turns the problems around—appears responsible and trustworthy in the eyes of the organization.

- *Use qualifiers and re-direction to soften what otherwise might be construed as harsh or accusatory language.* Use the classic business writing technique of the "you attitude." Turn the pointing finger back to yourself instead of to your message recipient. Instead of this, "Why don't you ever follow directions?" say this: "I am so sorry that my directions were not clear. Can you help me know where they led you astray so that I can revise them and help you understand?" Qualifying language—as opposed to categorical statements—can make your e-mails more logical and more effective. Contrast "Your department never works efficiently" to "Let's work together to find a strategy for increasing efficiency in your department."

▪ *Write each e-mail with the goal of leaving the recipient more informed and more integrated into your professional network than he or she was before your e-mail came.* You have the power to instill confidence, to boost morale, to strengthen the supportive net beneath your coworkers with every e-mail you send out. It is your choice whether to use that tool to maximize efficiency and goodwill, or to allow it to weaken your organization with misunderstandings and hurt feelings.

Squabbles that occur over a keyboard can escalate "hot" issues[28] and potentially land the sender in court.[29] Thinking about an emotionally charged e-mail for 24 hours instead of responding immediately allows both parties to gain perspective, and for at least one of them to make a peace offering.

Do not use e-comm when:[30]

▪ "information-rich" answers are solicited (those that require more than a "yes/no" answer);
▪ personal/confidential facts are communicated; or
▪ what you send may elicit an emotional response.

Offensive e-mails have fiscal implications for senders, employees, the organization, and even for stockholders. An offhand comment that originated from a Cerner Corporation CEO was posted on Yahoo. It contributed to a 22% stock drop in 3 days:

We are getting less than 40 hours of work from a large number of our K.C.-based EMPLOYEES. The parking lot is sparsely used at 8 a.m.; likewise at 5 p.m. As managers—you either do not know what your EMPLOYEES are doing; or you do not CARE. You have created expectations on the work effort which allowed this to happen inside Cerner, creating a very unhealthy environment. In either case, you have a problem and you will fix it or I will replace you.[31]

Another e-gaffe occurred at Hewlett-Packard, where a vice president inadvertently provided confidential information to competitors when he included details of an upcoming product launch on his LinkedIn profile.[32]

Electronic casualties can happen when people have insufficient training on how to construct e-mail and for the sake of time press either Send or Post without contemplating the content of their message, how it will be received, or if it was germane to send/post in the first place.

Lawful company policies prohibit the following:[33]

- online retaliation and harassment directed at coworkers from either their work or home computers, posted either during or outside official workplace hours;
- posts that harm an individual's reputation or are considered injurious or obscene, particularly if they might be construed as a violation of Title VII and create what employees perceive as a hostile work environment; and
- online discrimination and threats.

Unlawful policies, ones that violate employees' ability to discuss terms and conditions of employment or their ability to unionize as protected by the National Labor Relations Act, are ones that instruct them to[34]

- avoid making inappropriate remarks that may potentially disparage their employer;
- post in a "professional" fashion and to refrain from posting incendiary comments—because doing so may dissuade free and spirited discussion; and
- limit exercising their NLRA-protected rights by requiring them to report suspicious or unsolicited Internet correspondence.

Exercise:

How would you discourage cyberbullying and trolling at your place of employment? How would you sanction offenders, and what policies and practices would you promote? Formulate a comprehensive, detailed plan, and cite your sources.

_____

_____

_____

_____

_____

How to Curb Inappropriate Digital Activity

Pointing and clicking from behind a screen may enable accusatory, judgmental, base human correspondence.[35] Electronic devices can destroy empathy, erode character, and deter the hard work of reflective learning.[36]

It is simple to throw digital rocks at a screen-sized pellet, and not a living, breathing human being who feels shame and who experiences cringe-worthy, humiliating mental highlight reels in constant replay. Consider the following questions:

- Would you be proud if your name was attached to what you just wrote?
- Are there alternative and more mutual ways of resolving your grievance? Would you show your family what you have e-achieved, and would you say it to the target's face?
- Do you feel satisfied once you've posted a screed, as if you have somehow leveled the scales?

Respectful e-comm should adhere to organization-wide principles, or "ethics screens,"[37] that check if communication delivers the prescribed intent, benefits the greatest number of people, and respects individual rights and dignity.

Exercise:

Describe a time when you saw another person degraded in an e-forum. What actions did you take (or could you have taken) to help them and defuse the conflict? Search for articles that suggest the best ways to handle social-media attacks and for preventative software programs that ping online personal mentions.[38] The Air Force Web Posting Response Assessment (below) provides a decision tree for how to effectively deal with online trolls.

_____

_____

_____

_____

_____

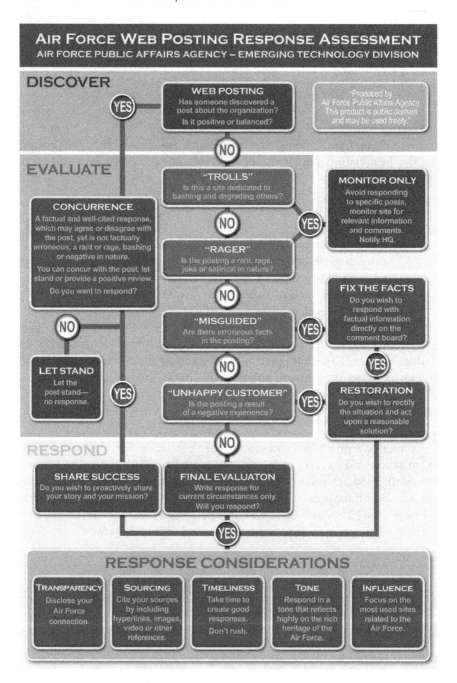

Source: Used with permission of Air Force Public Affairs website, http://www.publicaffairs
.af.mil/Portals/1/documents/AF%20web%20Posting%20Response%20Assessment.pdf

How Can People Handle E-Unthinkables?

In *The Civility Solution*, author P. M. Forni[39] includes an entire chapter on the best ways to handle disagreeable digital discourse, digital snipers, and people who are unaware of how they're perceived in an e-medium. For example:

- *You find an e-mail in your inbox that upsets you.*
  If you are the recipient of attack-mode, angry, accusatory e-comm, he suggests addressing the situation from an objective, fact-finding perspective instead of one that is seething with anger. Face-to-face or phone meetings, because they are media rich forms of interaction, might be preferable options.

  > **Example:** You have just received an e-mail from Sally Ann, your co-worker, who appears out of sorts.

  > **Sally Ann:** Why didn't you tell me about the user manual update? I've spent hours picking through code to determine how I should modify the wording.

  > **You:** It sounds to me like you missed the meeting where Stan explained Ed's markup. I'll forward you the annotated version. Let me know if you still have questions.

- *A friend or acquaintance sends you an e-mail that you consider both intrusive and inappropriate,* one that addresses sensitive topics about your family.
  Contact the sender and explain unequivocally that some things are not intended for e-comm, and more importantly, are not their personal concern.

- *An employee routinely copies you on correspondence that is solely the purview of another department or person (in this case, the production leader).* She copies you (the district vice president for production), the production leader's boss, along with the production leader on work orders that are processed by the production leader alone.
  To maintain an atmosphere of mutual respect, explain to the employee who originally copied you that doing so is unnecessary. Furthermore, consider affirming the capability, job competence, and responsibility of the employee/department they apparently wish you to monitor, so that they don't consider it necessary to copy you.

- *Someone posts confidential information about you online.*
  Contact the poster to stress the proprietary nature of personal exchange and request they let you have the final say in their future postings about you.

■ *You see people looking at their cell phones when they should be paying attention in a meeting.* Require workers to check their cell phones prior to meeting inception.[40] Shayne Hughes, CEO of Learning as Leadership, banned internal company e-mails for one week because of their usage as a sham conflict-resolution tool, and because they were a subsequent time waster. Intra-company e-mail can produce problems when it creates unnecessary work, and when people stop speaking to one another because they decide to communicate on their keyboards. [41]

Lack of face to face contact can distort information and cause interpersonal conflict.[42]

Digital citizenship is an antidote to "e-unthinkables." It consists of:

■ Addressing one another appropriately and responsibly online by:[43]
  – *Answer[ing] the question asked and keep[ing] it short.* This advice sounds obvious, but it is the cause of many a misunderstanding (not to mention frustration) in e-mail communications. If a coworker writes, "When do I need to get this back to you?" don't say, "You know, I thought that if I could have it by the middle of the month, I would be able to get that report finished and out to the stakeholders by the end of the fiscal year . . . so I think that we ought to try to get it done as soon as possible." Recognize that when you write a long and vague response you are not answering the question. Instead, just say, "June 18." Ah, what a relief to the recipient of your message! Remember that, like you, your coworkers are busy folks. Stay on task with efficient and effective language.
  – *Responding to the need, not the tone.* Re-read it carefully and take out any "loaded" language that could be interpreted as an attack or a criticism. When you receive a reply, you may be surprised to find that all the heat in the original e-mail was not intended for you but was a symptom of the writer's own frustration. Instead of creating friction and animosity, you have now made a new best friend.
  – *Consider[ing the] audience and the purpose of the e-mail.* Is it just a quick response to a simple question from a friend? Or is [it] a reply to an administrator that will later be used as documentation of protocol and sign-offs? Might it be printed and

filed in a folder as a reference document? If an e-mail will be used for future reference or documentation, you will want to use a more formal style and tone.

■ *Refraining from illegal and immoral online activity*,[44] such as (a) promulgation of viruses and worms that infiltrate computer systems to cause harm, (b) spam, (c) identity theft, and (d) plagiarism.

■ *Actively engaging in self-protection*. Chubb Insurance provides coverage for psychological injury that results from cyber-intrusion. It has added a cyberbullying rider to its existing policies that covers attorney fees, wages, relocation to another home, and treatment at behavioral health care providers. At work, the policy becomes effective when employees suffer wrongful termination, inappropriate school discipline, and/or mental turmoil due to cyber smear.[45] Apps such as ReThink scan e-messages for harmful content and issue a "reconsider" prompt if they find offensive language.[46] One day artificial intelligence (AI) may be able to identify cyberbullying before it morphs into full-blown electronic abuse.[47]

The Future of Digital Discourse

Because lawyers can subpoena IP addresses in alleged cases of Internet libel,[48] the Internet may be moving toward greater digital restraint. Eric Schmidt, ex-CEO of Google, suggests that web anonymity may become a thing of the past.[49] His prediction is particularly compelling in a 3D Internet where static point and click will be transformed into a virtual watering hole with avatars, or virtual representations of end users.[50]

Leaders can spare potential shame and online embarrassment[51] for employees through:

■ *Creating* a zero-tolerance, comprehensive, organization-wide online abuse policy. Microsoft's safety guidelines for young adults can also be applied to the workplace. They include:[52]
   – exemplifying good behavior online;
   – developing emotional self-awareness; and
   – thinking before posting, considering if online conduct reflects Golden Rule principles. Microsoft has committed resources to educate communities on Internet safety and to explain what steps people can take if and/or when they feel compromised online. The company has worked on cyber

issues and security with groups such as Lady Gaga's Born this Way Foundation, The Executive Women's Forum, and the European Commission.

- *Encouraging* conversation, instead of prolonging workplace conflict via keyboard. If employees use e-mail at work, they must carefully check their correspondence and consider the possible consequences before pressing Send. Talking to someone in a face-to-face confab creates rapport and prevents misunderstandings that can occur in a two-dimensional space.

- *Training* on the best response to cyberbullying. Balpreet Kaur,[53] an Ohio State University student, maintained her dignity when she was attacked on social media because of her visible facial hair and because she wore a turban. In a follow-up posting, she educated the Internet audience on her religion, and she explained that she did not feel embarrassed or self-conscious about her appearance. She later received an apology from the person who posted disparaging online commentary about her.

People do their best work in low-stress environments—ones free of harassment in any form.[54]

Communication Is a Continual Loop

✓ Message
✓ Interpretation
✓ Response
✓ Recalibration

Online, we can be easily offended. Cordial, understated, polite language leaves recipients more receptive and responsive to our message.[55]

Instead of a storehouse for unfiltered, stream-of-consciousness rhetoric, the Internet should be a location to inform, to persuade, and to educate. Businesses should monitor e-conduct, notify law enforcement when appropriate,[56] and, in general, raise awareness through workplace policies against cyberbullying.

Online Resources

- Gannett, A. K. (2013, June 8). At work: Cyberbullies graduate to workplace. Retrieved from http://www.usatoday.com/story/money/columnist/kay/2013/06/08/at-work-office-cyberbullies/2398671/
- Gilbert, J. A. (2011, February 25). E-mail: Efficiency gone haywire [Blog post]. Retrieved from https://organizedforefficiency.com/e-mail-efficiency-gone-haywire/
- Gilbert, J. A. (2011, March 28). Optimize your electronic office [Blog post]. Retrieved from https://organizedforefficiency.com/optimizing-your-electronic-office/
- Gilbert, J. A. (2011, April 1). Eliminate electronic interruptions [Blog post]. Retrieved from https://organizedforefficiency.com/eliminate-electronic-interruptions/
- Gilbert, J. A. (2011, July 24). The positiveness of a personal touch [Blog post]. Retrieved from https://organizedforefficiency.com/the-positiveness-of-a-personal-touch/
- Gilbert, J. A. (2014, April 14). Tip your electronic hat [Blog post]. Retrieved from https://organizedforefficiency.com/tip-your-electronic-hat/
- Gilbert, J. A. (2015, March 23). Communication without the electronics [Blog post]. Retrieved from https://organizedforefficiency.com/communication-without-the-electronics/
- Sanders, A. (2011, June 22). Respect in the electronic media, part I [Blog post]. Retrieved from https://organizedforefficiency.com/respect-in-the-electronic-media-part-i/
- Sanders, A. (2011, June 23). Respect in the electronic media, part II [Blog post]. Retrieved from https://organizedforefficiency.com/respect-in-the-electronic-media-part-ii/
- Wolchover, N. (2012, July 25). Why is everyone on the Internet so angry? *Scientific American*. Retrieved from https://www.scientificamerican.com/article/why-is-everyone-on-the-internet-so-angry/

Web Quests

1. After reading "Preventing Cyberbullying: Top Ten Tips for Adults Who are Being Harassed Online,"[57] and "UH Professor Garners Nationwide Recognition for Online Guideline for E-mail Etiquette,"[58] summarize the top four tips on digital etiquette. Why are these important to you, and what can happen if people don't adhere to these guidelines?

   _____

   _____

   _____

   _____

2. Forty percent of adults in a recent Pew sample of almost 3,000 people reported they received offensive, embarrassing online treatment, stalking, physical threats, and/or intentional harassment,[59] with an even greater percentage (75%) indicating they had seen other people bullied online. On the "State Cyberbullying Laws: A Brief Review of State Cyberbullying Laws and Policies"[60] website, locate your state and summarize cyberbullying legislation. Are these laws enough? If not, what other safeguards do you think are necessary?

   _____

   _____

   _____

   _____

3. Explain the four-prong threshold at which cyberbullying constitutes defamation; write a description in your own words of each "prong" and of the consequences for offenders. See "Is a Defamation Case a Good Remedy for Cyberbullying? An Atlanta Girl Tests the Law,"[61]

and "Online Harassment, Defamation, and Hateful Speech: A
Primer of the Legal Landscape"[62] web articles for starting points.

_____

_____

_____

_____

4. Read the following e-mail messages and suggest what is wrong in
each of them:[63]

First Scenario:	TEAM, WE ARE MEETING AT 9:00 O'CLOCK THIS MORNING. THE BOSS
Second Scenario:	When is the homework assignment due? Mary
Third Scenario:	The assignment would be easier if you'd just give us some instructions.

See page 161 for the key

_____

_____

_____

_____

5. Self-bullying occurs when people dedicate hours that should be
spent sleeping or on productive activity to indiscriminate web surf-
ing,[64] and when they view a smorgasbord of unedited information and lose sleep and time in the process. The average person
spends almost six hours per day on devices that have the capacity to
minimize human connection.[2] Nonstop Internet viewing can result
in depression,[65] loneliness, and self-focus. Internet addiction

disorder (IAD) has not yet been classified in the Diagnostic and Statistical Manual of Mental Disorders, although it reportedly affects as much as 8% of the U.S. and European populations.[66]

Research ways that people can curb their Internet addictions and limit time on the computer.

_____

_____

_____

_____

What Would You Do?

1. Several coworkers have posted negative comments about Dave, the lead software architect, on a website. You know that many of these were prompted by your company's restructure, over which Dave had no control. These remarks go beyond simply critiquing him as a boss. They denigrate his family, his character, and his personal work ethic.

   What should you do? Research "next steps" if you are victim of a cyberbullying attack. How can you refrain from being an online bystander?

_____

_____

_____

_____

2. Your manager has indicated that Carol, a teammate with whom you work closely on a large account, is not her favorite, but that *you* have the potential to be a favored in-group member if you follow "the rules." One of your boss's requirements for inclusion is using the "bcc" option to copy her on any correspondence either to or about Carol. How should you handle this situation? Support your rationale with web research. See Ramona Emerson's web

article "Bcc or Let Them See? The Etiquette of the Blind Carbon Copy."[67]

3. A colleague forwards your e-mails without your permission and posts them to social media. What is the best netiquette to address this person's behavior and to prevent a repeat episode?

Key: *E-mail Message Exercise*[68]

1. The communication is in all caps, which people may interpret as shouting.
2. The correspondence doesn't contain a salutation or letter closing, such as "Good morning" or "Best regards" respectively. E-mails are electronic letters. They should be treated with the same care as traditional correspondence because of their shelf life and potential repurposing.
3. Internet communication has contributed to sloppy, indiscreet, and aggressive interaction.

Notes

1. The Special Report "Digital in 2018: World's Internet Users Pass the 4 Billion Mark" provides a detailed analysis of digital users around the globe, delineated by their type of digital usage and time spent on their devices and social media platforms. McDonald, N. (2018, January 30). Digital in 2018: World's Internet users pass the 4 billion mark. *letstalk@wearesocial.com*. Retrieved from https://wearesocial.com/us/blog/2018/01/global-digital-report-2018

2. These devices include smart phones, computers, and gaming/streaming devices. Marvin, R. (2018, June 11). Tech addiction by the numbers: How much time we spend online. *PC Magazine.* Retrieved from https://www.pcmag.com/article/361587/tech-addiction-by-the-numbers-how-much-time-we-spend-online. The information on tech addiction was derived from Mary Meeker's 2018 Internet Trends Report.

8

Multiculturalism and Diversity Awareness

Scene: Blanche's friend Stan describes a situation at work.

"As a rule, Catug*n sticks to a profile. They'll keep outsiders *if* they do the following things: Number one, they keep their mouths shut; and number two, they agree with everything top management says. Equal opportunity only applies if you've made yourself equal in the eyes of the power brokers. Which means that standing up for your rights may get you a mark on your back. Just between you and me, I'm not sure how much more of this I can take."

Why Discrimination Occurs/The Problem and Definition

Employees who experience years of office abuse, exclusion, or lack of career development may feel helpless to protest inequity or to petition management for greater status at work.[1] Authors Rosabeth Moss Kanter and Barry A. Stein describe "Others" or minority "Os" as people who assimilate into the dominant "X" culture by playing expected, stereotypical roles, by taking sides against Os that challenge X employees, and by staying in the background and supporting X workers.[2] Os may appear invisible when they are stymied in dead-end jobs[3] and when they are deprived of training and apprenticeship opportunities. A 2015 Equal Employment Opportunity Commission report indicated that the largest percentage of executive/senior-level management positions in private industry held by a single racial minority group was only 5%.[4] Systemic abuse occurs when policies support exclusionary practices, and when bosses discriminate against minority employees and encourage other people to follow suit. At Texaco, for example, Bari-Ellen Roberts discovered that her annual performance rating was lowered after she had disagreed with an "Old X" Texaco employee.[5]

Toxic firms may eliminate Os who don't conform with unstated policy, even if terminating them decreases company profits.[6]

> "A 'Tale of O' depicts the exclusion and isolation that minority Others, or 'Os,' experience when [they work in] 'X' dominated [companies]. Os are viewed as unwanted interlopers, as unmistakable outsiders who by way of legislative mandate have crashed the company party. Xs regard their corporation as 'our house,' a place in which O presence [represents] encroachment."[7]

Minorities may experience a disproportionate share of workplace abuse. [8] In a 2017 Workplace Bullying Institute survey, African American and Hispanic employees reported bullying at higher rates than their White counterparts.[9] Selective disrespect occurs when minorities' seniority, credibility, rank, knowledge, or expertise are minimized or degraded by other people at work.

Scene: Dan, a disabled Catug*n employee, overhears a conversation about him.

Blanche: Dan has raised more money for our annual charity drive than any past chair at this company; he's putting in tons of effort.

Korie: That's great; but can he manage his group?

Micro-inequities are shaming, bullying, or belittling sentiments that may have been intended as nonthreatening, or even as friendly. Insults can be delivered in such a way that they appear free of sexually charged[10] or racist innuendo.

Example:

Albert: I'm an immigrant.
Korie: You speak English well for someone who arrived recently.

If O targets take umbrage, X coworkers may perceive that accusers have found a problem, or a problem person, who needs sanctions and/or attitudinal correction to be more "X" like.

> Micro-inequities include denigrating language and behavior toward Others that are difficult to pinpoint to a specific person as either intentional or harassing.[11]

Examples of everyday "cultural stoning"[12] include:

- condoning "machismo culture" that mandates women wear makeup, high heels, and skirts;[13]
- disrespecting "O" superiors through noncompliance, insubordination, discussing their alleged incompetence with coworkers, and undermining them in a way that makes tracing misbehavior back to the perpetrator difficult;[14]
- engaging in hostile stares and elevator eyes to reduce target status;
- exhibiting menacing attitudes that manifest in nonsupport;
- expecting women to outdo what's stated in their job description, without upstaging senior men;[15]
- making snide remarks only to those of "suspect" gender/race, which cannot be unequivocally pinned to either of those characteristics;
- pointing out minor infractions to a roomful of people;
- refusing to acknowledge "O" accomplishments;
- suggesting that Others do not act like "normal" persons of their race/heritage, and indicating they are more appropriately suited for certain roles;[16] and
- urging bullied men to find problem resolutions on their own, so they can present a strong, secure, unassailable "manly" approach to conflict management.[17]

Reflection

Have you heard or witnessed microaggressions, or subtle put-downs, of other people? How did these make you feel? How do you think the targets felt? How should you react when you hear micro-inequities hurled at women, racial minorities, the disabled, and other minority groups at work and/or school?

_____

_____

_____

_____

■────────

Discrimination May Be Abetted by the People Who Are Affected

Minority behavior and self-worth are influenced by organizational culture:[18]

- At Smith Barney, a female operations manager chided a woman who didn't excuse a more cavalier male coworker.[19] Related sentiments include "He doesn't mean any harm," "Lighten up," or "He just wants some attention."
- At "AAA" company, a Latina employee explained her female coworker's discomfort with office politics as an inability to roll with the punches.[20]
- Harassed female recruits at Astra Pharmaceutical received little empathy from women who had climbed the corporate ladder in a sexually permeated culture.[21]

Some minorities compete for status at work by sabotaging one another. Infighting can occur[22] when only select positions are available to Os, only a few token employees are promoted, and when direct competition with Xs is considered unacceptable. Unbalanced power differentials reinforce inequity at work.[23]

Reflection

Have you felt pressured to play along with the bully or boss, or to take sides against someone they viewed as different? The YouTube video "A Tale of O Video on Diversity" suggests that pressure to conform can result in Os taking the dominant group's side.

―――

―――

―――

―――

As a survival strategy, minorities may defer to the values and behavior of dominant group members, either through "code-switching"[24, 25, 26] or modifying their word choice, tone, dialect, mannerisms, or dress. They may even choose self-blame because they mistakenly believe they incited their abuse[27] and thus deserve company sanctions.[28] People who internalize racism and sexism want to be on the team that wields all the power and has the most status. Men and women take a harder stance against women in salary negotiations,[29] and Black-on-Black bias increases when community and media viewpoints emphasize White "mainstream Americana" and portray African Americans as a criminal element.[30] Protests of discriminatory treatment within toxic companies are either punished or ignored—a practice that preserves the corporate power structure and keeps potentially subversive employees in their place. People institutionalize dysfunctional behavior when they choose to appease the dominant coalition at work. Locker-room rituals that poison organizational culture can thus develop into hallowed traditions and accepted practices.

"...to obtain protection from the X in-group, Os must engage in conformance [and in activities that] Xs desire from their respective O group." "Internalized racism and sexism occur when hatred projected by society, employers, and the media takes root..."[31]

Exercise

List ways in which minorities are encouraged to assimilate, or to act more like the majority. How would you, as leader, change what is expected and encourage minorities to exhibit more authentic behavior?

_____

_____

_____

_____

Os may appear agreeable, congenial, noncontentious, and ultimately appealing to workers who exploit those characteristics to extract gains for themselves.[32]

Scene: Blanche describes troubling issues at Catug*n and the latent impact of her abusive upbringing.

Korie noticed I had a problem with politics at work—small things my co-workers took for granted, like office chit-chat and after-hours get-togethers at O'Chanahan's. They were both small hurdles compared to the departmental meeting that occurred bimonthly.

My first week at Catug*n she pulled me aside.

"Blanche, we need to get you some gumption. You just can't just sit there like a bump on a log and let the men do all the talking. They're going to think you don't know a thing."

My coworkers conversed seamlessly, almost on top of one another—barely pausing before the last one jumped into the fray, with Korie weaving in and out. So poised, so polished—she knew exactly what to say and when to say it, alternating between deference to the right people and piggybacking on their platforms. In a boardroom of ties and dark suits, we were the only two women.

Mental, verbal, and emotional abuse bound me tight and gagged me speechless. Memories that cemented my tongue to my palate permitted behavior that other people would consider encroachment.[1]

Standing outside the Old X network left me few options.

Employees within toxic firms face a choice between leaving and siding with their abusers.

In cultures where employees compete for attention by speaking their minds, silence may be misinterpreted as weakness, apathy, inadequate preparation, and disinterest. An inability or an unwillingness to communicate in the dominant style can result in missed opportunities—and in bullying from office politicians who perceive a quiet coworker as a weak-willed opponent.

From Reactive to Proactive

The overriding motive in toxic, reactive companies is to protect and preserve top management.[33] Managers and human resources professionals practice "pacification"[34] when they do the inclusionary bare minimum to appease outside stakeholders. The film *North Country* depicts a mining worker who complained about abuse only to find "employee friendly" services at her manager's disposal. In companies that place little importance on diverse perspectives, tokens may be sprinkled throughout but have little gravitas in crafting corporate policy.

A MODEL OF ORGANIZATIONAL DIPLOMACY

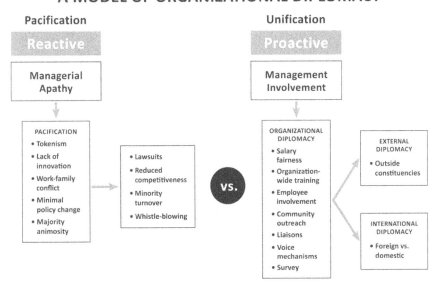

Gilbert, J. A., & Ivancevich, J. M. (1999). Organizational diplomacy: The bridge for managing diversity. *Human Resource Planning Journal, 22*(3), 29–39. Reprinted with permission of Human Resource Planning Society.

When bosses consider diversity an intrusion rather than a means of broadening the cognitive base and the resulting solution pool, workers may keep innovative ideas for improving products and services to themselves. Companies that operate from a "make the numbers" mandate and that use minority employees as window dressing[35] fail to mine the full range of perspectives from their employees.[36] Some reactive firms tarnish their reputations by enabling O failure.

Scene: Edwin thinks about recent diversity legislation.

These liberal politicians left us no place to hide, with "offender" companies thrown up on the Internet for everyone to see. I committed Catug*n in signage, but not spirit. I knew our round-robin approach to employee retention—you know, where we get rid of people who don't cotton to our practices—would catch notice. I had to choose something subtler, a more underhanded way to make sure that only people who played by "the rules" remained part of the crew.

In *Roberts vs. Texaco*, Bari-Ellen Roberts explained how top management at Chase orchestrated an assignment that could have ensured her failure and accelerated her exit.[37]

Proactive companies[38]

- eliminate people who display bullying or abusive behavior;
- encourage coworkers to treat one another with dignity;
- establish connections with internal customers;
- find ways to constructively address issues; and
- set an example, admit failings, and develop their employees.

Organizational diplomacy consists of "strategies used to minimize conflict in a diverse workplace" by "[using] differences to the organization's advantage."[39]

Diplomat Hall of Fame

Proactive companies change culture by encouraging their employees to act cooperatively and respectfully at work. Examples include:

- Tom's of Maine, which destroyed false barriers in the "Ups/ Downs"[40] diversity training exercise. Employees successively stood up and sat down in response to questions about their heritage, such as "Stand up if you are Christian...if you attended college...if you have children...if you are an only child." Employees shared the identities they had guarded for fear of being ridiculed, discriminated against, and/or ultimately eliminated from the next corporate rung. In a deconstructed safe space, workers feel free to shed their false selves and to embrace who they are in front of supporters.[41] Tom Chappell (Tom's of Maine ex-CEO) realized that employees are a complex mix of attitudes, feelings, and emotions who come with rich histories that most times remain hidden.
- Herman Miller Inc., which embraced diversity through creating a civil culture and by encouraging workers to participate in problem solving with leadership. Max De Pree (former Herman Miller CEO) argued that each person's unique gift is what contributes to a unifying corporate effort, one that capitalizes on and depends on the talents of many employees.[42]
- Marriott International Inc. (number seven on the Fortune/Great Place to Work 2017 "Best Places for Diversity List"[43]), which promotes inclusion and fosters a climate where every member of its diverse workforce can thrive. CEO Arne Sorenson's open LinkedIn letter to then President-elect Donald Trump about LGBT rights is an example of Marriott's values and outreach efforts:

  "Use your leadership to minimize divisiveness around these areas [e.g., identity, gender, race, religion, disability, ethnicity]...by ensuring that [people] are treated equally in the public square."[44]

Diversity exists on multiple dimensions, which include personality, self-expression, family origin, and foreign culture. Group-oriented collectivists who emphasize "face," or saving oneself and others from embarrassment, are at a disadvantage in companies that promote unfettered expression and unbridled self-interest.

The following e-mails contrast the collectivist expression of face saving and the value of high context—where people pay attention not only to what is said, but to how it is said, with individualists using a more me-centered approach. The first e-mail example is from a collectivist whose emphasis is on preserving the relationship, whereas the second is from an individualist who wants to get down to business. Conflicts can arise when a no-frills style is misinterpreted as brusque, and when a deferential tone is perceived as timid.

Dear Mr. D,

I hope this correspondence finds you well, and that you had a wonderful weekend! I wanted you to know how much I enjoyed our conversation the other day, and how the information helped me to solve an accounting problem. Thank you again for taking time out of your busy day to assist me.

When you have time, could we set up a meeting to discuss the financials? I want to ensure that I have all the paperwork ready before the auditors arrive.

I look forward to hearing from you, and I look forward to our upcoming meeting. Thank you again for your attention.

My very best,

Kano

Hi Ed,

Could we schedule a meeting to discuss the financials? The auditors arrive at the office next week.

Thanks,

Jane

The term "saving face" refers to eliminating the possibility of embarrassment or discomfort and to maintaining people's dignity. In collectivist society, individual needs are subordinated to group interests and people are careful not to offend their peers, extended family, or their nation-state. Mexico, for example, legislated face-saving measures to ban attack ads after its 2006 presidential election.

Although individualists in theory may support mutual respect and collegial dialogue, these concepts may be forgotten in a heated exchange. The desire to trounce an opponent, to win an argument, or to score points for themselves may cause them to forget the Golden Rule, along with the Platinum Rule®—which suggests that we should treat people not how we wish to be treated, but how they wish to be treated.

The following reflection points may ease conflict within a diverse, multicultural workplace: [45]

1. *Refrain* from using insulting, derogatory, or demeaning words. Although verbal bullets may temporarily ease frustration, they may leave people feeling small and embarrassed when they consider their behavior from the recipients' perspectives. Remember that coworkers have a cultural history, fragile egos, past abuses, and challenging personal situations. Consider their feelings.
2. *Let* the other person speak, and listen to their story. Perhaps you don't have all the facts, and heaven forbid, perhaps you are the one at fault! Apologize—not only to people you think are powerful, well-connected, and could cause you trouble, but to everyone else in your line of fire. Making an act of contrition when you realize you've bruised someone's spirit is a sign of character.
3. *Don't grandstand* over minor issues, particularly when large disparities or persistent inequities exist.
4. *Cut* the other person some slack. Everyone at work is juggling multiple responsibilities and you may not be aware of a coworkers' personal situations. It is possible that a procedural element slipped someone's mind. Remember that no one lives, eats, and breathes the organization 24 hours a day. Don't be so dogged in proving yourself right.
5. *Give* the other person the benefit of the doubt. Assume that instead of committing a deliberate act of disobedience, they have simply forgotten. Pick up the telephone and talk. This gesture will in many cases clear up misunderstandings and prevent them from escalating into full-blown incidents. Find out the other person's preferred mode of interaction.
6. *Approach* people like someone on a fact-finding mission, rather than someone who wants to engage in an accusatory monologue. Recuse yourself from the position of jury, judge, and executioner. Approach situations as collaborative, win–win encounters rather than opportunities to showcase your positional strength.
7. *Create* an atmosphere of equals. Furniture placement, for example, may seem insignificant, but how your body is positioned in relation to another person creates tone. If you are a manager, have you tried sitting next to another person, rather than across a desk? How people feel they have been treated when they leave your office is what is going to leave a lasting impression.

8. *Ask* for suggestions. If there is a conflict, invite people to express opinions on how they would perform operations differently. Some fruitful discussion and plans for improvement that you had not considered may ensue.

Corporate communalism, or the idea of family superimposed at work, suggests that caring for other people precedes effective business relationships. How can you create workplace inclusion at work?

- *Try the velvet-glove approach,* in which a leader's priority is to develop relationships. Friendly back-and-forth, as opposed to interrogation or accusation, is more likely to produce loyalty, enhanced connection, and faster problem resolution at work.
- *Don't assume that people can discern your intentions through two-dimensional contact alone.* Because e-mail lacks tonality and emotion, electronic communication has the potential to create misunderstandings.
- *Exercise your EQ.* The ability to read nonverbal behavior enables leaders to ascertain (quickly) if they have hurt someone's feelings or if other people feel uncomfortable. Soliciting employees' opinions (and acting on their suggestions) can help managers capitalize on diverse employee perspectives. The ability to see things from multiple viewpoints is an acquired skill, one that can be learned from diverse interaction. If you feel hamstrung by a cloistered upbringing, consider:[46]
  - *Making friends.* Serve on a board of directors where you are in a minority race/gender/age or other characteristic, or lead a committee of a group in which you are a minority. Learning about culture can be accomplished in fun, exploratory ways by experiencing new food, places, or music. Eating in ethnic restaurants, conversing with strangers, volunteering to welcome new arrivals to the United States, teaching ESL classes, visiting international food fairs, experimenting with new recipes, and learning unfamiliar dialects are all ways to experience multiculturalism. An enlarged hippocampus and enhanced memory are added benefits of foreign language training.[47]
  - *Traveling.* Group rates and youth hostels make foreign trips affordable. Check out the "Fifteen Ways to Travel for Free"

website, which lists how to visit other countries for a fraction of the cost. These include:

- House sitting
- House swapping
- Volunteering
- Crewing a yacht/cruise ship (can you teach a valuable skill, like bridge?)
- Capitalizing on credit card, airline, and hotel rewards

Activities that initially create discomfort may, over time, seem like second skin and create a more cosmopolitan "we." [48]

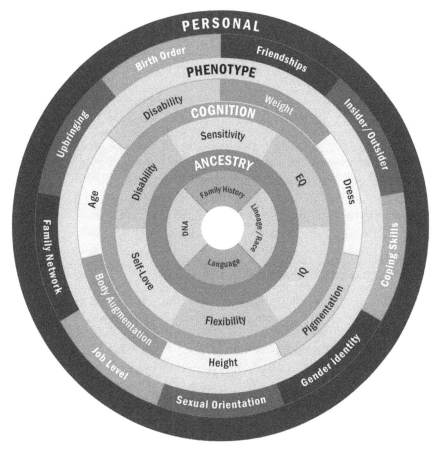

Ancestral, Cognitive, Phenotypic, and Personal Dimensions of Diversity. Source: Adapted from Loden, M., & Rosener, J. B. (1991). *Workforce America!* Homewood, IL: Business One Irwin. Illustration by Middle Tennessee State University.

Proactive leadership can facilitate diversity inclusion. Fear of the unknown prompts some LGBT employees to change jobs rather than approach their coworkers and human resource officers to discuss their treatment at work.[49] A reported 90% of transgender workers experience harassment or bullying due to their transition or transitional status.[50] Suggestions to prevent discrimination and to promote acceptance at work include:

- forming an LGBT community at work,
- providing time off so employees can engage in associated therapies and reconstructive processes, along with
- reacting in a supportive manner to employees who are contemplating transition.[51]

> "We sustain false empowerment from a manufactured 'us vs. them' distinction."[52]

The degree to which companies encourage façade, "false consciousness," and/or "false consensus"[53] is the degree to which employees are asphyxiating. Love brings forth the "living" organization,[54] whose growth results from the combined force of employees seeking to promote goodwill. An atmosphere of loving acceptance at work destroys façade.

In the children's story *The Velveteen Rabbit*, a toy becomes real through the act of being loved—at which point its veneer and trappings of "newness" eroded.[55]

How to Start the Proactive Ball Rolling?

Appreciation of diversity begins at school, when students are encouraged to practice civility among campus factions and religious sects.[56] An understanding and respect of how people's varied life experiences influence their perspectives improves student reactions. Universities and colleges that promote civility encourage student organizations to[57]

- award accolades for exemplary citizenship;
- engage in exploratory debates;
- find common ground;
- forge meta-communities that foster an integrative worldview and promote learning about people different from oneself;
- invite speakers from different faiths;

- offer classes that engender cognitive restructure and myriad ways of problem solving;
- prompt interfaith dialogue;
- provide educational workshops; and
- work with one another.

Whether on campus or at work, hierarchy *with* equality increases cognitive complexity, or "the ability to employ multiple frames of reference in an unstructured, complex, or novel situation."[58] Workers who are trained to appreciate diverse perspectives can rapidly shift their positions to explore pan-cultural issues,[59] which they might face in multinational companies that employ expatriates, host-country nationals, and third-country nationals working in teams.

"In a unifying effort, all employees work toward mutually acceptable solutions, with the overriding objective of maximizing organizational profitability."[60]

Online Resources

- Gilbert, J. A. (2011, April 28). Silence and self-injure [Blog post]. Retrieved from https://organizedforefficiency.com/silence-and -self-injure/
- Gilbert, J. A. (2016, November 26). Objectification at the office [Blog post]. Retrieved from https://organizedforefficiency.com/ objectification-at-the-office/
- Gilbert, J. A. (2017, March). Managing surface-level diversity as a business imperative. *Oxford Research Encyclopedias: Business and Management*. Retrieved from http://business.oxfordre.com/view/ 10.1093/acrefore/9780190224851.001.0001/acrefore-978019022 4851-e-43
- On sexual harassment in Japan (Part 1). (2014, June 23) [Blog post]. *This Japanese Life*. Retrieved from https://thisjapaneselife .org/2014/06/23/sexual-harassment-sekuhara/
- Stead, B. A. (2011, July 23). The quiet generation [Blog post]. Retrieved from https://organizedforefficiency.com/the-quiet -generation/

Web Quests

1. Diversity training has the potential to derail if it embarrasses employees or if it pits them against one another. Research diversity training within companies that negatively impacted employees. What type of training is most effective in creating acceptance? See the article by Frank Dobbin and Alexandra Kalev,[61] "Why Diversity Programs Fail: And What Works Better." The authors contrast effective and ineffective diversity programs to highlight successful change efforts.

   _____

   _____

   _____

   _____

2. What type of discrimination/negative stereotypes do disabled people face? Include "EEOC and disability discrimination" in your web search.

   _____

   _____

   _____

   _____

3. Federal legislation to prevent "lookism," or discrimination based on height, weight, and facial appearance, does not exist. Why does lookism occur, and what are some practical hiring techniques that could help leaders sidestep their personal biases? See the web article "Will Lookism Ever End? A Possible Way out of Our Most Stubborn and Ugly Prejudice."[62]

   _____

   _____

   _____

   _____

What Would You Do?

1. How would you, as a supervisor, prevent LGBT mistreatment at work, educate your workforce on LGBT issues, and sanction offenders?

_____

_____

_____

_____

2. Ann, a Singaporean immigrant, was raised in a collectivistic culture that emphasizes polite behavior and deference to the group. Her background in a high-power distance country also emphasized respect and deference to authority. At the office she often is a target for practical jokes, malicious gossip, and coworker exploitation. How can managers help Ann to acclimate at work, and how can they change policy and practice to promote her inclusion? Management researchers Kathryn J. L. Jacobson, Jacqueline N. Hood, and Harry J. Van Buren[63] imply that assertiveness can be associated with bullying incidents at work, particularly if workers are on opposite ends of the assertiveness spectrum.

_____

_____

_____

_____

3. You have been appointed the new CEO at X*YZ Company. The "Old X network" is well entrenched. There are, in fact, few "Os" within top level spots and a dearth of O opinions at departmental meetings. How can you transform your company so that it is more democratic, representative, and inclusive? In your search, identify companies, such as Denny's,[64] that have successfully changed office culture to embrace diversity.

_____

_____

_____

_____

Assessment: Does Your Organization Value Diversity?

Goal: Organizational policies and planning processes recognize and incorporate diversity objectives and contribute to establishing a more inclusive and welcoming community.

Scoring:

4 | **full** action taken   **3** | **substantial** action taken   **2** | **partial** action taken   **1** | **minimal** action taken   **0** | **no** action taken

INDICATORS	EVIDENCE	SCORE
1. Organizational policies have incorporated goals to address diversity and eliminate access barriers for newcomers.		
2. These goals are communicated to and discussed with staff.		
3. The organization is developing expertise and resources to implement inclusionary practices.		
4. Organizational strategic planning and annual business planning and budgeting have incorporated diversity and inclusionary objectives.		
5. Inclusionary objectives are built into the job descriptions and performance development of all staff.		
6. Relevant demographic and community data are used to inform and review policy and planning activities.		
7. The outcomes in implementing inclusionary policies and practices are regularly analyzed and used to review and update policies and programs.		
8. Inclusionary goals are integrated in reporting to executive and governing bodies.		
Leadership/Governance TOTAL SCORE		**0** /32

Source: From "Strengthening Diversity in Your Organization: A Self-Assessment Tool." (n.d.). Retrieved from http://www.yorkwelcome.ca/wps/wcm/connect/immigration/b4fd0295 -4f20-4941-8a6e-e1cc76d30a2e/SelfAssessmentTool.pdf?MOD=AJPERES. The higher the score, the greater the diversity acceptance. Reprinted with permission.

Notes

1. Kathy Caprino in the Forbes web article "5 Glaring Signs that your Childhood has Negatively Impacted Your Career" suggests that childhood emotional abuse surfaces much later. Adults who were abused as children may feel unable to articulate their needs at work, speak freely in group forums, or self-advocate if they sense unfairness. Caretakers who blame children for not feeling "the correct way," who tell them what to think and what to say, and who punish them harshly for a minor infraction foster timid adults. See Caprino, K. (2018, January 23). 5 glaring signs that your childhood has negatively impacted your career. [Blog post]. Retrieved from https://www.forbes.com/sites/kathycaprino/2018/01/23/5-glaring-signs-that-your-childhood-has-negatively-impacted-your-career/#62e1ac2253fa

9

Conflict and Top Leadership Support

The Problem and Definition

Disagreements can unleash breakthrough innovation. On the flip side, they can also produce factions that would prefer "winning" over finding a mutually acceptable fix. A singular approach to settling an issue may be contentious. A short fuse can burn through in a split second before rational "thinking" brains have an opportunity to intervene. Coworkers may be surprised when their mode of delivery offends other people or falls flat. A diverse team of employees needs guidance on how to avoid intractable, relationship-destroying conflict so they can respectfully solve problems and so they can reach an agreement to facilitate a superior product.

Inquiry (not inquisition), requests (not requirements), and mea culpas (as opposed to "my way or the highway") are methods of communicating that make coworkers feel like equal partners. Communication styles that lead to problem resolution, mutually acceptable outcomes, and positive interaction occur when people can express how they feel, and when they can respectfully disagree with anyone at any hierarchical level without incurring negative repercussions. Collegial employees emphasize concepts other than "I," ascertain what is best for everyone despite their individual wishes,

How to Transform Workplace Bullies Into Allies, pages 183–198
Copyright © 2020 by Information Age Publishing
All rights of reproduction in any form reserved.

and refrain from conversational bullying. Members of a team feel a sense of cohesion, or affinity, when they are included, valued, and appreciated by their coworkers. Community cultivated in a supportive work culture buoys employees' spirits.[1]

Take the following "Conflict Handling" assessment to learn your personal style:

Assessment

Rate the following items on a 1–5 scale (1 = *almost never*, 5 = *mostly always*).

1. _____ I try to learn something from other people, even if I disagree with them.
2. _____ I contact my workplace allies when I feel I've been wronged so that we can develop a revenge strategy.
3. _____ I visit my colleague's supervisor when I have an issue instead of speaking to them directly.
4. _____ It's difficult for me to forgive other people.
5. _____ When a person I don't like is attacked, I jump on the bandwagon.
6. _____ I devise roundabout ways to get back at people who have hurt me.
7. _____ I ask the opinion of other people before deciding how to act.
8. _____ I coax quiet members to offer their perspectives.
9. _____ I usually ask trusted colleagues for advice before I address a prickly issue.
10. _____ Sometimes scare tactics are a necessary cost of doing business.
11. _____ I don't make a big deal out of conflicts because doing so might damage my relational capital.
12. _____ I engage in gang taunting to score points with powerful workgroup members.
13. _____ I refuse to talk to people who have wronged me.
14. _____ I try to sabotage my enemies.
15. _____ The end justifies the means, even if someone else gets trampled.
16. _____ I modify my speech and mannerisms to obtain agreement.
17. _____ I encourage behavior that makes everyone in a meeting feel comfortable.
18. _____ I hold grudges.
19. _____ I butter up to the abuser (after he/she emotionally mutilated someone else) to gain their protection. I take the abuser's side in front of their targets and other people.

20. _____ I think that I can gain people's trust by being pleasant.
21. _____ I bulldoze tentative coworkers.
22. _____ I am sometimes hesitant to address colleagues with whom I have a disagreement.
23. _____ I search the web for negative information on people I don't like.
24. _____ I think frequently about how other people have hurt me.
25. _____ I speak "with" other people, not at them; I ask clarifying questions to promote understanding.
26. _____ Even after I speak to someone about the best way to handle a problem, I'm sometimes tentative about what to do.
27. _____ I go along to get along.
28. _____ I rarely speak to my coworkers when I have an issue with them. I instead post about my feelings on social media.
29. _____ I'm dogged unless I receive pushback.
30. _____ I ask my mentor to role-play before approaching "problem" people.
31. _____ I find it difficult to work with colleagues with whom I have a conflict.
32. _____ I engage in negative gossip so that I can build a case against someone else.
33. _____ Before I decide on a course of action, I include everyone who might be affected.
34. _____ I keep the lines of communication open by frequently stopping by my colleagues' offices.
35. _____ Might makes right when it comes to making a deal.

Scoring: Place your numbers in the spaces that correspond to the matching column items. Add the columns. The highest column score indicates your primary conflict handling preference.

Battling*	Mobbing	Sneaking	Unyielding	Schmoozing	Soliciting	Coproducing*
10.	2.	3.	4.	11.	7.	1.
15.	5.	6.	13.	16.	9.	8.
21.	12.	14.	18.	20.	22.	17.
29.	19.	23.	24.	27.	26.	25.
35.	32.	28.	31.	34.	30.	33.

* Dimensions adapted from Thomas, K. W., & Kilmann, R. H. (1974). *Thomas-Kilmann Conflict Mode Instrument.* Mountain View, CA: Xicom, a subsidiary of CPP, Inc.

Conflict-Handling Preferences

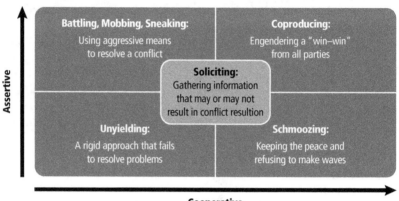

- *Battling:* a "my way or the highway" approach to vanquish competitors. A domineering style may win the battle but win few friends in the process.
- *Mobbing:* Strength in numbers is a mobber's primary approach. In their mind, a duo or a threesome of like-minded people creates a firewall from attacks and presents a unified front on issues important to the clique. Although mobbers may succeed in obtaining their objectives, they create casualties and people who are isolated from and afraid of the wolf pack.
- *Sneaking:* Underhanded, scheming, devious methods of dealing with other people that sabotage relationships. Colleagues will learn how to avoid office snitches and carefully edit their speech.
- *Schmoozing:* Politically savvy, smooth-spoken employees minimize conflict to advance their standing and their reputations. They realize that making colleagues feel good about themselves is a surefire way to increase their popularity and to advance up the ranks. Because schmoozers sidestep important workplace issues, problems may linger.
- *Unyielding:* Psychologist and author Kevin Leman[2] explains that forgiveness is essential to moving on with our lives and to repairing relationships. Although a grudge match and an ice out may create barriers against future mistreatment, they do little to encourage office rapport.
- *Soliciting:* It's never a bad idea to gather opinions. But when someone is hamstrung in decision making because they feel they must always consult with other people, little may be accom-

plished. Soliciting takes additional time and may annoy coworkers if it is too frequent.

- *Coproducing:* using exceptional communication skills to broker a win–win that leaves all parties to the conflict fully satisfied. [3]

Exercise:

What behaviors represent your conflict-handling style? Would you change any of these? How would you change them? Is your style more representative of the battling or the co-producing end of the conflict-handling spectrum?

_____

_____

_____

_____

How Can Leaders Create Alchemy Within a Random Mix of People?

Competitive conflict-handling styles can arise from abusive leader role modeling or from lack of a civility policy and community-centered culture at work.

Laissez-faire, or anything-goes, leaders ignore workplace conflict. Toxic bosses encourage it.

Toxic manager	Laissez-faire manager
Inappropriate role modeling	lack of standards
⬇	⬇
bullies	confusion on what constitutes acceptable behavior
⬇	⬇
workplace havoc	employees who don't know what behavior is appropriate or expected

A competing style, in which people overcompensate with aggression,[4] predominates in companies where managers are reluctant to address conflict between coworkers,[5] or when they encourage it. Consider whether the following conditions exist at your office:

- Bosses micromanage and closely monitor employees; "[a] practice [that] is . . . offensive to highly trained professionals who are accustomed to working [with little supervision]. 'Bossy and overbearing' . . . leaves [employees] who feel helpless and emotionally hogtied."[6]
- Managers circumvent human resources and direct employees to interface with their immediate supervisors (who may have initiated their problem).
- Aggressive parties rule at meetings, even encourage members to attack certain persons. Managers do not provide definitions of acceptable conduct or what they expect of coworkers.[7]
- Managers and others "[act] as if abuse did not occur. Business as usual following office [bullying] sends a message that 'delinquency is welcome here.' Probationary members follow suit, using the example provided by senior management."[8]
- Passive-aggressive behaviors substitute for more open, direct, matter-of-fact ways of problem-solving.
- "Abusers . . . digress into mobbers and proceed without sanction."[9]

Reflection:

Recall a workplace incident that made you feel uncomfortable. Examples include the enactment of policy that railroaded employees or procedures that were formulated without worker input. Did your company provide any means for employees to voice their dissatisfaction? After managers received your input, did they take follow-up measures?

See the web articles "Social Media and Employee Voice: The Current Landscape"[10] and "How to Get Employees to Voice their Opinions"[11] for ways to encourage workers to contribute.

Seventy-two percent of surveyed workers indicated the highest contributing factor to job satisfaction was respect at work.[12]

Transforming Conflict Into Constructive Dialogue

Fearful workers may fail to fully utilize their skills.[13] People-centered leaders create a safe space, one where employees showcase their talents, engage with coworkers, and feel they can "tinker" with projects[14] (and sometimes fail) without having to engage in game playing or compulsive checking. Exemplary leaders and organizations include:

Exemplary Leaders

- Richard Knowles, former DuPont plant manager who constructed a "safe container" (or "bowl") where employees who opposed corporate policy could express themselves.[15] Knowles walked the factory floor 5 hours each day, conversing with and getting to know his employees.
- Tony Morgan, former chief executive at the Industrial Society who initiated a radical change in his company's culture when he encouraged employees to speak their minds.[16]
- Ex-CEO Tom Chappell, who fought an urge to closely monitor or hoard his power—a choice that led to innovation and creativity at Tom's of Maine. Chappell admitted that leaders can stagnate if they fail to incorporate worker input[17] and if they create cultures in which they "[carry] out instructions, closely follow orders, and [receive] reprimands for anything less than perfect job completion."[18]
- John Kopicki, former CEO and president at Muhlenberg Medical Center who recalls the relief his employees felt when they had permission to act on their intuition and the freedom he felt when he displayed vulnerability at work.[19]
- Andy Law and David Abraham, who founded St. Luke's Advertising agency, collapsed organizational hierarchy so that the ideas of employees and supervisory personnel were accessible.[20] Flattened, egalitarian structures create an intrinsic motivation to excel and a desire to perform exemplary work because they reflect a higher, employee-centered purpose.

■ Former Verifone CEO Hatim Tyabji, who logged 500,000 miles in a single year to nurture the connective fiber among himself, his branch offices, and Verifone customers. Employee care was a core set of principles that he enacted daily, not something that he practiced solely in a crisis or at review time. Tyabji created connection with his employees when he let down his guard and when he treated coworkers like family. At Verifone, Tyabji acted as an ethical North Star.[21] Managers who lack morality and who use coercion as their primary management tool contribute to employee mistreatment, persecution, and abuse.[22]

■ Rich Sheridan, CEO of Menlo Innovations (and author of *Joy Inc.*) who describes an open learning environment where pairs of employees collaborate, share, and learn from one other. Joy is, according to Menlo Innovations' CEO, the outgrowth of focused value creation in a culture that uses nonhierarchical teams. The employee-centric company has won multiple accolades, including five *Inc. Magazine* growth awards. In 2013, Menlo Innovations was named one of Inc.'s 25 "most audacious" firms. Others include a distinction from the Chief Happiness Officer in Denmark as one of the 10 happiest companies on earth and annual recognition by WorldBlu as one of the most democratic workplaces in the world.[23]

Exemplary Organizations

■ HubSpot, which was chosen as the 2020 best tech company to work for in a Glassdoor.com survey based on its commitment to inclusion, diversity, and its positive work culture. [24]

■ Zappos, which delivers the "WOW" factor to both coworkers and customers by emphasizing honesty, congeniality, and civility.[25]

■ The National Security Agency (NSA), which encourages good manners. It distributes challenge cards that employees can use to nominate their peers for organizational perks and/or recognition. Complimenting other people and fostering respect creates a positive workplace culture.[26]

The counterintuitive strategy of encouraging workers to buck the system can produce positive benefits.

Employee-centric firms dissolve "us vs. them" distinctions through:

- displaying an interest in employees as persons;[27]
- holding anti-bullying education workshops;
- initiating town hall meetings to discuss issues;
- instigating informal departmental activities;
- making a concerted effort to know employees;
- mandating open-door policy from leaders;
- presenting awards to employees for considerate behavior; and
- requiring training on cultural differences, peer respect, and considerate ways of expressing opinions and questioning others' platforms.

"The 'new millennium worker' [wishes] to be viewed as partner. [They] will respond positively to [a] facilitative leadership style, ... [one] which is supportive, empathic, compassionate, and encouraging." "[Participative management] requires an element of trust, and a faith in employees' determination to provide quality work."[28] "Handling" people is a world apart from giving them the tools to solve their own problems.

When employees arrive at work, what they experience determines whether they feel comfortable in speaking their minds and if they are expected to do so in a respectful fashion. Timely, accurate, unambiguous communication, and a mandate that people keep their emotions in check, can prevent nasty disagreements.[29] People-centered leaders encourage functional disruption and airing of oppositional viewpoints through:[30]

- *Job rotation.* If you walked in someone's shoes for a month, a week, or even one day—would you see them differently? Would you be less likely to criticize them if you had a more complete understanding of what they accomplished? A well-rounded perspective contributes to joint resolution of differences, instead of to unfounded critiques and complaints.

- *Leadership development.* "Dean's disease," or the possession of an exalted position (over time), creates managers who are more concerned with keeping their position than with developing their employees.[31] A leadership development program based on feedback helps bosses to accurately view their blind spots and to become more respected and affable leaders in the process.
- *Debate.* Hearing both sides of an argument can positively affect decision-making. Because offices are comprised of different personas (introverted/extroverted, open to experience/more conservative in approach), debates should occur in verbal and nonverbal formats. Some companies use a horseshoe configuration and a computer screen positioned at the front of a room to display responses, and to allow feedback to occur simultaneously and anonymously.
- *Team building.* Outdoor exercises, adventure games, and off-site communication training[32] stimulate problem-solving behaviors through a dissolution of job labels and organizational hierarchy.
- *Direct interaction.* Workers should be encouraged to speak *with* one another. In the "How We Manage Conflict at Google" YouTube video,[33] Liane Hornsey explains that boss intervention (between feuding parties) at Google is rare, because meddling might alienate at least one party involved in the conflict. Googlers are encouraged to handle differences among themselves and to use honesty and the Golden Rule as their guiding principles [see the Appendix for a multi-step process to encourage diplomacy and a more collaborative style[34] when speaking with a coworker].

Leaders can promote healthy give and take by using the STATE (share, tell, ask, talk tentatively, encourage testing)[35] model, where leaders use a conversational style that promotes equity and sharing among participants, and where they follow up using gentle encouragement. The STATE model (described below) can uncover potentially counterproductive workplace issues in a non-threatening manner.

STATE

1. *Share* what happened using objective, fact-based descriptions.
2. *Tell* your version of events by suggesting what you think may have contributed to the problem. (Acknowledging factors outside of someone's

control eases tension, encourages dialogue, and demonstrates an openness to alternative interpretations and problem resolution.)

3. *Ask* the other party to share their viewpoints and their version of events.
4. *Talk tentatively,* using questioning tags like "I wonder," "Correct me if I'm wrong, but . . . ," and "Am I on the right path . . . ?" to mitigate defensiveness.
5. *Encourage testing* (using solicitation, as opposed to shellacking) with language like, "I'd love to hear what you have to say; I think the solution could benefit from your perspectives. Would you mind sharing them with me?"

STATE Example (a supervisor is speaking to an employee about an expense report anomaly at work):

> **Share:** In the past month, I've noticed some unusual charges on your expense account, ones that exceeded your budget.
>
> **Employee:** I wasn't aware of these.
>
> **Tell:** Lately, the Accounting Department has been slammed with expense accounts from several regional divisions; there have been reports of receivables clerks inadvertently mixing up itemized accounts. We have a new hire in that department, so they might not be up to speed. [Tentative]
>
> **Ask:** Do you think someone else could have made a mistake?
>
> **Employee:** I'd have to go through my paperwork, but no one has ever questioned my expense reports before.
>
> **Encourage testing:** You have a sterling reputation, so I imagine this snafu is a mix-up (a contrast of the initial inquiry with an affirmation). Could you shed some light on this? I know that together, we can get to the bottom of things and clear this up quickly.

If someone appears reluctant to share, then "priming" (a technique that casts you, the questioner, as more vulnerable in the exchange) is a good way to discern how other people feel. The supervisor in the above example might use the statement below to draw information from her employee:

> "I sense that you feel I'm scrutinizing your expense reports. The last thing I'd want is for you to feel micromanaged. Is that how you feel? All I'm trying to do is ensure accuracy for our year-end report."

Reaching the crux of a problem by acknowledging other perspectives results in future dialogue where people are less likely to either clam up or lash out. Conflict and misunderstandings are more likely to occur when people behave in a forceful, single-minded, and doggedly persistent fashion. To avoid a ruckus at work, ask yourself, "What is the endgame?" Do you want to control, to "win" at all costs, to put someone in their place? Or do you instead wish for mutual understanding and esteem among conflicted parties? Collaborators rise above their knee-jerk responses, their hair-trigger feelings of offense, passive aggression, vindictiveness, and intractable grudges to solve problems.

Reflection

Think back to a conflict where you or a coworker mishandled communication and created long-lasting negative feelings between you. Considering the conflict-management techniques discussed in this chapter, what could you (or he/she) have done differently to eliminate the tension?

_____

_____

_____

_____

> What leaders say should support and empower their employees. A learning community will be far superior to one where individuals are continually infighting.[36]

Online Resources

- Bunashe, J., & Broder, L. (2015, June 12). How leaders can best manage conflict within their teams. Retrieved from https://www.entrepreneur.com/article/247275
- Gilbert, J. A. (2016, June 30). Excavate your personal plank [Blog post]. Retrieved from https://organizedforefficiency.com/excavate-your-personal-plank/

- Lipman, V. (2013, April 3). How to manage conflict at work. Retrieved from https://www.forbes.com/sites/victorlipman/2013/04/03/how-to-manage-conflict-at-work/#1205d4c65ee5
- Shonk, K. (2019, May 27). Negotiation case studies: Google's approach to dispute resolution [Blog post]. Retrieved from https://www.pon.harvard.edu/daily/dispute-resolution/googles-approach-to-dispute-resolution/

Appendix
Process to Encourage Give-and-Take in a Discussion[*]

1. *Invite* someone else to have a conversation in a mutually designated place to discuss issues.
2. *Use* respectful behavior[37]—like non-accusatory language, reciprocal dialogue,[38] and positive facial expressions.
3. *Scan* for negative nonverbal communication and check to see if your message was received in the intended manner. If you sense confusion or disagreement, query the other party's take on what was said, and ask for clarity when you misunderstand what the other person has stated.[*]
4. *Correct* the erroneous statements and behavior of other people in a gentle, tactful fashion.

> **Scene: Someone sees that another person is using the computer in his assigned time.**
>
> Hi! You may have overlooked this, but there is a computer sign-up sheet at the front desk. My session began at 2:00. Would you mind if I used the computer now?

5. *Avoid* making assumptions. Ask questions and maintain an open mind before you arrive at a decision.
6. *Refrain* from dwelling on past events that are unrelated to the issue. Victim status creates a defensive attitude in other people.
7. *Offer* an olive branch, even if you are not the one who has made a mistake.
8. *Affirm* the positive qualities of your conversation partner and thank them for sharing their perspectives.[*]

[*] Adapted from Lytle, T. (2015, July 13). How to resolve workplace conflicts. *SHRM*. Retrieved from https://www.shrm.org/hr-today/news/hr-magazine/pages/070815-conflict-management

.aspx

Web Quests

1. Search the Internet for some of the worst ways to handle conflict at work. What could managers do to improve these? (See "4 Ways Leaders Effectively Manage Employee Conflict," [39] which suggests that getting to know employees and treating them with respect are key to maintaining positivity at work.)

_____

_____

_____

_____

2. Read the web article "A Practical Guide for Defusing Conflict" [40] How do the suggestions inform you, as a leader, to behave? In what situations will you use face-to-face communication instead of electronic methods? (See "Conflict Escalation: Dispute Exacerbating Elements of E-mail Communication." [41])

_____

_____

_____

_____

3. How can leaders increase cultural harmony without creating friction? Check out some recommendations, such as keeping a "cultural journal" to document perceptions of other people, in the web article "How Cultural Conflict Undermines Workplace Creativity." [42]

_____

_____

_____

_____

What Would You Do?

1. A coworker avoids you. When you catch her eye, she says the bare minimum, averts her gaze, and takes the long way back to her office. In the spirit of *Non-Violent Communication* (see Rosenberg's suggestions in Chapter 2), what is the best way to approach her?

    _____

    _____

    _____

    _____

2. Marj, your coworker, is a renowned sycophant and conflict avoider. You have just been promoted to a leadership position, and now you are the one supervising Marj. How can you encourage her to share information that is not just what she thinks managers want to hear, but that includes honest opinions and a realistic appraisal of the workplace situation? See "Strong Leaders Encourage Dissent, and Gain Commitment,"[43] which suggests that a confluence of ideas makes for the best final product, and "Why Great Leaders Don't Take Yes for an Answer."[44]

    _____

    _____

    _____

    _____

3. Your team lead has just cursed a coworker in a heated debate. Subsequently, both members' productivity drops significantly, and other people in your department are dragged into the office conflict. What should the team lead do? In your response, cite research that suggests the power of a leaderful apology. See "Courageous Leaders Don't Make Excuses . . . They Apologize"[45] for some specifics on an "apology primer," "When Should a Leader Apologize—and

When Not?"[46] and "On Apology"[47] for an explanation of the importance of apologizing.

_____

_____

_____

_____

10

Epilogue

Opportunities to Enact Change

Why Employee-Centered Firms Are Important

> *"One day in 2001, [Daniel] Raess became angry because [Joseph] Doescher had complained to the administration about how Raess treated coworkers. Testifying at a later trial, Doescher claimed that Raess 'aggressively and rapidly advanced on him with clenched fists, piercing eyes, beet-red face, popping veins, and screaming and swearing at him.'"[1]*

The cost of employing egotistical, haughty, and exploitative employees—"bad apples" who steal the spotlight and disrupt the office culture[2]—is high. Although some may be above-average performers, they can undermine workplace harmony through self-centeredness,[3] irritability, low EQ,[4] and elitism. This also can result in them using mercenary, self-serving pricing and pay tactics.[5]

Bullies who are promoted to bosses are able to manipulate their peers. [6] Research has found that abusive managerial behavior affects employees two levels down. Managers can influence what supervisors consider

---

How to Transform Workplace Bullies Into Allies, pages 199–208
Copyright © 2020 by Information Age Publishing
All rights of reproduction in any form reserved.

acceptable behavior at work, encourage inappropriate role modeling,[7] and influence teammates who behave badly toward one another.[8]

abusive managers

abusive supervisors

teammates who embarass, humiliate, and bully each other

Because negligent bosses make decisions that affect a multitude of stakeholders, they have a multiplier effect on customers, company image, and product sales. Forty percent of surveyed consumers stated they would not buy products if they knew they had originated from companies they didn't like[9]—a finding that may incite firms to be more circumspect in the image they project. Impact is now as important as profit. One criterion on which potential customers evaluate companies—and make their purchasing decisions—is how managers treat their employees.[10]

> Setting positive standards can change dysfunctional culture. People rise to a high level of expectation, or oppositely, sink to inarticulate norms.

Proactive companies take the bullies by the horns through posting a zero-tolerance policy that sends an unmistakable signal.

Bully-Busting Hall of Fame[11]

- *ServiceMaster* doesn't tolerate abuse, no matter how high-ranking the offender.
- *DuPont Memphis'* focus has shifted from command and control to preserving and promoting people-centered practice.
- *Tom's of Maine* ex-CEO Tom Chappell fired employees who were insensitive, who abused their authority, or who mistreated co-workers.
- *Southwest Airlines* refused to hire a pilot after he was rude to a receptionist,[12] despite his exceptional credentials.
- *Zappos* makes potential new hires pass the "nice guy" test, which measures how interviewees from out of town treat the shuttle driver. If the report is unfavorable, they don't get the job.[13]

Noxious bosses may create expectations of bad experiences and behavior[14] within toxic companies. Conversely, cooperative work cultures can provide endorphin release and a stress buffer.

In reactive firms, workers experience the following sequence of events:

1. Attack! Bullies on the rampage choose targets. They are joined by gawkers—a crowd of onlookers who seek protection through shared silence—and the bullies' minions.
2. Run for cover. Targets assume outsider status, and coworkers steer clear of future contact with them.
3. Pretend like nothing happened. Bosses continue business as usual. Employees learn that abusive conduct will be sidestepped, tolerated, and possibly condoned.
4. Blame the victim. Abusers and bystanders explain how targets annoyed the abuser. Managers enable bullies when they say nothing, or worse, when they feel that only inappropriate behavior from the target could have instigated an attack.[15] Bullying is seen as "provocation of the victim or a strategic leadership behavior that is a temporary jolt to the target designed to assist their long-term success."[16] Unbalanced power dynamics between bullies and their targets create an unfair cataloging of events.

To be effective, leaders must confront serial abusers, analyze the evidence, notify top leadership at the company, and obtain an agreement from the bully that bad behavior will not recur.[17] Abusers who are unable to amass followers may move elsewhere.

The Results

Concerted effort can produce impressive outcomes.

- In a study of 16,898 dual-earner employee couples, family-friendly policies such as taking time off and telework, along with high-performance work practices such as autonomous work teams and on-the-job discretion, were associated with increased job satisfaction and a feeling of work life/family balance.[18]
- At Harley-Davidson, market share rose by 35% and output increased threefold when employees became partners in determining company policy.[19]
- At the former Dupont Belle Plant, Richard Knowles' "shoe leather" campaign led to a 95% injury rate decline and a reduction in environmental emissions of more than 87%. EPE (earnings per employee) increased threefold.[20]
- In a sample of 968 firms, a one standard deviation increase in high-performance work practices—quality circles, worker training, profit-sharing, and employee voice—decreased turnover by 7.05%. It also increased sales by an average of $27,044, market value by $18,641, and profits by $3,814 per employee.[21]
- High-quality relationships or a *participative community*, where relics of rank like large offices are eliminated, resulted in a "sixfold increase in earnings" in the first year of their implementation at Oticon.[22]
- In a survey of 1,064 employees, 96% of Googlers reported that they were proud to tell outsiders the name of their employer.[23] Their pride reflects Alphabet's "Do the right thing" core value: "follow the law, act honorably, treat each other with respect." The parent company creates positive culture through collaboration with employees and by encouraging them to support one another in a bully-free environment.[1] Google claimed the number one spot in the 2017 Fortune 100 Best Companies to Work for Report, followed (in order) by Wegman's Food Markets, The Boston Consulting Group, Baird, and Edward Jones.

Workers who are treated as partners and empowered as owners create workplace equanimity. Low employee turnover and exemplary annualized stock market returns result when supervisors communicate often and with respect, solicit employee opinion, and delegate and motivate workers to accomplish organizational meta-goals. Civility emanates from top-leader role modeling and trickle-down acts of kindness that take root at all company levels.

Trust (I feel like I can depend on people), engagement (my work is more than a job), transparency (I feel comfortable speaking to my leader), communication (continuous conversation between leaders and employees), and intention (everyone is on board with the plan) round out the top company attributes of companies that foster positivity[24] and engender loyalty, collegiality, and a contagion effect that spreads compassionate behavior. Cultures that encourage feedback[25] elicit more civil behavior and create a scaffolding of kindness as well.

> When employees feel buoyant, they produce better work.[26]

The CareerBliss "50 Happiest Companies in America"[27] report notes that pay is only *one* equally weighted factor that contributes to a perception of workplace greatness. Other dimensions that affect overall employee happiness include leader-member relations, work environment/office culture, job satisfaction, and opportunities for career development.

Does Culture Affect Firm Performance or Vice Versa?

In a study of 95 car dealerships (over a 6-year period), Anthony Boyce, Levi Nieminen, Michael Gillespie, Ann Marie Ryan, and Daniel Denison[28] found that departmental culture positively and significantly affected both customer satisfaction and vehicle sales. Culture, as defined in their study, consisted of the following four components:

- *Employee involvement:* Leadership encouraged democratic participation and individual growth across hierarchical levels.
- *Internal consistency:* Managers and employees cooperated by jointly determining policy.
- *Adaptability:* Employees took advantage of learning opportunities.
- *Mission:* Strategy trickled down to operating levels and enhanced performance metrics.

Can Cultures That Discourage Abuse and Model Top Leadership Support Reduce Bullying?

In zero-tolerance companies:

- Employees who hold implicit biases and who outwardly support women and minorities, but who overtly discriminate, may cease their exclusionary practice if their organization makes continuous, proactive attempts to educate employees and to promote inclusion [29]; and

- Employees who overtly discriminated against women and minorities (and who, in an inclusive culture find no avenues to express their dissatisfaction) may choose to leave the company.

In people-centered companies:

- Employees know where leaders stand and that they respect employee rights. Cooperative leaders behave as partners who are open to critique and self-improvement.[30] They inspire civil behavior from customers and coworkers when they show concern for freedom, decency, and fairness.[31]

"Cooperative" Firm Exemplars

- At *Southwest Airlines*, employees demonstrate goodwill by volunteering to help customers and coworkers, by modeling considerate behavior, and by going above and beyond what is expected. [32] When a colon cancer patient was separated from her luggage that contained her chemotherapy medication, a Southwest service agent drove over 20 miles to deliver the needed supplies—which arrived at 3:00 a.m.![33]
- In her book *Managing With the Wisdom of Love: Uncovering Virtue in People and Organizations,* Dorothy Marcic describes New Management Virtues of trustworthiness, unity, respect, justice, and humility,[34] which are reflected in *Hewlett Packard's* "trust and respect for individuals" credo.
- Leaders at *ServiceMaster* stress empowerment, flexibility, servant leadership, dignity, and life-long learning[35] to create an employee-centric culture. The common thread linking individuals is unity, a belief that suggests people can reach their potential by confronting and eliminating discrimination at work so that everyone can move forward with a more informed perspective.

CEOs, whether they are in a proactive, reactive, or turnaround mode, have the power to shape policy, folklore, norms, and organizational culture through an overhaul of the way they do business.

> Inclusive leadership—or its absence—produces a domino effect that permeates the surrounding community and affects recruitment, stock price, customer goodwill, and, ultimately, company image.

A MODEL OF EFFECTIVE DIVERSITY MANAGEMENT

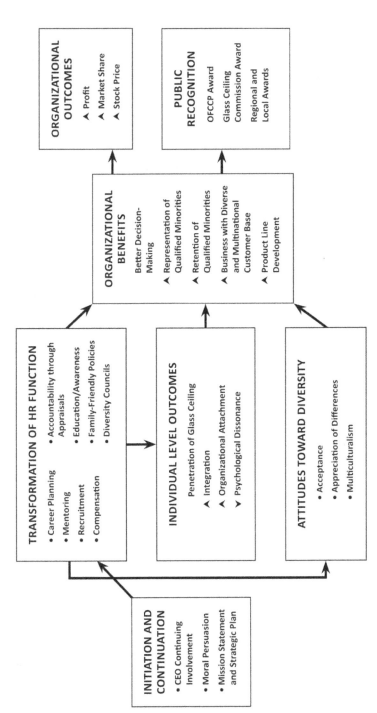

ORGANIZATIONAL OUTCOMES
- ▲ Profit
- ▲ Market Share
- ▲ Stock Price

PUBLIC RECOGNITION
- OFCCP Award
- Glass Ceiling Commission Award
- Regional and Local Awards

ORGANIZATIONAL BENEFITS
- Better Decision-Making
- ▲ Representation of Qualified Minorities
- ▲ Retention of Qualified Minorities
- ▲ Business with Diverse and Multinational Customer Base
- ▲ Product Line Development

TRANSFORMATION OF HR FUNCTION
- Career Planning
- Mentoring
- Recruitment
- Compensation
- Accountability through Appraisals
- Education/Awareness
- Family-Friendly Policies
- Diversity Councils

INDIVIDUAL LEVEL OUTCOMES
Penetration of Glass Ceiling
- ▲ Integration
- ▲ Organizational Attachment
- ▼ Psychological Dissonance

ATTITUDES TOWARD DIVERSITY
- Acceptance
- Appreciation of Differences
- Multiculturalism

INITIATION AND CONTINUATION
- CEO Continuing Involvement
- Moral Persuasion
- Mission Statement and Strategic Plan

Reprinted with permission from *Springer Journal of Business Ethics Diversity Management: A New Organizational Paradigm, 21*(1), (1999), 61–76, Gilbert, J. A., Stead, B. A., & Ivancevich. J. M. ©1999 Kluwer Academic Publishers. Printed in the Netherlands.

To shift from a problem-based to an outcome-based workplace, bosses need to study exemplars, set the stage for why change is necessary, and then jointly craft a plan to foster new, empowering behaviors that contribute to an inclusive workplace culture.

How to Create People-Centered Bosses

Companies must reexamine the criteria for promotion to ensure that responsibility and emotional maturity exist at the executive level.[36] Max De Pree, the former CEO of Herman Miller, argues that performance appraisal criteria should encompass principles[37] from what Mahatma Gandhi describes as "the seven social sins." These are wealth without work, pleasure without conscience, knowledge without character, commerce without morality, science without humanity, worship without sacrifice, and politics without principle. If technical skills and goal achievement are solely rewarded, employees may think that people-centered skills are unimportant. PepsiCo—which, according to Grote Consulting, bases 40% of employee bonus on how well individuals develop their coworkers[38]—realized that employees may plateau if they are unable to work well with others. Some criteria for consideration to be considered an "unleader," or democratic boss, include a willingness to:

- *act* as a mentor;
- *carefully monitor* their communications for embedded racist/sexist attitudes, and constructively address workplace abuse;[39]
- *initiate* projects with newcomers;
- *communicate* empathically;
- *contribute* to ideas that promote inclusion;
- *defuse* tension within interpersonal situations;
- *focus* on self-improvement;
- *offer* helping behaviors to the lesser-experienced and to those who are the most dependent on others for their success; and
- *volunteer* for employee mentoring and orientation.

Employees who are solicited for their opinions often feel embedded within the company fabric.[40]

The Legacy of Bully-Busters at Work[41]

Opposition to powerful others can be taught—but the problem of conformance persists [42] because few are teaching an alternative. Behaviors and practices that set resistance leaders apart from the "I got mine; you get yours any way you can" mindset and encourage them to oppose bad policy can be learned.

> [Resistance leaders] are nothing like bystanders who stand to the side. Their behavior is 180 degrees from the concept of mobbing—in which half the people are delighted to bully another person and the remaining half hide behind the bully's skirt.
> Bully resistors think outside the box of self-protection to enact change. In contrast to coworkers who may easily fold and become part of the crowd, they are difficult to break. Resistors are their own persons who possess an immutable moral compass. They follow their conscience, eschew ill-gotten gains, and assist empathetic, principled employees who refuse to capitulate.[43]
> If enough people confronted abuse (and named it), organizational weasels, snakes, and jerks[44] would cease and desist. Better yet, many of them would never see the light of day. Tolerance of small abuses can lead to groupthink, whether in a nation, state, community, or a single meeting. People who are willing to act as lightning rods could, over time, revolutionize their firms. Abused targets could reframe their role as resistance leaders and behave as both exemplars and change agents. Organizational dissidents can prevent the rule of yes men/women within their companies, and they can preempt the rise of bullies within their schools.

We can take a stand within our unique sphere of influence.

Today, take a chance, risk discomfort.

A more courteous future is within our reach.

Online Resources

- Cable, D. (2018, April 23). How humble leadership really works [Blog post]. Retrieved from https://hbr.org/2018/04/how-humble -leadership-really-works?referral=03759&cm_vc=rr_item_page .bottom
- Gilbert, J. A. (2011, August 23). Defiance in the face of opposition [Blog post]. Retrieved from https://organizedforefficiency .com/defiance-in-the-face-of-opposition/

- Gilbert, J. A. (2011, May 10). The makings of a movement [Blog post]. Retrieved from https://organizedforefficiency.com/the -makings-of-a-movement/
- Gilbert, J. A. (2011, June 29). Non-violent militancy to mend fences [Blog post]. Retrieved from https://organizedforefficiency .com/non-violent-militancy-to-mend-fences/
- Gilbert, J. A. (2011, December 22). Reframing the anti-bullying movement [Blog post]. Retrieved from https://organizedfor efficiency.com/reframing-the-anti-bullying-movement/
- Gilbert, J. A. (2012, January 28). The personality of change [Blog post]. Retrieved from https://organizedforefficiency.com/the -personality-of-change/
- Gilbert, J. A. (2013, December 29). Defiance and disruptors [Blog post]. Retrieved from https://organizedforefficiency.com/ defiance-and-disruptors/

Note

1. In a reflection of how conditions at work can change quickly, workers protested what they thought were unfair employment practices at Google.

   See the web article "Google Reportedly Has a Massive Culture Problem that's Destroying it from the Inside."

   Gilbert, B. (2019, August 13). Google reportedly has a massive culture problem that's destroying it from the inside. *Business Insider.* Retrieved from https://www.businessinsider.com/google-culture-problems-eric-schmidt-aberrant -geniuses-2019-8

References

Chapter 1

[1] Porath, C., & Pearson, C. (2013). The price of incivility: Lack of respect hurts morale—and the bottom line, *91*(1–2), 114–121. Retrieved from https://hbr.org/2013/01/the-price-of-incivility

[2] Namie, G. (2014, April 24). Estimating the costs of workplace bullying [Blog post]. Retrieved from http://www.workplacebullying.org/costs/

[3] Gunsalus, C. K. (2006). *The college administrator's survival guide.* Cambridge, MA: Harvard University Press. (p. 122)

[4] Mukherjee, S. (2011). *A life interrupted: The story of my battle with bullying and obsessive-compulsive disorder.* Bloomington, IN: Xlibris Corporation.

[5] Tracy, S. J., Lutgen-Sandvik, P., & Alberts, J. K. (2006). Nightmares, demons, and slaves: Exploring the painful metaphors of workplace bullying. *Management Communication Quarterly, 20*(2), 148–185.

[6] Wlassoff, V. (2015, January 24). How does post-traumatic stress disorder change the brain? [Blog post]. Retrieved from http://brainblogger.com/2015/01/24/how-does-post-traumatic-stress-disorder-change-the-brain/

[7] Otten, M., & Jonas, K. J. (2014). Humiliation as an intense emotional experience: Evidence from the electro-encephalogram. *Social Neuroscience, 9*(1), 23–35. http://dx.doi.org/10.1080/17470919.2013.855660

[8] Schmitz, T. W., Correia, M. M., Ferreira, C. S., Prescot, A. P., & Anderson, M. C. (2017). Hippocampal GABA enables inhibitory control over

How to Transform Workplace Bullies Into Allies, pages 209–246
Copyright © 2020 by Information Age Publishing
All rights of reproduction in any form reserved.

unwanted thoughts. *Nature Communications, 8*(1), 1–12. https://doi.org/10.1038/s41467-017-00956-z

[9] Namie, G. (2012, December 3). Workplace bullying drives Annette Prada, NM gov't worker, to suicide [Blog post]. Retrieved from http://www.workplacebullying.org/prada/

[10] Sanchez, R. (2010, August 17). Did depression or an alleged bully boss prompt editor's suicide? [Blog post]. Retrieved from http://abcnews.go.com/Business/MindMoodResourceCenter/editors-suicide-draws-attention-workplace-bullying/story?id=11421810

[11] Walton, A. G. (2012, July 5). Bully psychology: Where evolution and morality collide [Blog post]. (Retrieved from https://www.forbes.com/sites/alicegwalton/2012/07/05/bully-psychology-why-bullying-is-one-of-evolutions-big-snafus/#2f1725dd6559). Christopher Boehm, whom Walton references, is the author of *Moral Origins: The Evolution of Virtue, Altruism, and Shame.* See Boehm, C. (2012). *Moral origins: The evolution of virtue, altruism, and shame.* New York, NY: Basic Books.

[12] The bad news: Derailment happens. (2001). *Center for Creative Leadership.* Retrieved from http://myccl.ccl.org/leadership/pdf/publications/badNewsGoodNews.pdf

[13] Zenger, J., & Folkman, J. (2013, May 2). I'm the boss! Why should I care if you like me? [Blog post]. Retrieved from https://hbr.org/2013/05/im-the-boss-why-should-i-care

[14] ibid.

[15] Wilfert, M. (2007). *Building new traditions: Hazing prevention in college athletics.* Retrieved from NCAA website: https://www.ncaa.org/sites/default/files/hazing%20prevention%20handbook%2057315.pdf

[16] Rosenberg, M. B. *Non-Violent Communication.* (2015). Encinitas, CA: PuddleDancer Press.

[17] Ni, P. (2015, October 11). 14 signs of psychological and emotional manipulation [Blog post]. Retrieved from https://www.psychologytoday.com/blog/communication-success/201510/14-signs-psychological-and-emotional-manipulation

[18] Rosenberg, M. B. *Non-violent communication.* (2015). Encinitas, CA: PuddleDancer Press.

[19] Gibson, L. C. (2015). *Adult children of emotionally immature parents: How to heal from distant, rejecting, or self-involved parents.* Oakland, CA: New Harbinger.

[20] Namie, G., & Namie, R. (2009). *The bully at work: What you can do to stop the hurt and reclaim your dignity on the job.* Naperville, IL: Sourcebooks.

[21] Chapman, D. (2009). Best responses to a bully. *kickbully.com.* Retrieved from http://www.kickbully.com/best.html

[22] Vonk, R. (1998). The slime effect: Suspicion and dislike of likeable behavior toward superiors. *Journal of Personality and Social Psychology, 74*(4), 849–864. https://doi.org/10.1037/0022-3514.74.4.849 (p. 857)

[23] How to Find and Stop the Workplace Snitch. (2016, May 13). (Retrieved from http://www.comparebusinessproducts.com/fyi/how-to-find-and-stop-the-workplace-snitch). For a description of workplace honesty and the value of directly expressing oneself to coworkers, see *Powerful* by Patty McCord, Netflix former Chief Talent Officer. McCord, P. (2017). *Powerful: Building a culture of freedom and responsibility.* Jackson TN: Silicon Guild. Also see Gilbert, J. A. (2016, March 14). Behind your back "bully-lites" [Blog post]. (Retrieved from https://organizedforefficiency.com/behind-your-back-bully-lites/). Author Fred Kofman describes his method of dealing with conflict between employees as "escalating collaboration." If a subordinate walked into his office to complain, his first question might be, "Have you discussed this with your coworker?" He suggests that conversations about (and not with) other people undermine a spirit of mutual respect. If negotiations with one's fellow worker(s) are unsuccessful, he holds a meeting with feuding parties. Boss-buddy interactions leave at least one person feeling alienated, isolated, and maligned for the duration of the working relationship. See Kofman, F. (2018). *The meaning revolution: The power of transcendent leadership.* New York, NY: Currency.

[24] Jordan, P. J., Ashkanasy, N. M., & Härtel, C. E. J. (2002). Emotional intelligence as a moderator of emotional and behavioral reactions to job insecurity. *Academy of Management Review, 27*(3), 361–372. https://doi.org/10.2307/4134384

[25] Sternberg, R. J. (2003). WICS: A model of leadership in organizations. *Academy of Management Learning & Education, 2*(4), 386–401. https://doi.org/10.5465/AMLE.2003.11902088

[26] McCain, J., & Salter, S. (2004). *Why courage matters: The way to a braver life.* New York, NY: Random House.

[27] Gilbert, J. A. (2011, November 21). Modern day resistance [Blog post]. Retrieved from https://organizedforefficiency.com/modern-day-resistance/

[28] Amanda, G. (2010). Coping with seven disruptive personality types in the classroom [White paper]. Retrieved from http://www.northwestms.edu/library/Library/Web/magna_wp7.pdf

[29] Gilbert, J. A. (2017, April 25). The doggedness of OCPD [Blog post]. Retrieved from https://organizedforefficiency.com/the-doggedness-of-ocpd/

Chapter 2

[1] Richardson, J. E., & McCord, L. B. (2001). Are workplace bullies sabotaging your ability to compete? *Graziadio Business Review, 4*(4), 1–16. (Retrieved from https://frrl.files.wordpress.com/2012/07/gbr-pepperdine-edu_2010_08_are-workplace-bullies-sabotag.pdf). This quote is adapted from Namie, G., & Namie, R. (2000). *The bully at work: What you can do to stop the hurt and reclaim your dignity on the job.* Naperville, IL: Sourcebooks;

and Davenport, N., Schwartz, R. D., & Elliott, G. P. (1999). *Mobbing: Emotional abuse in the American workplace*. Ames, Iowa: Civil Society.

[2]   Dizik, A. (2010, October 18). What to do if you're cursed out at work. *CNN*. (Retrieved from http://www.cnn.com/2010/LIVING/10/18/cb.cursed.out. work/). If you do find yourself in a volley of cursing/profanity/indignation, Dizik suggests temporarily removing yourself—then later explaining your desire for respectful interaction at work.

[3]   Bedeian, A. G. (2002). The dean's disease: How the darker side of power manifests itself in the office of dean. *Academy of Management Learning and Education, 1*(2), 164–173. http://dx.doi.org/10.5465/AMLE.2002.8509359

[4]   Gilbert, J. A. (2016, October 15). Pets on parade [Blog post]. (Retrieved from https://organizedforefficiency.com/pets-on-parade/). Modified and adapted from the original post.

[5]   Parker, D., & Parker, M. (2017, September 15). Sick of sycophants [Blog post]. Retrieved from https://www.psychologytoday.com/us/blog/sucking/201709/sick-sycophants

[6]   Gilbert, J. A. (2014, April 11). Bullying and the boss's buddy [Blog post]. (Retrieved from https://organizedforefficiency.com/bullying-and-the-bosss-buddy/). Bullet points were modified and adapted from the original post.

[7]   Gilbert, J. A. (2013, August 24). The case for reverse snitching [Blog post]. Retrieved from https://organizedforefficiency.com/the-case-for-reverse-snitching/

[8]   Gilbert, J. A. (2014, April 11). Bullying and the boss's buddy [Blog post]. Retrieved from http://organizedforefficiency.com/bullying-and-the-bosss-buddy/

[9]   Gilbert, J. A. (2013, August 24). The case for reverse snitching [Blog post]. (Retrieved from https://organizedforefficiency.com/the-case-for-reverse-snitching/). Modified and adapted from the original post.

[10]   ibid.

[11]   Brass, D. J. (1984). Being in the right place: A structural analysis of individual influence in an organization. *Administrative Science Quarterly, 29*(4), 518–539.

[12]   Wang, S., Hu, Q., & Dong, B. (2015). Managing personal networks: An examination of how high self-monitors achieve better job performance. *Journal of Vocational Behavior, 91*, 180–188. https://doi.org/10.1016/j.jvb.2015.10.005

[13]   Kristof-Brown, A., Barrick, M. R., & Franke, M. (2002). Applicant impression management: Dispositional influences and consequences for recruiter perceptions of fit and personality. *Journal of Management, 28*(1), 27–46. https://doi.org/10.1177/014920630202800103

[14]   Politicking and Power Seeking. (1991, January). *SPIRIT*. 22 & 28–29.

[15]   Yu, L., Duffy, M. K., & Tepper, B. J. (2018). Consequences of downward envy: A model of self-esteem threat, abusive supervision, and supervisory leader self-improvement. *Academy of Management Journal, 61*(6), 2296–2318. https://doi.org/10.5465/amj.2015.0183

[16]   Osborne, H. (2010, June 18). Envy in the workplace: Jealous guise [Blog post]. Retrieved from https://www.theguardian.com/money/2010/jun/19/envy-workplace-recession

[17]   Rosenberg, M. B. (2015). *Non-violent communication: A language of life.* Encinitas, CA: PuddleDancer Press.

[18]   ibid.

[19]   Kraft, R. N. (2017, April 28). Restoring our selves and others after personal injustices [Blog post]. Retrieved from https://www.psychologytoday.com/us/blog/defining-memories/201704/restoring-our-selves-and-others-after-personal-injustices

[20]   Menon, T., & Thompson, L. (2010). Envy at work. *Harvard Business Review, 88*(4), 74–79.

[21]   Gilbert, J. A. (2015, October 16). The inner workings of a stalker [Blog post]. Retrieved from https://organizedforefficiency.com/the-inner-workings-of-a-stalker/

[22]   Stalking Resource Center. (n.d.). Retrieved from http://victimsofcrime.org/our-programs/stalking-resource-center/stalking-information

[23]   Vaknin, S. (2011, May 19). *Stalker psychology* [Video file]. Retrieved from https://www.youtube.com/watch?v=Ol2RM135ZHI&feature=youtu.be

[24]   ibid.

[25]   Saunders, R. B., & Michaud, S. G. (2008). *Whisper of fear: The true story of the prosecutor who stalks the stalkers.* New York, NY: Berkley Books. (p. xii).

[26]   Vaknin, S. (2011, May 19). *Stalker psychology.* [Video file]. Retrieved from https://www.youtube.com/watch?v=Ol2RM135ZHI&feature=youtu.be

[27]   Peirce, P. (1997). *The intuitive way: The definitive guide to increasing your awareness.* New York, NY: Atria.

[28]   Saunders, R. B., & Michaud, S. G. (2008). *Whisper of fear: The true story of the prosecutor who stalks the stalkers.* New York, NY: Berkley Books. (p. xii).

[29]   Logan, T. K., Cole, J., & Shannon, L., & Walker, R. (2006). *Partner stalking: How women respond, cope, and survive.* New York, NY: Springer. (p. 31). Information regarding phone calls is from a study by Mary Brewster, who in a study of 187 women who were targets of intimate stalking found that 90.4 percent reported stalking via phone call. See Brewster, M. P. (1999). An exploration of the experiences and needs of former intimate stalking victims. Retrieved from https://www.ncjrs.gov/pdffiles1/nij/grants/175475.pdf

[30]   Characteristics of a stalker. (2019). *Marshall Women's Center.* Retrieved from the Women's Center website: https://www.marshall.edu/wcenter/stalking/characteristic-of-a-stalker/

[31]   Gilbert, J. A. (2011, February 21). Ways to recognize stalking at work [Blog post]. (Retrieved from http://organizedforefficiency.com/ways-to-recognize-stalking-at-work/). Bullet points were modified and adapted from the original post.

[32]   Pasquella, D. (2010, May 20). Is it "stalking" or "peeking"? [Blog post]. Retrieved from http://www.debrapasquella.com/2010/05/is-it-stalking-or-peeking.html

[33]   Saunders, R. B., & Michaud, S. G. (2008). *Whisper of fear: The true story of the prosecutor who stalks the stalkers.* New York, NY: Berkley Books.

[34]   Vaknin, S. (2011, May 19). *Stalker psychology* [Video file]. Retrieved from https://www.youtube.com/watch?v=Ol2RM135ZHI&feature=youtu.be

[35]   ibid.

[36]   Samenow, S. E. (2017, December 15). The thinking processes of sexual predators [Blog post]. Retrieved from https://www.psychologytoday.com/us/blog/inside-the-criminal-mind/201712/the-thinking-processes-sexual-predators

[37]   Gilbert, J. A. (2015, October 16). The inner workings of a stalker [Blog post]. (Retrieved from https://organizedforefficiency.com/the-inner-workings-of-a-stalker/). Modified and adapted from the original post.

[38]   Gilbert, J. A. (2017, August 31). What you don't know about stalking [Blog post]. (Retrieved from https://organizedforefficiency.com/what-you-dont-know-about-stalking/). Modified and adapted from the original post.

[39]   Morrison, K. A. (2001). Predicting violent behavior in stalkers: A preliminary investigation of Canadian cases in criminal harassment. *Journal of Forensic Science, 46*(6), 1403–1410.

[40]   Vaknin, S. (2011, May 19). *Stalker psychology* [Video file]. Retrieved from https://www.youtube.com/watch?v=Ol2RM135ZHI&feature=youtu.be

[41]   Purcell, R., Pathé, M., & Mullen, P. E. (2001). A study of women who stalk. *American Journal of Psychiatry, 158*(12), 2056–2060.

[42]   Harmes, L., & Forde, E. (2018, January 7). Male stalking victim: "People don't take you seriously." *BBC.* Retrieved from https://www.bbc.com/news/uk-42582820

[43]   Blaauw E., Winkel, F. W., Arensman, E., Sheridan, L., & Freeve, A. (2002). The toll of stalking: The relationship between features of stalking and psychopathology of victims. *Journal of Interpersonal Violence, 17*(1), 50–63.

[44]   ibid.

[45]   Vaknin, S. (2011, May 19). *Stalker psychology* [Video file]. Retrieved from https://www.youtube.com/watch?v=Ol2RM135ZHI&feature=youtu.be. The information on stalking laws is derived from the Bureau of Justice Statistics, located at https://www.bjs.gov/index.cfm?ty=tp&tid=973

[46]   Forrell, C. A., & Matthews, D. M. (2000). *A Law of Her Own: The Reasonable woman as a measure of man.* New York, NY: New York University Press. (p. 141). (The quote is from a court ruling in Ellison vs. Gray, Supreme Court of Oklahoma, 1985).

[47]   Engel, B. (2017, November 16). Why don't victims of sexual harassment come forward sooner? [Blog post]. Retrieved from https://www.psychologytoday.com/us/blog/the-compassion-chronicles/201711/why-dont-victims-sexual-harassment-come-forward-sooner

[48]   Gilbert, J. A. (2017, November 22). Peering inside the mind of a predator [Blog post]. Retrieved from https://organizedforefficiency.com/peering-inside-the-mind-of-a-predator/

[49] Kanter, R. M., & Stein, B. A. (1980). *A tale of "O:" On being different in an organization.* New York, NY: Harper & Row.

[50] Ragins, B. R., Townsend, B., & Mattis, M. (1998). Gender gap in the executive suite: CEOs and female executives report on breaking the glass ceiling. *Academy of Management Executive, 12*(1), 28–42. https://doi.org/10.5465/AME.1998.254976

[51] Hakim, C. (2011). *Erotic capital: The power of attraction in the boardroom and the bedroom.* New York, NY: Basic Books.

[52] Melamed, T. (1995). Barriers to women's career success: Human capital, career choices, structural determinants, or simply sex discrimination. *Applied Psychology: An International Review, 44*(4), 295–314. https://doi.org/10.1111/j.1464-0597.1995.tb01082.x

[53] Kantor, J. S. (2017, March 11). Four key benefits of workplace mentoring initiatives [Blog post]. Retrieved from https://www.huffingtonpost.com/julie-kantor/four-key-benefits-of-work_b_9432716.html

[54] Emrich, C., Livingston, M. H., Oberfeld, L., Page, S., & Pruner, D. (2017). *Creating a culture of mentorship.* Retrieved from http://www.heidrick.com/Knowledge-Center/Publication/Creating_a_culture_of_mentorship

[55] Burt, R. S. (1995, August). *The contingent value of social capital.* Paper presented at The Annual Meeting of the Academy of Management: Vancouver, Canada.

[56] Snook, A. (n.d.). Stalking in the workplace. The complete guide to prevention and investigation. *i-Sight.* (Retrieved from https://i-sight.com/resources/stalking-in-the-workplace-the-complete-guide-to-prevention-and-investigation/). Bullet points 2 and 4 were adapted from this source.

[57] Achor, S. (2010). *The happiness advantage: The seven principles of positive psychology that fuel success and performance at work.* New York, NY: Crown Business.

[58] Simone, R. (2010). *Asperger's on the job: Must-have advice for people with Asperger's or high functioning autism and their employers, educators, and advocates.* Arlington, TX: Future Horizons.

[59] Meltdowns in adults with Asperger's & high-functioning autism. (n.d.). [Blog post]. Retrieved from http://www.adultaspergerschat.com/2012/09/meltdowns-in-adults-with-aspergers-high.html

[60] Marshack, K. (2013, November 12). Why Aspies struggle with apologies [Blog post]. Retrieved from http://www.kmarshack.com/_blog/Kathy_Marshack_News/post/why-do-those-with-aspergers-syndrome-struggle-with-apologies/

[61] Holmes, L. (2015, February 22). How to stop a jealous thought in its tracks [Blog post]. Retrieved from https://www.huffpost.com/entry/managing-jealousy_n_6700474

[62] Bauer, P. (2016, April 26). Dealing with envy: What envy teaches you [Blog post]. Retrieved from https://www.huffingtonpost.com/pam-bauer/dealing-with-envy-what-en_b_9774594.html

[63] Gilbert, J. A. (2014, April 11). Bullying and the boss's buddy [Blog post]. Retrieved from https://organizedforefficiency.com/bullying-and-the-bosss-buddy/

[64] Kislik, L. (2017, May 19). Being the boss's favorite is great, until it's not [Blog post]. Retrieved from https://hbr.org/2017/05/being-the-bosss-favorite-is-great-until-its-not

[65] Gilbert, J. A. (2013, April 24). The case for reverse snitching [Blog post]. Retrieved from https://organizedforefficiency.com/the-case-for-reverse-snitching/

[66] de Dios, M. A., Kuo, C., Hernandez, L., Clark, U. S., Wenze, S. J., Boisseau, C. L., . . . Zlotnick, C. (2013). The development of a diversity mentoring program for faculty and trainees: A program at the Brown Clinical Psychology Training Consortium. *Behavioral Therapy, 36*(5), 121–126. https://www.ncbi.nlm.nih.gov/pmc/articles/PMC4207083/

Chapter 3

[1] Social Form of Bullying Linked to Depression, Anxiety in Adults. (2008, April 22). *ScienceDaily*. Retrieved from http://news.ufl.edu/archive/2008/04/social-form-of-bullying-linked-to-depression-anxiety-in-adults.html

[2] Bowes, L., Joinson, C., Wolke, D., & Lewis, G. (2015). Peer victimisation during adolescence and its impact on depression in early adulthood: Prospective cohort study in the United Kingdom. *British Medical Journal, 350*, h2469. Retrieved from https://www.bmj.com/content/350/bmj.h2469

[3] Blanchard, L. (2017, April 15). My worst nightmare—What if I accidentally raise the bully? [Blog post]. Retrieved from http://www.huffingtonpost.com/leslie-blanchard/where-helicopter-parents-need-to-hover_b_9628142.html

[4] Aquire, S. (2015, November 30). Bullying may have caused my OCD: A case study [Blog post]. Retrieved from http://www.ocdsymptoms.co.uk/can-bullying-cause-ocd-case-study.html

[5] Streep, P. (2017, January 27). The brutal truth about 6 types of "quiet" verbal abuse [Blog post]. Retrieved from https://www.psychologytoday.com/us/blog/tech-support/201701/the-brutal-truth-about-6-types-quiet-verbal-abuse

[6] Meyer, A., Proudfit, G. C., Bufferd, S. J., Kujawa, A. J., Laptook, R. S., Torpey, D. C., & Klein, D. N. (2015). Self-reported and observed punitive parenting prospectively predicts increased error-related brain activity in six-year-old children. *Journal of Abnormal Child Psychology, 43*(5), 1201–1202. https://doi.org/10.1007/s10802-014-9918-1. Also see Peck, M. E. (2015, May 1). Harsh, critical parenting may lead to anxiety disorder symptoms. "Tiger" parents may cause kids' brains to overreact to errors (Retrieved from https://www.scientificamerican.com/article/harsh-critical-parenting-may-lead-to-anxiety-disorder-symptoms/). Research that Morgen Peck discusses suggests that authoritarian parenting may lead to perceived powerlessness, and an inability to handle unexpected life events.

[7]   Caprino, K. (2016, July 9). How being raised by a narcissist damages your life and self-esteem [Blog post]. Retrieved from https://www.forbes.com/sites/kathycaprino/2016/07/09/how-being-raised-by-a-narcissist-damages-your-life-and-self-esteem/#21a00ef42c67

[8]   Teicher, M. H., Samson, J. A., Polcari, A., & Mcgreenery, C. E. (2006). Sticks, stones, and hurtful words: Effects of various forms of childhood maltreatment. *American Journal of Psychiatry, 163*(6), 993–1000. https:/doi.org/10.1176/appi.ajp.163.6.993 (p. 994)

[9]   Damour, L. (2016). *Untangled: Guiding teenage girls through the seven transitions into adulthood.* New York, NY: Ballantine Books.

[10] Gerschoff, E. T., & Grogan-Kaylor, A. (2016). Spanking and child outcomes: Old controversies and new meta-analyses. *Journal of Family Psychology, 30*(4), 453–469.

[11] Lazelere, R. E., & Kuhn, B. R. (2005). Comparing child outcomes of physical punishment and alternative disciplinary tactics: A meta-analysis. *Clinical Child and Family Psychology Review, 8*(1), 1–37.

[12] Seamands, D. A. (1981). *Healing for damaged emotions.* Colorado Springs, CO: David C. Cook. *The Slap* is a novel that tells the story of a boy who was slapped by a neighbor at a backyard barbecue. His parents subsequently file charges. Tsiolkas, C. (2010). *The slap.* New York, NY: Penguin Books.

[13] Cummins, D. (2014, September 19). This is what happens when you hit your kids [Blog post]. Retrieved from https://www.psychologytoday.com/blog/good-thinking/201409/is-what-happens-when-you-hit-your-kids

[14] Child abuse is wrong: What can I do? (n.d). *Department of Justice: Canada.* Retrieved from http://www.justice.gc.ca/eng/rp-pr/cj-jp/fv-vf/caw-mei/p4.html

[15] Violent discipline. (2019, October). Retrieved from https://data.unicef.org/topic/child-protection/violence/violent-discipline/

[16] Sege, R. D., & Siegel, B. S. (2018). Effective discipline to raise healthy children. *Pediatrics, 142*(6), 1–10, e20183112. https://doi.org/10.1542/peds.2018-3112

[17] Coloroso, B. (2003). *The bully, the bullied, and the bystander.* New York, NY: HarperResource. Both the arguments and results are adapted from this source.

[18] Cloud, H., & Townsend, J. (1992). *Boundaries: When to say yes, how to say no to take control of your life.* Grand Rapids, MI: Zondervan.

[19] Wyatt, J., & Hare, C. (1997). *Work abuse: How to recognize and survive it.* Rochester, VT: Schenkman Books.

[20] Gilbert, J. A. (2015, June 8). The legacy of power imbalance and emotional abuse [Blog post]. (Retrieved from https://organizedforefficiency.com/the-legacy-of-power-imbalance-and-emotional-abuse/). Modified and adapted from the original post.

[21] Leman, K., & Carlson, R. (1989). *Unlocking the secrets of your childhood memories.* Nashville, TN: Thomas Nelson. (p. 172)

[22] Roberts, B. E., & White, J. E. Jr. (1998). *Roberts vs. Texaco.* New York, NY: Avon Books. (p. 22)

[23]   Sapolsky, R. M. (2017). *Behave: The biology of humans at our best and worst.*
       New York, NY: Penguin Books. In *Unlocking the Secrets of Your Childhood
       Memories,* Leman and Carlson suggest some parents may harm children
       through "smother love." Recipients of "little emperor/empress" treatment
       are potentially explosive, with parental largesse (and zero limits) that foster
       a lack of consideration for others. In *Generation Me,* author Jean Twenge
       argues that millennials may behave with disrespect and non-deference to
       authority figures because they expect instant gratification, and because they
       feel an equality that entitles them to tell people—regardless of their age
       or status—what they want and how they want it. See Twenge, J. M. (2006).
       *Generation me: Why today's young Americans are more confident, assertive, and
       entitled–and more miserable than ever before.* New York, NY: Free Press.

[24]   Leman, K. (1984). *The birth order book: Why you are the way you are.* Old
       Tappan, NJ: Fleming H. Revell Company.

[25]   Leman, K. (1989). *Growing up first born: The pressure and privilege of being
       number one.* New York, NY: Delacorte Press.

[26]   ibid.

[27]   ibid.

[28]   Leman, K. (1984). *The birth order book: Why you are the way you are.* Old
       Tappan, NJ: Fleming H. Revell Company.

[29]   Gilbert, J. A. (2011, March 7). Birth order: For the sake of expediency [Blog
       post]. (Retrieved from https://organizedforefficiency.com/birth-order-for-
       the-sake-of-expediency/). Modified and adapted from the original post.
       The post references Leman, K. (1989). *Growing up first born: The pressure and
       privilege of being number one.* New York, NY: Delacorte Press.

[30]   Leman, K. (1984). *The birth order book: Why you are the way you are.* Old
       Tappan, NJ: Fleming H. Revell Company.

[31]   Whitson, S. (2013, August 26). What does assertiveness have to do with
       stopping bullying? [Blog post]. Retrieved from https://www.huffingtonpost.
       com/signe-whitson/what-does-assertiveness-h_b_3812926.html

[32]   Lafair, S. (2009). *Don't bring it to work: Breaking the family patterns that limit
       success.* San Francisco, CA: Jossey-Bass.

[33]   Leman, K., & Carlson, R. (1989). *Unlocking the secrets of your childhood
       memories.* Nashville, TN: Thomas Nelson.

[34]   Caprino, K. (2014, January 16). 7 crippling parenting behaviors that keep
       children from growing into leaders [Blog post]. Retrieved from https://
       www.forbes.com/sites/kathycaprino/2014/01/16/7-crippling-parenting-
       behaviors-that-keep-children-from-growing-into-leaders/#20d830285957

[35]   Campbell, S. (2014, March 29). 8 guaranteed ways to emotionally f*ck
       up your kids [Blog post]. Retrieved from https://www.huffingtonpost.
       com/sherrie-campbell-phd/8-guaranteed-ways-to-emotionally-fck-up-your-
       kids_b_4619389.html

[36]   Caprino, K. (2018, January 23). 5 glaring signs that your childhood has
       negatively impacted your career [Blog post]. Retrieved from https://www.

forbes.com/sites/kathycaprino/2018/01/23/5-glaring-signs-that-your-childhood-has-negatively-impacted-your-career/#4cb8f9d353fa

[37] Campbell, S. (2015, April 23). 8 advantages highly sensitive people bring to business. Retrieved from https://www.entrepreneur.com/article/245293

[38] Tirado, B. (2011, September 26). Birth order in the workplace [Blog post]. Retrieved from https://www.psychologytoday.com/blog/digital-leaders/201109/birth-order-in-the-workplace

[39] Dattner, B. (2008, June 2). Is your workplace personality out of (birth) order? [Blog post]. Retrieved from https://www.psychologytoday.com/blog/credit-and-blame-work/200806/is-your-workplace-personality-out-birth-order-1

[40] Sullivan, A. (2010, May 17). Woman berates clerk with Down syndrome. *abcNEWS*. Retrieved from http://abcnews.go.com/WhatWouldYouDo/syndrome-grocery-clerk-scenario/story?id=10648284

[41] Gilbert, J. A. (2014, March 8). Highly sensitive persons and employment [Blog post]. Retrieved from https://organizedforefficiency.com/highly-sensitive-persons-and-employment/

[42] Namie, G., & Namie, R. (2000). *The bully at work: What you can do to stop the hurt and reclaim your dignity on the job.* Naperville, IL: Sourcebooks. (p. 63)

[43] Gilbert, J. A. (2011, February 14). Conducting a meeting—the civil way [Blog post] (Retrieved from https://organizedforefficiency.com/conducting-a-meeting-the-civil-way/). For the full story on Exxon Baytown, see Sheridan, J. H. (1994, September 19). Dividends from diversity. *Industry Week, 243*(17), 23.

[44] Cain, S. (2013). *Quiet: The power of introverts in a world that can't stop talking.* New York, NY: Broadway Books.

[45] Roberts, L. M., Spreitzer, G., Dutton, J., Quinn, R., Heaphy, E., & Barker, B. (2005). How to play to your strengths. *Harvard Business Review, 83*(1), 74–81.

[46] Gilbert, J. A. (2018, June 20). Quiet in a world of talk [Blog post]. Retrieved from https://organizedforefficiency.com/quiet-in-a-world-of-talk/

Chapter 4

[1] Gilbert, J. A. (2015, May 20). Navigating the narrow corridors of office politics [Blog post] (Retrieved from https://organizedforefficiency.com/navigating-the-narrow-corridors-of-office-politics/). Modified and adapted from the original post.

[2] Namie, G. (2017, June 23). 2017 WBI U.S. Workplace Bullying Survey. Retrieved from https://www.workplacebullying.org/2017-prevalence

[3] Gilbert, J. A. (2015, May 20). Navigating the narrow corridors of office politics [Blog post] (Retrieved from https://organizedforefficiency.com/navigating-the-narrow-corridors-of-office-politics/). Modified and adapted from the original post.

[4] Kampen, J. (2015). *Emotional abuse and neglect in the workplace.* London, England: Palgrave Macmillan.

[5] Gilbert, J. A. (2018, January 31). Highlight culture to harness abusers [Blog post]. Retrieved from https://organizedforefficiency.com/highlight-culture-to-harness-abusers/

[6] Glazer, R. (2016, April 13). Do nice businesses finish first? The perils of a toxic culture. *Business.com.* Retrieved from http://www.business.com/company-culture/do-nice-businesses-finish-first-the-perils-of-a-toxic-culture/

[7] Ringer, R. J. (1974). *Winning through intimidation: How to be the victor instead of the victim in all areas of life.* New York, NY: Skyhorse. Also see Gilbert, J. A. (2011, March 31). Machiavelli meet civility [Blog post]. Retrieved from https://organizedforefficiency.com/machiavelli-meet-civility/ which explains Ringer's philosophy.

[8] Kanter, R. M., & Stein, B. A. (1980). *A tale of "O:" On being different in organizations.* New York, NY: Harper & Row.

[9] Martinuzzi, B. (2013, August 16). 7 signs you're working in a toxic office [Blog post]. Retrieved from https://www.americanexpress.com/us/small-business/openforum/articles/7-signs-youre-working-in-a-toxic-office/

[10] Peck, M. S. (1978). *The road less traveled: A new psychology of love, traditional values, and spiritual growth.* New York, NY: Simon & Schuster.

[11] Adizes, I. (1979). *How to solve the mismanagement crisis: Diagnosis and treatment of management problems.* Santa Monica, CA: Adizes Institute.

[12] Perrow, C. (1986). *Complex organizations: A critical essay.* Glenview, IL: Scott, Foresman, and Company.

[13] Verschoor, C. C. (2015, October 30). Toshiba's toxic culture *questia.* Retrieved from http://sfmagazine.com/post-entry/october-2015-toshibas-toxic-culture/

[14] Peck, M. S. (1978). *The road less traveled: A new psychology of love, traditional values, and spiritual growth.* New York, NY: Simon & Schuster. Kampen and Henken (2018) draw a parallel between neglectful organizations and families that neglect the emotional needs of their children. See Kampen, J., & Henken, A. (2018). Organizational neglect: The toxic triangle of deficits. *Organizational Dynamics, 47*(4). 241–249 (https://doi.org/10.1016/j.orgdyn.2017.11.001). Caregivers may not always realize the harm they inflict, and the resulting negative outcomes of perfectionism, trouble accepting blame, obsessive/compulsive tendency, stinginess, and selfishness that emanate from children of authoritarian parents. See Rosenthal, K. (1987). Rituals of undoing in abused and neglected children. *Child and Adolescent Social Work Journal, 4*(3&4), 78–88.

[15] Boddy, C. R. (2014). Corporate psychopaths, conflict, employee affective well-being and counterproductive work behaviour. *Journal of Business Ethics, 121*(1), 107–121. http://dx.doi.org/10.1007/s10551-013-1688-0

[16] Babiak, P., & Hare, R. D. (2006). *Snakes in suits: When psychopaths go to work.* New York, NY: HarperCollins.

[17] Gilbert, J. A. (2017, May 26). How to prevent hazing [Blog post]. Retrieved from https://organizedforefficiency.com/how-to-prevent-hazing/

[18] Maremont, M. (1996, May 13). Abuse of power: The astonishing tale of sexual harassment at Astra USA. *Business Week*, 86–98.

[19] Thomas, C. W. (2002, March 31). The rise and fall of Enron. *Journal of Accountancy*. Retrieved from http://www.journalofaccountancy.com/issues/2002/apr/theriseandfallofenron.html

[20] Gilbert, J. A., Carr-Ruffino, N., Ivancevich, J. M., & Konopaske, R. (2012). Toxic versus cooperative behaviors at work: The role of organizational culture and leadership in creating community centered organizations. *International Journal of Leadership Studies*, 7(1), 29–47. Retrieved from http://www.regent.edu/acad/global/publications/ijls/new/vol7iss1/IJLS_Vol7Iss1_Winter2011.pdf

[21] Branden, N. (1998). *Self-esteem at work: How confident people make powerful companies*. San Francisco, CA: Jossey-Bass.

[22] Kennedy, M. M. (1980). *Office politics: Seizing power, wielding clout*. Chicago, IL: Follett.

[23] Rodriguez, S. (2019, January 8). Inside Facebook's 'cult-like' workplace, where dissent is discouraged and employees pretend to be happy all the time. *CNBC*. Retrieved from https://www.cnbc.com/2019/01/08/cnbcs-salvador-rodriguez-inside-facebooks-cult-like-workplace-where-dissent-is-discouraged-and-employees-pretend-to-be-happy-all-the-time.html

[24] Kantor, J., & Streitfeld, D. (2015, August 15). Inside Amazon: Wrestling big ideas in a bruising workplace. *The New York Times*. Retrieved from https://www.nytimes.com/2015/08/16/technology/inside-amazon-wrestling-big-ideas-in-a-bruising-workplace.html

[25] Howland, D. (2016, November 15). Amazon overhauls controversial 'rank-and-yank' employee review program. *RETAILDIVE*. Retrieved from https://www.retaildive.com/news/amazon-overhauls-controversial-rank-and-yank-employee-review-program/430426/

[26] Arnott, D. (2000). *Corporate cults: The insidious lure of the all-consuming organization*. New York, NY: AMACOM.

[27] McCord, P. (2017). *Powerful: Building a culture of freedom and responsibility*. Jackson, TN: Silicon Guild.

[28] Cancialosi, C. (2014, June 7). The dark side of bonus and incentive programs [Blog post]. Retrieved from http://www.forbes.com/sites/groupthink/2014/06/07/the-dark-side-of-bonus-and-incentive-programs/#313a36d96f23

[29] Han, M. (2016, January 20). Large trader bonuses breed arrogance, risky market behaviour. *Financial Review*. Retrieved from http://www.afr.com/news/large-trader-bonuses-breed-arrogance-risky-market-behaviour-20160118-gm8ri8

[30] Mawritz, M. B., Mayer, D. M., Hoobler, J. M., Wayne, S. J., & Marinova, S. V. (2012). A trickle-down model of abusive supervision. *Personnel Psychology*,

65(2), 325–357 (https://doi.org/10.1111/j.1744-6570.2012.01246.x). (p. 328)

[31] Rynes, S. L., Trank, C. Q., Lawson, A. M., & Ilies, R. (2003). Behavioral coursework in business education: Growing evidence of a legitimacy crisis. *Academy of Management Learning & Education, 2*(3), 269–283. https://doi. org/10.5465/AMLE.2003.10932135

[32] Gilbert, J. A. (2011, March 31). Machiavelli meet civility [Blog post] (Retrieved from https://organizedforefficiency.com/machiavelli-meet-civility/). Modified and adapted from the original post.

[33] Dobbin, F., & Kalev, A. (2016). Why diversity programs fail: And what works better. *Harvard Business Review, 94*(7/8), 52–60.

[34] Rempel, W. C. (1987, January 28). Year after disaster: Challenger's wake: Rage, pain, guilt. *Los Angeles Times*. Retrieved from http://articles.latimes .com/1987-01-28/news/mn-1361_1_engineers

[35] DeBatto, D. (2004, December 9). Whitewashing torture? *Salon*. Retrieved from http://www.salon.com/2004/12/09/coverup_3/

[36] McCook, A. (2017, January 18). How a dispute at Harvard led to a grad student's forced mental exam and an extraordinary restraining order against a prominent scientist. *Science*. Retrieved from http://www. sciencemag.org/news/2017/01/how-dispute-harvard-led-grad-student-s-forced-mental-exam-and-extraordinary-restraining

[37] Carreyrou, J. (2018, May 21). A new look inside Theranos' dysfunctional corporate culture. *WIRED*. Retrieved from https://www.wired.com/story/a-new-look-inside-theranos-dysfunctional-corporate-culture/

[38] Markman, A. (2014, July 23). Ask the experts: I like my job but the culture is toxic—Should I quit? *Fast Company*. (Retrieved from https://www. fastcompany.com/3033240/ask-the-experts-i-like-my-job-but-the-culture-is-toxic-should-i-quit). Statement 4 is adapted from this source.

[39] Wyatt, J., & Hare, C. *Work abuse: How to recognize and survive it*. Rochester, VT: Schenkman Books. Bullets points were adapted from this source.

[40] Gilbert, J. A., Carr-Ruffino, N., Ivancevich, J. M., & Konopaske, R. (2012). Toxic versus cooperative behaviors at work: The role of organizational culture and leadership in creating community centered organizations. *International Journal of Leadership Studies, 7*(1), 29–47 (Retrieved from http://www.regent.edu/acad/global/publications/ijls/new/vol7iss1/IJLS_Vol7Iss1_Winter2011.pdf). (p. 31)

[41] Bridges, W. (1994, September 19). THE END OF THE JOB. *Fortune*. Retrieved from http://archive.fortune.com/magazines/fortune/fortune_archive/1994/09/19/79751/index.htm

[42] Barnard, J. W. (2008). Narcissism, over-optimism, fear, anger, and depression: The interior lives of corporate leaders. *University of Cincinnati Law Review, 77*(2), 405–430.

[43] Lubit, R. (2004). *Coping with toxic managers, subordinates, and other difficult people*. Upper Saddle River, NJ: Financial Times Prentice Hall.

[44] Austin, R., & Larkey, P. (1992). The unintended consequences of micromanagement: The case of procuring mission critical computer resources. *Policy Sciences, 25*(1), 3–28.

[45] Kim, H., & Yuki, G. (1995). Relationships of managerial effectiveness and advancement to self-reported and subordinate-reported leadership behaviors from the multiple-linkage mode. *The Leadership Quarterly, 6*(3), 361–377. https://doi.org/10.1016/1048-9843(95)90014-4

[46] Khatri, N., & Tsang, E. W. K. (2003). Antecedents and consequences of cronyism in organizations. *Journal of Business Ethics, 43*(4), 289–303. https://doi.org/10.1023/A:1023081629529

[47] Taylor, M. S., Tracy, K. B., Renard, M. K., Harrison, J. K., & Carroll, S. J. (1995). Due process in performance appraisal: A quasi-experiment in procedural justice. *Administrative Science Quarterly, 40*(3), 495–523. https://doi.org/10.2307/2393795

[48] Volberda, H. W. (1996). Toward the flexible form: How to remain vital in hypercompetitive environments. *Organization Science, 7*(4), 359–374. https://doi.org/10.1287/orsc.7.4.359

[49] Branden, N. (1998). *Self-esteem at work: How confident people make powerful companies.* San Francisco, CA: Jossey-Bass.

[50] Carse, J. (1986). *Finite and infinite games: A vision of life as play and possibility.* New York, NY: Free Press.

[51] Marcic, D. (1997). *Managing with the wisdom of love: Uncovering virtue in people and organizations.* San Francisco, CA: Jossey-Bass.

[52] Peck, M. S. (1987). *The different drum: Community making and peace.* New York, NY: Simon & Schuster.

[53] Semler, R. (1993). Maverick: The success behind the world's most unusual workplace. New York, NY: Warner Books. (p. 206)

[54] Hannan, C. (2013, January 3). Dish Network: The meanest company in America. *Bloomberg.* Retrieved from https://www.bloomberg.com/news/articles/2013-01-02/dish-network-the-meanest-company-in-america

[55] Sutton, R. (2007). *The no asshole rule: Building a civilized workplace and surviving one that isn't.* New York, NY: Warner Business Books.

[56] Sutton, R. I. (2007, March 17). Why I wrote the no asshole rule [Blog post]. Retrieved from https://hbr.org/2007/03/why-i-wrote-the-no-asshole-rule

[57] Lipman, V. (2015, June 22). The strong business case for civility in management [Blog post]. Retrieved from https://www.forbes.com/sites/victorlipman/2015/06/22/the-strong-business-case-for-civility-in-management/#5514af6537b9

[58] Karl Albrecht International. (n.d.). Self-assessment quiz: Are you "toxic" or "nourishing?" Retrieved from https://www.karlalbrecht.com/downloads/Albrecht-ToxicNourishingQuiz.pdf

[59] Kantor, J., & Streitfeld, D. (2015, August 15). Inside Amazon: Wrestling big ideas in a bruising workplace. *New York Times.* Retrieved from https://www.nytimes.com/2015/08/16/technology/inside-amazon-wrestling-big-ideas-in-a-bruising-workplace.html

Chapter 5

[1] Lacayo, R., & Ripley, A. (2002, December 30). Persons of the year 2002: The whistleblowers. *TIME*. Retrieved from http://content.time.com/time/subscriber/article/0,33009,1003998-3,00.html

[2] Solomon, R. C., & Higgins, K. M. (1996). *A short history of philosophy*. New York, NY: Oxford University Press. (p. 94)

[3] Romm, C. (2015, January 28). Rethinking one of psychology's most infamous experiments. *The Atlantic*. (Retrieved from http://www.theatlantic.com/health/archive/2015/01/rethinking-one-of-psychologys-most-infamous-experiments/384913/). "Diffusion of responsibility" occurs as greater numbers of people inversely impact our willingness to intervene. "Situationism" is driven by a desire to "fit" within a given set of circumstances.

[4] Jarvis, C. (2011, October 5). Workplace bullying—the triad: Bullies, victims, and bystanders [Blog post]. Retrieved from http://www.workplacebullying.org/workplace-bullying-the-triad-bullies-victims-and-bystanders/

[5] Gilbert, J. A. (2011, May 10). The makings of a movement [Blog post] (Retrieved from https://organizedforefficiency.com/the-makings-of-a-movement/). The information within the post is adapted from Lentz, R., & Gateley, E. (2003). *Christ in the Margins*. Maryknoll, NY: Orbis Books.

[6] Gilbert, J. A. (2011, June 3). Facing the angry mob at work [Blog post]. Retrieved from https://organizedforefficiency.com/facing-the-angry-mob-at-work/

[7] ibid.

[8] Davenport, N., Schwartz, R. D., & Elliott, G. P. (1999). *Mobbing: Emotional abuse in the American workplace*. Ames, Iowa: Civil Society.

[9] Duffy, M. (2009). Preventing workplace mobbing and bullying with effective organizational consultation, policies, and legislation. *Consulting Psychology Journal: Practice and Research, 61*(3), 242–262.

[10] Frost, P. J. (2003). *Toxic emotions at work: How compassionate managers handle pain and conflict*. Boston, MA: Harvard Business School Press.

[11] Adizes, I. (1979). *How to solve the mismanagement crisis: Diagnosis and treatment of management problems*. Santa Monica, CA: Adizes Institute.

[12] Fuller, R. W. (2003). *Somebodies and nobodies: Overcoming the abuse of rank*. Gabriola Island, BC Canada: New Society.

[13] Staub, E. (2012, January 27). Our power as active bystanders: Acting to prevent suffering and creating a better world [Blog post]. Retrieved from https://www.psychologytoday.com/blog/in-the-garden-good-and-evil/201201/our-power-active-bystanders

[14] Gilbert, J. A. (2011, February 18). Communicate, don't desecrate [Blog post]. Retrieved from https://organizedforefficiency.com/communicate-dont-desecrate/

[15] Gilbert, J. A. (2011, June 3). Facing the angry mob at work [Blog post]. Retrieved from https://organizedforefficiency.com/facing-the-angry-mob-at-work/

[16] Coloroso, B. (2003). *The bully, the bullied, and the bystander.* New York, NY: HarperResource. Bullet points were adapted from this source.

[17] Shamay-Tsoory, S. G., Ahronberg-Kirschenbaum, D., & Bauminger-Zviely, N. (2014). There is no joy like malicious joy: Schadenfreude in young children. *PLOS ONE, 9*(7), e100233. https://doi.org/10.1371/journal.pone.0100233

[18] Police: As Many as 20 Present at Gang Rape Outside School Dance. (2009, October 28). (Retrieved from http://www.cnn.com/2009/CRIME/10/27/california.gang.rape.investigation/). When bystanders are available, even the willingness of five-year-olds to help adults drops from about half, to approximately twelve percent. Given that children as young as three engage in prosocial helping behaviors (and age five is typically when children begin preschool), could bystanding be a byproduct of school yard socialization? See Plötner, M., Over, H., Carpenter, M., & Tomasello, M. (2015). Young children show the bystander effect in helping situations. *Psychological Science, 26*(4), 499–506. https://doi.org/10.1177/0956797615569579

[19] Gilbert, J. A. (2011, June 3). Facing the angry mob at work [Blog post] (Retrieved from https://organizedforefficiency.com/facing-the-angry-mob-at-work/). This paragraph was modified and adapted from the original post.

[20] Gilbert, J. A. (2011, July 29). Secret societies in the office [Blog post]. Retrieved from https://organizedforefficiency.com/secret-societies-in-the-office/

[21] Everyday Sadists Take Pleasure in Others' Pain. (2013, September 12). *Science Daily.* Retrieved from http://www.psychologicalscience.org/news/releases/everyday-sadists-take-pleasure-in-others-pain.html

[22] Gilbert, J. A. (2011, July 29). Secret societies in the office [Blog post] (Retrieved from https://organizedforefficiency.com/secret-societies-in-the-office/). Bullet points were modified and adapted from the original post.

[23] Roberts, B. E., & White, J. E. Jr. (1998). *Roberts vs. Texaco.* New York, NY: Avon Books.

[24] Castillo, M. (2013, October 29). Study reveals people physically take pleasure in others' pain. *CBS News.* Retrieved from http://www.cbsnews.com/news/study-reveals-people-physically-take-pleasure-in-others-pain/

[25] Gilbert, J. A. (2011, June 3). Facing the angry mob at work [Blog post]. Retrieved from https://organizedforefficiency.com/facing-the-angry-mob-at-work/

[26] Emmons, R. A., & McCullough, M. E. (2003). Counting blessings versus burdens: An experimental investigation of gratitude and subjective well-being in daily life. *Journal of Personality and Social Psychology, 84*(2), 377–389. https://doi.org/10.1037/0022-3514.84.2.377

[27] Scully, M., & Rowe, M. (2009). Bystander training within organizations. *Journal of the International Ombudsman Association, 2*(1), 89–95. The bullet points were adapted from this source.

[28] Porath, C. (2016). Creating a more human workplace where employees and business thrive. Alexandria, VA: Society for Human Resource Management. Retrieved from https://www.shrm.org/hr-today/trends-and-forecasting/special-reports-and-expert-views/Documents/Human-Workplace.pdf

[29] Equal Employment Opportunity Commission. (2015, October 23). *Multi-prong strategy essential to preventing workplace harassment* [News release]. Retrieved from https://www.eeoc.gov/eeoc/newsroom/release/10-23-15.cfm

[30] Some information in the "Bystanders can demonstrate" section was modified and adapted from the following blog posts:

Gilbert, J. A. (2011, March 30). Encourage meeting participation [Blog post]. Retrieved from https://organizedforefficiency.com/encourage-meeting-participation/ and

Gilbert, J. A. (2013, May 24). Unseemly behaviors in side conversations [Blog post]. Retrieved from https://organizedforefficiency.com/unseemly-behaviors-in-side-conversations/

[31] Gilbert, J. A., & Ivancevich, J. M. (2000). Valuing diversity: A tale of two organizations. *Academy of Management Executive, 14*(1), 93–105.

[32] Foote, D. (2011, March 11). Leadership is not about getting things done [Blog post]. Retrieved from https://organizedforefficiency.com/leadership-is-not-about-getting-things-done%e2%80%a6/

[33] Porath, C., & Pearson, C. (2013, January/February). The price of incivility: Lack of respect hurts morale—and the bottom line. *Harvard Business Review, 91*(1–2), 114–121. Retrieved from https://hbr.org/2013/01/the-price-of-incivility

[34] Whitbourne, S. K. (2010, September 28). How and why do we help? From one-ness to we-ness: The courage needed to be a hero [Blog post]. Retrieved from https://www.psychologytoday.com/blog/fulfillment-any-age/201009/why-and-how-do-we-help

[35] Davenport, N., Schwartz, R. D., & Elliott, G. P. (1999). *Mobbing: Emotional abuse in the American workplace.* Ames, Iowa: Civil Society.

[36] Duffy, M. (2009). Preventing workplace mobbing and bullying with effective organizational consultation, policies, and legislation. *Consulting Psychology Journal: Practice and Research, 61*(3), 242–262.

[37] Gilbert, J. A. (2011, June 3). Facing the angry mob at work [Blog post]. Retrieved from https://organizedforefficiency.com/facing-the-angry-mob-at-work/

[38] Gillman, O. (2015, October 23). Would YOU help a child being bullied? Experiment tests the compassion of bystanders as two teenagers pick on young girl at bus stop... and the result will restore your faith in humanity. *DailyMail.com.* Retrieved from http://www.dailymail.co.uk/news/article-3285767/Would-help-child-saw-bullied-Experiment-tests-bystanders-intervene-two-teenagers-pick-young-girl-bus-stop.html

[39] What Makes First Responders Run Toward Danger? (2013, April 20).
      CBC. Retrieved from http://www.cbc.ca/news/world/what-makes-first-
      responders-run-toward-danger-1.1324458

[40] Tervooren, T. (2015, August 24). Bystander effect: If you need help, you'd
      better ask for it [Blog post]. Retrieved from https://www.huffingtonpost.
      com/tyler-tervooren/bystander-effect-if-you-need-help-youd-better-ask-for-
      it_b_8026328.html

[41] Triffin, M. (2014, May 7). How to ask for a raise—and get it [Blog post].
      Retrieved from https://www.forbes.com/sites/learnvest/2014/05/07/how-
      to-ask-for-a-raise-and-get-it/#4dac3a281cb3

[42] Krznaric, R. (2012, November 27). Six habits of highly empathic people.
      Greater Good Magazine. Retrieved from https://greatergood.berkeley.edu/
      article/item/six_habits_of_highly_empathic_people1

[43] Reeder, H. (2014, August 13). The witness: 6 steps to take if you
      see workplace bullying [Blog post]. Retrieved from https://www.
      psychologytoday.com/us/blog/i-can-relate/201408/the-witness-6-steps-take-
      if-you-see-workplace-bullying

Chapter 6

[1]   Gilbert, J. A. (2011, February 18). Communicate, don't desecrate [Blog
      post]. Retrieved from https://organizedforefficiency.com/communicate-
      dont-desecrate/

[2]   ibid.

[3]   Robinson, J. (2009, June). Bullying: the "B" word that won't go away.
      State Magazine. Retrieved from http://workplacebullying.org/multi/pdf/
      StateMag0609.pdf

[4]   Quast, L. (2016, June 27). Co-worker's bad mood ruined other people's
      day [Blog post]. Retrieved from http://www.forbes.com/sites/
      lisaquast/2016/06/27/coworkers-bad-mood-ruined-other-peoples-
      day/#36fd311b7831

[5]   Gilbert, J. A. (2011, February 18). Communicate, don't desecrate [Blog
      post]. Retrieved from https://organizedforefficiency.com/communicate-
      dont-desecrate/

[6]   NiCarthy, G., Gottlieb, N., & Coffman, S. (1993). *You don't have to take it!: A
      woman's guide to confronting emotional abuse at work.* Seattle, WA: Seal Press.
      The first four bullet points in the list of "aggressive speech" were adapted
      from this source.

[7]   Aslett, D. (2005). *The office clutter cure: Get organized, get results.* Avon, MA:
      Adams Media.

[8]   Pallotta, N. (2010, October 14). Gossip kills possibility [Blog post].
      Retrieved from https://hbr.org/2010/10/gossip-kills-possibility

[9]   Leu, L. (2015). *Non-violent communication companion workbook.* Encinitas, CA:
      PuddleDancer Press.

[10]   Quast, L. (2016, June 27). Co-worker's bad mood ruined other people's day [Blog post]. Retrieved from http://www.forbes.com/sites/lisaquast/2016/06/27/coworkers-bad-mood-ruined-other-peoples-day/#36fd311b7831

[11]   Gibson, L. C. (2015). *Adult children of emotionally immature parents: How to heal from distant, rejecting, or self-involved parents.* Oakland, CA: New Harbinger.

[12]   ibid.

[13]   Carnegie, D. (1936). *How to win friends and influence people.* New York, NY: Simon & Schuster.

[14]   Gibson, L. C. (2015). *Adult children of emotionally immature parents: How to heal from distant, rejecting, or self-involved parents.* Oakland, CA: New Harbinger.

[15]   Wilkie, D. (2016, June 30). Tried-and-true ways to deal with a workplace bully. *SHRM.* Retrieved from https://www.shrm.org/ResourcesAndTools/hr-topics/employee-relations/Pages/Handling-Bullies.aspx

[16]   Gilbert, J. A. (2015, October 27). Immersion and memory implant [Blog post]. Retrieved from https://organizedforefficiency.com/immersion-and-memory-implant/

[17]   Robinson, J. (2009, June). Bullying: the "B" word that won't go away. *State Magazine.* Retrieved from http://workplacebullying.org/multi/pdf/StateMag0609.pdf

[18]   Gibson, L. C. (2015). *Adult children of emotionally immature parents: How to heal from distant, rejecting, or self-involved parents.* Oakland, CA: New Harbinger.

[19]   Rosenberg, M. B. (2015). *Non-violent communication: A language of life.* Encinitas, CA: PuddleDancer Press.

[20]   Gilbert, J. A. (2014, January 19). An ironman approach to interpersonal relationships [Blog post]. Retrieved from https://organizedforefficiency.com/an-ironman-approach-to-interpersonal-relationships/

[21]   Carse, J. (1986). *Finite and infinite games: A vision of life as play and possibility.* New York, NY: Free Press.

[22]   Gilbert, J. A. (2016, June 30). Excavate your personal plank [Blog post]. Retrieved from https://organizedforefficiency.com/excavate-your-personal-plank/

[23]   Towers Watson. (2013). *Change and communication ROI—The 10th anniversary report. How the fundamentals have evolved and the best adapt.* https://www.willistowerswatson.com/

[24]   ibid.

[25]   Finney, J. (2008). Six secrets of top performers. *Communication World,* 25(3), 23–27. Retrieved from https://www.iabc.com/wp-content/uploads/2014/10/Six-Secrets-of-Top-Performers.pdf

[26]   Trahant, B. (2008). Six communication secrets of top-performing organizations: Through better communication, government executives and human capital professionals engage employees to improve organizational

performance. *The Public Manager, 37*(3), 68–75. Bill Trahant describes a 2007/2008 Watson Wyatt (Willis Towers Watson) survey that suggests a positive correlation between organizational communication and enhanced firm performance (also see Finney [2008] for an explanation of these results).

[27] Baldoni, J. (2009, November 19). New study: How communication drives performance [Blog post]. Retrieved from https://hbr.org/2009/11/new-study-how-communication-dr (Baldoni shares data from the 2009/2010 Watson Wyatt Communication ROI Study Report).

[28] Towers Watson. (2013). *Change and communication ROI—The 10th anniversary report. How the fundamentals have evolved and the best adapt.* https://www.willistowerswatson.com/

[29] Guisbond, A. (2017, May 1). Four corporate best practices to learn from GE [Blog post]. Retrieved from https://www.forbes.com/sites/forbescommunicationscouncil/2017/05/01/four-corporate-communications-best-practices-to-learn-from-ge/#41d350913b87

[30] Baldoni, J. (2009, November 19). New study: How communication drives performance [Blog post]. Retrieved from https://hbr.org/2009/11/new-study-how-communication-dr data from the 2009/2010

[31] Finney, J. (2008, May/June). Six secrets of top performers. *Communication World, 25*(3), 23–27.

[32] Towers Watson. (2010). *Capitalizing on effective communication. How courage, innovation, and discipline drive business results in challenging times.* https://www.willistowerswatson.com/

[33] Towers Watson. (2011). *Clear direction in a complex world. How top companies create clarity, confidence, and community to build sustainable performance.* https://www.willistowerswatson.com/

[34] Towers Watson. (2013). *Change and communication ROI—The 10th anniversary report. How the fundamentals have evolved and the best adapt.* (Top performers were companies that responded to survey questions with a "four" or "five" on a five-point Likert scale—agree/strongly agree, effective/highly effective, or a "yes"). https://www.willistowerswatson.com/

[35] Gilbert, J. A., Carr-Ruffino, N., Ivancevich, J. M., & Konopaske, R. (2012). Toxic versus cooperative behaviors at work: The role of organizational culture and leadership in creating community-centered organizations. *International Journal of Leadership Studies, 7*(1), 29–47.

[36] Information in this section was modified and adapted from the following blog posts:

Gilbert, J. A. (2011, February 14). Conducting a meeting the civil way [Blog post]. Retrieved from https://organizedforefficiency.com/conducting-a-meeting-the-civil-way/

Gilbert, J. A. (2011, March 30). Encourage meeting participation [Blog post]. Retrieved from https://organizedforefficiency.com/encourage-meeting-participation/

Gilbert, J. A. (2013, March 24). Unseemly behaviors in side conversations [Blog post]. Retrieved from https://organizedforefficiency.com/unseemly-behaviors-in-side-conversations/

[37] Tuck, P. (2014, March 1). A failure to communicate. *Training Journal.* Retrieved from https://www.trainingjournal.com/articles/feature/failure-communicate

[38] Fukuda, M. (2015, November 16). Thriving cultures are built with recognition and praise. *Entrepreneur.* Retrieved from https://www.entrepreneur.com/article/252850

[39] Smith, J. (2013, February 15). 13 things you should never say at work [Blog post]. Retrieved from https://www.forbes.com/sites/jacquelynsmith/2013/02/15/13-things-you-should-never-say-at-work/#5e7261612632

[40] Giang, V. (2013, November 24). 10 etiquette rules for meetings that every professional should know. *Business Insider.* Retrieved from http://www.businessinsider.com/10-etiquette-rules-for-meetings-that-every-professional-needs-to-know-2013-11

[41] Kruse, K. (2013, July 25). 6 ways to get people to open up [Blog post]. Retrieved from https://www.forbes.com/sites/kevinkruse/2013/07/25/get-people-to-open-up/#5bf983e07ddd

[42] Andersen, E. (2013, August 9). 5 simple things you can do to get people to speak up in meetings [Blog post]. Retrieved from https://www.forbes.com/sites/erikaandersen/2013/08/09/5-simple-things-you-can-do-to-get-people-to-speak-up-in-meetings/#24aca13fbe85

[43] Morin, A. (January 22, 2016). Study reveals a conversation trick that motivates people to change their behavior [Blog post]. Retrieved from https://www.forbes.com/sites/amymorin/2016/01/22/study-reveals-a-conversation-trick-that-motivates-people-to-change-their-behavior/#40cedc2e6ff0

[44] Barth, F. D. (2012, April 22). 5 steps for dealing with people who talk too much [Blog post]. Retrieved from https://www.psychologytoday.com/blog/the-couch/201204/5-steps-dealing-people-who-talk-too-much

Chapter 7

[1] Internet live stats. (n.d.). Retrieved from http://www.internetlivestats.com/

[2] Brown, N. W. (2008). *Children of the self-absorbed: A grown-up's guide to getting over narcissistic parents.* Oakland, CA: New Harbinger.

[3] Farley, S., Coyne, I., Sprigg, C., Axtell, C., & Subramanian, G. (2015). Exploring the impact of workplace cyberbullying on trainee doctors. *Medical Education, 49*(4), 436–443. https://doi.org/10.1111/medu.12666

[4] Cyberbullying in the workplace. (2012, November 30). Northeastern University. Retrieved from http://www.northeastern.edu/securenu/cyberbullying-in-the-workplace/

[5] Faucher, C., Jackson, M., & Cassidy, W. (2014). Cyberbullying among university students: Gendered experiences, impacts, and perspectives. *Education Research International.* Retrieved from http://dx.doi.org/10.1155/2014/698545

[6] Adele's baby welcomed with insults and taunts from Twitter trolls. (2012, October 22) [Blog post]. Retrieved from http://www.huffingtonpost.com/2012/10/22/adeles-baby-welcomed-with-insults-taunts-twitter-trolls_n_2002156.html

[7] Buckels, E. E., Trapnell, P. D., & Paulhus, D. L. (2014). Trolls just want to have fun. *Personality and Individual Differences, 67,* 97–102. https://doi.org/10.1016/j.paid.2014.01.016

[8] Patil, S. B. (2014, August 2). 10 celebs who were victims of cyber bullying & web trolling. *TheRichest.* Retrieved from http://www.therichest.com/rich-list/nation/10-celebrities-who-were-victims-of-cyber-bullying-web-trolling/

[9] Cary, M. K. (2010, May 6). Nothing good can come of Formspring, cyber bullying's newest venue. *U.S. News.* Retrieved from https://www.usnews.com/opinion/blogs/mary-kate-cary/2010/05/06/nothing-good-can-come-of-formspring-cyber-bullyings-newest-venue

[10] Chapman, P. (2010, November 18). Academic cyberbully is sentenced to jail in Dead Sea Scrolls case. *The Chronicle of Higher Education.* Retrieved from https://www.chronicle.com/article/Cyberbully-Is-Found-Guilty-on/124762

[11] Brenoff, A. (2017, July 27). How a billion-dollar Internet scam is breaking hearts and bank accounts [Blog post]. Retrieved from https://www.huffingtonpost.com/entry/romance-scams-online-fbi-facebook_us_59414c67e4b0d318548666f9

[12] Queally, J. (2011, February 13). Newark teen's online identity stolen and used to destroy her reputation. *NJ.com.* Retrieved from http://www.nj.com/news/index.ssf/2011/02/someone_had_stolen_a_newark_te.html

[13] Taran, R. (2013, September 18). Cyberbullying apps — Why are we allowing anonymous cruelty? [Blog post]. Retrieved from http://www.huffingtonpost.com/randy-taran/cyberbullying-apps_b_3941599.html

[14] Fonrouge, G. (2017, September 22). Inside the twisted revenge porn site that's ruining people's lives. *New York Post.* Retrieved from https://nypost.com/2017/09/22/revenge-porn-site-leaves-trail-of-innocent-victims/

[15] Snyman, R., & Loh, J. M. I. (2015). Cyberbullying at work: The mediating role of optimism between cyberbullying and job outcomes. *Computers in Human Behavior, 53,* 161–168. https://doi.org/10.1016/j.chb.2015.06.050

[16] Interview With Dr. Christine MacDonald, Ph.D., on the Effects of Cyberbullying. (n.d.). *Online MSW Programs.* Retrieved from https://www.onlinemswprograms.com/in-focus/interview-with-dr-christine-macdonald-on-cyberbullying.html

[17] Farley, S., Coyne, I., Sprigg, C., Axtell, C., & Subramanian, G. (2015). Exploring the impact of workplace cyberbullying on trainee doctors. *Medical Education, 49*(4), 436–443. https://doi.org/10.1111/medu.12666

[18] Faucher, C., Jackson, M., & Cassidy, W. (2014). Cyberbullying among university students: Gendered experiences, impacts, and perspectives. *Hindawi Education Research International*. Retrieved from https://www.hindawi.com/journals/edri/2014/698545/

[19] Cyberbullying facts. (n.d.). Retrieved from http://cyberbullying.org/facts

[20] Harary, C. (2016, April 15). 5 ways to cope with online haters. *Entrepreneur*. Retrieved from https://www.entrepreneur.com/article/272138

[21] Gilbert, J. A. (2011, February 21). The hidden facet of organizational culture [Blog post]. Retrieved from https://organizedforefficiency.com/the-hidden-facet-of-organizational-culture/

[22] Olson, G. A. (2014, October 6). E-mails are forever [Blog post]. Retrieved from http://www.huffingtonpost.com/gary-a-olson/emails-are-forever_b_5932854.html

[23] Poe, A. C. (2001). Don't touch that 'send' button! *HRMagazine, 46*(7), 74–80.

[24] ibid.

[25] Gilbert, J. A. (2011, February 25). E-mail: Efficiency gone haywire [Blog post] (Retrieved from https://organizedforefficiency.com/e-mail-efficiency-gone-haywire/). Information is adapted from Goleman, D. (1995). *Emotional intelligence: Why it can matter more than IQ*. New York, NY: Bantam Books.

[26] Gilbert, J. A. (2011, February 25). E-mail: Efficiency gone haywire [Blog post]. Retrieved from https://organizedforefficiency.com/e-mail-efficiency-gone-haywire/

[27] Information in the "Before you press the Send button" bullet points is from:

Sanders, A. (2011, June 22). Respect in the media, Part I [Blog post]. Retrieved from https://organizedforefficiency.com/respect-in-the-electronic-media-part-i/

Sanders, A. (2011, June 23). Respect in the media, Part II [Blog post]. Retrieved from https://organizedforefficiency.com/respect-in-the-electronic-media-part-ii/

[28] Poe, A. C. (2001). Don't touch that 'send' button. *HR Magazine, 46*(7), 74–80.

[29] McCarthy, D. (2012, January 13). Are you managing or just nagging? [Blog post]. Retrieved from http://www.greatleadershipbydan.com/2012/01/are-you-managing-or-just-nagging.html

[30] Effective E-Mail Communication. (n.d.). *The Writing Center University of North Carolina at Chapel Hill*. Retrieved from http://writingcenter.unc.edu/handouts/effective-e-mail-communication/ (The three bullet points were adapted from this source.)

[31] Wong, E. (2001, April 5). A stinging office memo boomerangs; chief executive is criticized after upbraiding workers by e-mail. *The New York Times*. Retrieved from http://www.nytimes.com/2001/04/05/business/

stinging-office-memo-boomerangs-chief-executive-criticized-after-upbraiding.html

[32] Hickey, A. R. (2011, May 4). HP public cloud strategy leaked by VP on LinkedIn. *CRN*. Retrieved from http://www.crn.com/news/cloud/229402748/hp-public-cloud-strategy-leaked-by-vp-on-linkedin.htm

[33] Schenk, L. B. (2012, October 5). Employers beware: Cyber-bullying could wreak havoc in your workplace. *Lexology*. (Retrieved from https://www.lexology.com/contributors/frost-brown-todd-llc). The information on unlawful and lawful policies was derived from the National Labor Relations Board (NLRB) Acting General Counsel's Memorandum on Social Media Policies. Smith (2016) explains that when supervisors send harassing text messages outside of normal work hours, they may create a hostile work environment. In addition, employers may be liable for their subordinate's abusive online activity. See Smith, A. (2016, February 10). Employers may be held liable for employees' cyberbullying. *SHRM*. Retrieved from https://www.shrm.org/resourcesandtools/legal-and-compliance/employment-law/pages/employers-cyberbullying.aspx

[34] ibid.

[35] Belkin, L. (2010, January 27). When mommies are bullies [Blog post]. Retrieved from http://parenting.blogs.nytimes.com/2010/01/27/when-mommies-are-bullies/

[36] Gilbert, J. A. (2016, February 10). In memoriam of EQ [Blog post]. Retrieved from https://organizedforefficiency.com/in-memoriam-of-eq/ (Information is from Turkle, S. [2015]. *Reclaiming conversation: The power of talk in a digital age*. New York, NY: Penguin Books.)

[37] Gilbert, J. A., Stead, B. A., & Ivancevich, J. M. (1999). Diversity management: A new organizational paradigm. *Journal of Business Ethics, 21*(1), 61–76. https://doi.org/10.1023/A:1005907602028

[38] Angelotti, E. (2013, August 20). How to handle personal attacks on social media. *Poynter*. Retrieved from http://www.poynter.org/2013/how-to-handle-personal-attacks-on-social-media/219452/

[39] Forni, P. M. (2008). *The civility solution: What to do when people are rude*. New York, NY: St. Martin's Press. The bulleted examples are adapted from this source.

[40] Hedges, K. (2014, June 5). How to get people off their phones in meetings without being a jerk [Blog post]. Retrieved from http://www.forbes.com/sites/work-in-progress/2014/06/05/how-to-get-people-off-their-phones-in-meetings-without-being-a-jerk/#1437de304c45

[41] Hughes, S. (2012, October 25). I banned all internal e-mails at my company for a week [Blog post]. Retrieved from http://www.forbes.com/sites/forbesleadershipforum/2012/10/25/i-banned-all-internal-e-mails-at-my-company-for-a-week/#72061af2adcb

[42] Gilbert, J. A., & Ivancevich, J. M. (1999). Organizational diplomacy: The bridge for managing diversity. *Human Resource Planning Journal, 22*(3), 29–39. (p. 33)

[43] Information in the three sub-bullet points under "Addressing one another appropriately and responsibly online" is from:

Sanders, A. (2011, June 22). Respect in the media, Part I [Blog post]. Retrieved from https://organizedforefficiency.com/respect-in-the-electronic-media-part-i/

Sanders, A. (2011, June 23). Respect in the media, Part II [Blog post]. Retrieved from https://organizedforefficiency.com/respect-in-the-electronic-media-part-ii/

[44] Ribble, M. (n.d.). Nine themes of digital citizenship. *Digital Citizenship*. Retrieved from http://www.digitalcitizenship.net/nine-elements.html

[45] Reuters. (2016, March 30). You can now get covered for cyberbullying with your home insurance. Retrieved from http://fortune.com/2016/03/30/cover-cyber-bullying-home-insurance/

[46] Caspari, S. (2015, August 20). How one teen's app could stop cyberbullying at its source. Retrieved from https://www.csmonitor.com/Technology/2015/0820/How-one-teen-s-app-could-stop-cyberbullying-at-its-source

[47] Hinduja, S. (n.d.). How machine learning can help us combat online abuse: A primer [Blog post]. Retrieved from https://cyberbullying.org/machine-learning-can-help-us-combat-online-abuse-primer

[48] Neal, S. T. (2018, June 22). Fighting back against anonymous defamation on the Internet: Ten steps to take (United States). *Association of Corporate Counsel*. Retrieved from https://www.acc.com/resource-library/fighting-back-against-anonymous-defamation-internet-ten-steps-take-united-states

[49] Ms. Smith. (2010, August 9). Google CEO Schmidt: No anonymity is the future of web. *CSO*. Retrieved from http://www.csoonline.com/article/2231573/microsoft-subnet/google-ceo-schmidt—no-anonymity-is-the-future-of-web.html

[50] Malewar, A. (2016, December 7). 3D Internet: The future of the Internet [Blog post]. Retrieved from https://www.techexplorist.com/future-internet-3d-internet/

[51] Cyberbullying in the Workplace. (2012, November 30). *SECURENU*. Retrieved from http://www.northeastern.edu/securenu/cyberbullying-in-the-workplace/

[52] Beauchere, J. F. (2014). Preventing online bullying: What companies and others can do. *International Journal of Technoethics*, *5*(1), 69–77. https://doi.org/10.4018/ijt.2014010106

[53] Balpreet Kaur, Sikh Woman, Receives Remarkable Apology From Redditor Who Posted Her Photo. (2012, September 27). [Blog post]. Retrieved from https://www.huffingtonpost.com/2012/09/27/balpreet-kaur-receives-recieves-remarkable-apology-from-redditor_n_1919336.html

[54] Beauchere, J. F. (2014). Preventing online bullying: What companies and others can do. *International Journal of Technoethics*, *5*(1), 69–77. https://doi.org/10.4018/ijt.2014010106

[55] Draves, W. A. (2002). *Teaching online*. River Falls, WI: LEARN Books.

[56] Beauchere, J. F. (2014). Preventing online bullying: What companies and others can do. *International Journal of Technoethics, 5*(1), 69–77. https://doi.org/10.4018/ijt.2014010106

[57] Hinduja, S., & Patchin, J. W. (n.d.). Preventing cyberbullying: Top ten tips for adults who are being harassed online. *Cyberbullying Research Center.* Retrieved from http://cyberbullying.org/preventing-cyberbullying-adults

[58] Garvin, K. (2017, May 16). UH professor garners nationwide recognition for online guideline for email etiquette. *Click2Houston.com.* Retrieved from http://www.click2houston.com/news/uh-professor-garners-nationwide-recognition-for-online-guideline-for-email-etiquette

[59] Hegman, S. (2014, October 23). Study: 40% of adults experience cyberbullying. *ADWEEK.* Retrieved from https://www.adweek.com/digital/new-study-finds-40-adults-cyberbullying/

[60] Hinduja, S., & Patchin, J. W. (n.d.). State cyberbullying laws: A brief review of state cyberbullying laws and policies. *Cyberbullying Research Center.* Retrieved from https://cyberbullying.org/state-cyberbullying-laws-a-brief-review-of-state-cyberbullying-laws-and-policies

[61] Hilden, J. (2012, June 11). Is a defamation case a good remedy for cyberbullying? An Atlanta girl tests the law. *VERDICT.* Retrieved from https://verdict.justia.com/2012/06/11/is-a-defamation-case-a-good-remedy-for-cyberbullying

[62] Marwick, A. E., & Miller, R. (2014). Online harassment, defamation, and hateful speech: A primer of the legal landscape. New York, NY: Fordham Center on Law and Information Policy. Retrieved from http://ir.lawnet.fordham.edu/cgi/viewcontent.cgi?article=1002&context=clip

[63] Gilbert, J. A. (2006). Communication. *Middle Tennessee State University.* Retrieved from http://mtweb.mtsu.edu/jgilbert/Electronic%20Course%20Notes/Communication.htm. Information is adapted from the original post.

[64] Greenfield, S. (2015, May 1). Is searching the Internet addictive? [Blog post]. Retrieved from https://www.psychologytoday.com/blog/mind-change/201504/is-surfing-the-internet-addictive

[65] Streussy, L. (2016, December 22). Your social media addiction is giving you depression. *New York Post.* Retrieved from https://nypost.com/2016/12/22/your-social-media-addiction-is-giving-you-depression/

[66] Gregory, C. (2018, May 15). Internet addiction disorder. *PSYCOM.* Retrieved from https://www.psycom.net/iadcriteria.html

[67] Emerson, R. (2012, January 23). Bcc or let them see? The etiquette of the blind carbon copy [Blog post]. Retrieved from http://www.huffingtonpost.com/2012/01/22/email-etiquette-bcc_n_1221901.html

[68] Gilbert, J. A. (2006). Communication. *Middle Tennessee State University.* Retrieved from http://mtweb.mtsu.edu/jgilbert/Electronic%20Course%20Notes/Communication.htm. Information is adapted from the original post.

Chapter 8

[1]   Roberts. B. E., & White, J. E. Jr. (1998). *Roberts vs. Texaco.* New York, NY: Avon Books.

[2]   Kanter, R. M., & Stein, B. A. (1980). *A tale of O: On being different in an organization.* New York, NY: Harper & Row.

[3]   Youngblood, M. D. (2000). *Life at the edge of chaos: Creating the quantum organization.* Dallas, TX: Perceval.

[4]   2015 Job Patterns for Minorities and Women in Private Industry (EEO-1). (2015). *U.S. Equal Employment Opportunity Commission.* Retrieved from https://www1.eeoc.gov/eeoc/statistics/employment/jobpat-eeo1/2015/index.cfm#select_label

[5]   Roberts. B. E., & White, J. E., Jr. (1998). *Roberts vs. Texaco.* New York, NY: Avon Books.

[6]   Antilla, S. (2002). *Tales from the boom-boom room.* Princeton, NJ: Bloomberg Press.

[7]   Gilbert, J. A. (2011, March 9). How to recognize discrimination in the new millennium [Blog post]. Retrieved from https://organizedforefficiency.com/how-to-recognize-discrimination-in-the-new-millenium/

[8]   Merritt, A. C., Effron, D. A., & Monin, B. (2010). Moral licensing: When being good frees us to be bad. *Social and Personality Psychology Compass, 4*(5), 344–357.

[9]   Namie, G. (2017). *2017 Workplace Bullying Institute U.S. Workplace Bullying Survey.* Retrieved from https://www.workplacebullying.org/multi/pdf/2017/Gender.pdf

[10]   Sobre-Denton, M. S. (2012). Stories from the cage: Autoethnographic sense-making of workplace bullying, gender discrimination, and white privilege. *Journal of Contemporary Ethnography, 41*(2), 220–250. https://doi.org/10.1177/0891241611429301

[11]   Rowe, M. (2008). Micro-affirmations & micro-inequities. *Journal of the International Ombudsperson Association, 1*(1), 45–48.

[12]   Pearce, J. C. (2002). *The biology of transcendence: A blueprint of the human spirit.* Rochester, VT: Park Street Press.

[13]   Sobre-Denton, M. S. (2012). Stories from the cage: Autoethnographic sense-making of workplace bullying, gender discrimination, and white privilege. *Journal of Contemporary Ethnography, 41*(2), 220–250. https://doi.org/10.1177/0891241611429301

[14]   Jones, E. E. (1964). *Ingratiation, a social psychological analysis.* New York, NY: Appleton-Century Crofts.

[15]   Ragins, B. R., Townsend, B., & Mattis, M. (1998). Gender gap in the executive suite: CEOs and female executives report on breaking the glass ceiling. *Academy of Management Executive, 12*(1), 28–42. https://doi.org/10.5465/AME.1998.254976

[16]   Nigatu, H. (2013, December 9). 21 racial microaggressions you hear on a daily basis [Blog post]. Retrieved from https://www.buzzfeed.com/

hnigatu/racial-microagressions-you-hear-on-a-daily-basis?utm_term=.
ffNDVx1LX#.ayRwyzONG

[17]   O'Donnell, S. M., & MacIntosh, J. A. (2016). Gender and workplace
        bullying: Men's experiences of surviving bullying at work. *Qualitative Health
        Research, 26*(3), 351–366. https://doi.org/10.1177/1049732314566321

[18]   NiCarthy, G., Gottlieb, N., & Coffman, S. (1993). *You don't have to take it!: A
        woman's guide to confronting emotional abuse at work.* Seattle, WA: Seal Press.

[19]   Antilla, S. (2002). *Tales from the boom-boom room.* Princeton, NJ: Bloomberg
        Press.

[20]   Sobre-Denton, M. S. (2012). Stories from the cage: Autoethnographic
        sense-making of workplace bullying, gender discrimination, and white
        privilege. *Journal of Contemporary Ethnography, 41*(2), 220–250. https://doi
        .org/10.1177/0891241611429301

[21]   Maremont, M. (1996, May 13). Abuse of power: The astonishing tale of
        sexual harassment at Astra USA. *Business Week,* 86–98.

[22]   Gilbert, J. A. (2016, January 20). Female bullying: The gender divide [Blog
        post]. Retrieved from https://organizedforefficiency.com/female-bullying
        -the-gender-divide/

[23]   Kanter, R. M., & Stein, B. A. (1980). *A tale of O: On being different in an
        organization.* New York, NY: Harper & Row.

[24]   Ely, R. J. (1994). The effects of organizational demographics and social
        identity on relationships among professional women. *Administrative Science
        Quarterly, 39*(2), 203–238. https://doi.org/10.2307/2393234

[25]   Cross, W. E., Jr., Smith, L., & Payne, Y. (2002). Black identity: A repertoire
        of daily enactments. In P. B. Pedersen, J. G. Draguns, W. J. Loner, & J. E.
        Trimble (Eds.), *Counseling across cultures* (5th ed., pp. 93–107). Thousand
        Oaks, CA: SAGE.

[26]   Peacock, L. (2013, September 13). Women feel need to 'act like men' to get
        ahead at work. *The Telegraph.* Retrieved from http://www.telegraph.co.uk/
        women/womens-business/10306864/Women-feel-need-to-act-like-men-to-
        get-ahead-at-work.html

[27]   NiCarthy, G., Gottlieb, N., & Coffman, S. (1993). *You don't have to take it!: A
        woman's guide to confronting emotional abuse at work.* Seattle, WA: Seal Press.

[28]   Antilla, S. (2002). *Tales from the boom-boom room.* Princeton, NJ: Bloomberg
        Press.

[29]   Babcock, L., & Laschever, S. (2007). *Women don't ask: The high cost of avoiding
        negotiation and positive strategies for change.* New York, NY: Bantam Books.

[30]   Johnson, T. R. (2014, December 26). Black-on-Black racism: The hazards of
        implicit bias: How the politics of respectability twists society. Retrieved from
        https://www.theatlantic.com/politics/archive/2014/12/black-on-black-
        racism-the-hazards-of-implicit-bias/384028/

[31]   Gilbert, J. A. (2011, March 9). How to recognize discrimination in the new
        millennium [Blog post]. Retrieved from https://organizedforefficiency.
        com/how-to-recognize-discrimination-in-the-new-millenium

[32] Dahl, J. (2015, January 21). The shocking truth about emotional abuse in the workplace [Blog post]. Retrieved from https://www.huffpost.com/entry/the-shocking-truth-about-_4_b_6181574

[33] Namie, G., & Namie, R. (2009). *The bully at work: What you can do to stop the hurt and reclaim your dignity on the job.* Naperville, IL: Sourcebooks.

[34] Gilbert, J. A., & Ivancevich, J. M. (1999). Organizational diplomacy: The bridge for managing diversity. *Human Resource Planning Journal, 22*(3), 29–39. (pp. 30, 31)

[35] Gilbert, J. A., & Ivancevich, J. M. (2000). Valuing diversity: A tale of two organizations. *Academy of Management Executive, 14*(1), 93–105.

[36] Thomas, D. A., & Ely, R. J. (1996). Making differences matter: A new paradigm for managing diversity. *Harvard Business Review, 74*(5), 79–91.

[37] Roberts. B. E., & White, J. E., Jr. (1998). *Roberts vs. Texaco.* New York, NY: Avon Books.

[38] Sobre-Denton, M. S. (2012). Stories from the cage: Autoethnographic sense-making of workplace bullying, gender discrimination, and White privilege. *Journal of Contemporary Ethnography, 41*(2), 220–250 (https://doi.org/10.1177/0891241611429301). Bullet points 2, 4, and 5 were derived from this source, in which Sobre-Denton addresses efforts that individual employees can take to eliminate abusive interaction within organizations.

[39] Gilbert, J. A., & Ivancevich, J. M. (1999). Organizational diplomacy: The bridge for managing diversity. *Human Resource Planning Journal, 22*(3), 29–39. (pp. 30, 31)

[40] Chappell, T. (1993). *The soul of a business: Managing for profit and the common good.* New York, NY: Bantam Books.

[41] ibid.

[42] De Pree, M. (1989). *Leadership is an art.* New York, NY: Bantam Dell.

[43] Best Places for Diversity 2017. (2017). *Great Place to Work.* Retrieved from https://www.greatplacetowork.com/best-workplaces/diversity/2017

[44] Sorenson, A. (2016, November 11). An open letter to president-elect Trump [LinkedIn status update]. Retrieved from https://www.hospitalitynet.org/opinion/4079373.html

[45] Gilbert, J. A. (2011, January 22). Eight ways to save face for someone else [Blog post] (Retrieved from https://organizedforefficiency.com/eight-ways-to-save-face-for-someone-else/). The eight points and the two paragraphs preceding them were modified and adapted from the original post.

[46] Gilbert, J. A. (2017, June 3). Why does bullying feel so bad? [Blog post] (Retrieved from https://organizedforefficiency.com/why-does-bullying-feel-so-bad/). The preceding three bullets and the sentence on corporate communalism were modified and adapted from the original post.

[47] Graven, A. R. (2012, October 16). Language studies trigger brain growth [Blog post]. Retrieved from sciencenordic.com/language-studies-trigger-brain-growth

[48] Gilbert, J. A. (2018, March 14). Adapting by developing an affinity for culture [Blog post] (Retrieved from https://organizedforefficiency.com/

adapting-by-developing-an-affinity-for-culture/). The preceding two sub-bullet points were modified and adapted from the original post.

[49]   Ross, E. (2015, March 5). Transgender: Is there still fear in the workplace? *Center for American Progress.* Retrieved from https://www.theguardian.com/sustainable-business/2015/mar/05/transgender-fear-workplace-business

[50]   Burns, C., & Krehely, J. (2011, June 2). Gay and transgender people face high rates of discrimination and harassment. Retrieved from https://www.americanprogress.org/issues/lgbt/news/2011/06/02/9872/gay-and-transgender-people-face-high-rates-of-workplace-discrimination-and-harassment/

[51]   Ross, E. (2015, March 5). Transgender: Is there still fear in the workplace? *Center for American Progress.* Retrieved from https://www.theguardian.com/sustainable-business/2015/mar/05/transgender-fear-workplace-business. The three bulleted points are adapted from this source.

[52]   Gilbert, J. A. (2019, June 29). What is inclusion? [Blog post]. Retrieved from https://organizedforefficiency.com/archives/

[53]   Morrison, E. W., & Milliken, F. J. (2000). Organizational silence: A barrier to change and development in a pluralistic world. *Academy of Management Review, 25*(4), 706–725. https://doi.org/10.2307/259200

[54]   Wheatley, M. J. (1999). *Leadership and the new science: Discovering order in a chaotic world.* San Francisco, CA: Berrett-Koehler.

[55]   Gilbert, J. A. (2010, December 6). The circle of luv [Blog post] (Retrieved from https://organizedforefficiency.com/the-circle-of-luv/). Information in the two paragraphs was modified and adapted from the original post.

[56]   Hayden, J. M. (2010). Developing civility at the deepest levels of difference. *AboutCampus, 15*(4), 19–25. https://doi.org/10.1002/abc.20031

[57]   ibid.

[58]   Gilbert, J. A. (2001). From stereotypes to sociotypes: The impact of multicultural education. *Journal on Excellence in College Teaching, 12*(2), 55–76. (p. 57)

[59]   Triandis, H. C., Kurowski, L. L., & Gelfand, M. J. (1994). Workplace diversity. In H. C. Triandis, M. D. Dunnette, & L. M. Hough (Eds.), *Handbook of industrial and organizational psychology* 2 (Vol. 4, pp. 769–827). Palo Alto, CA: Consulting Psychologists Press.

[60]   Gilbert, J. A., & Ivancevich, J. M. (1999). Organizational diplomacy: The bridge for managing diversity. *Human Resource Planning Journal, 22*(3), 29–39. (p. 34)

[61]   Dobbin, F., & Kalev, A. (2016). Why diversity programs fail: And what works better. *Harvard Business Review, 94*(7–8), 52–60.

[62]   Sherman, J. E. (2017, December 27). Will lookism ever end? A possible way out of our most stubborn and ugly prejudice [Blog post]. Retrieved from https://www.psychologytoday.com/us/blog/ambigamy/201712/will-lookism-ever-end

[63]   Jacobson, K. J. L., Hood, J. N., & Van Buren III, H. J. (2014). Workplace bullying across cultures: A research agenda. *International Journal of Cross*

Cultural Management, 14(1), 47–65. https://doi.org/10.1177/147059581 3494192

[64]   Rice, F. (1996, May 13). Denny's changes its spots: Not so long ago, the restaurant chain was one of America's most racist companies. Today it is a model of multicultural sensitivity. Here is the inside story of Denny's about-face. *Fortune*. Retrieved from http://archive.fortune.com/magazines/ fortune/fortune_archive/1996/05/13/212386/index.htm

Chapter 9

[1]   Some information in the "The Problem and Definition" section was modified and adapted from the following blog posts:

> Gilbert, J. A. (2018, March 12). Optimum performance through team input [Blog post]. Retrieved from https://organizedforefficiency.com/ optimum-performance-through-team-input/
>
> Gilbert, J. A. (2017, September 30). What is emotional intelligence? [Blog post]. Retrieved from https://organizedforefficiency.com/what-is-emotional-intelligence/
>
> Gilbert, J. A. (2016, April 29). Positive team building for continuity [Blog post]. Retrieved from https://organizedforefficiency.com/positive-team-building-for-continuity/

[2]   Leman, K. (1989). *Growing up first born: The pressure and privilege of being number one*. New York, NY: Delacorte Press.

[3]   Baillien, E., Notelaers, G., De Witte, H., & Matthiesen, S. B. (2011). The relationship between the work unit's conflict management styles and bullying at work: Moderation by conflict frequency. *Economic and Industrial Democracy, 32*(3), 401–419. https://doi.org/10.1177/0143831X10377929

[4]   ibid.

[5]   Comaford, C. (2014, March 12). How to stop workplace bullies in their tracks [Blog post]. Retrieved from http://www.forbes.com/sites/ christinecomaford/2014/03/12/bust-workplace-bullies-and-clear-conflict-in-3-essential-steps/#38224af3188b

[6]   Gilbert, J. A. (2011, October 31). Dissension in the ranks [Blog post]. Retrieved from https://organizedforefficiency.com/dissension-in-the-ranks/

[7]   Comaford, C. (2014, March 12). How to stop workplace bullies in their tracks [Blog post]. Retrieved from http://www.forbes.com/sites/ christinecomaford/2014/03/12/bust-workplace-bullies-and-clear-conflict-in-3-essential-steps/#38224af3188b

[8]   Gilbert, J. A. (2017, July 28) What is restorative bullying? [Blog post]. Retrieved from https://organizedforefficiency.com/what-is-restorative-bullying/

[9]   Gilbert, J. A. (2016, January 20). Female bullying: The gender divide [Blog post]. Retrieved from https://organizedforefficiency.com/female-bullying-the-gender-divide/

[10]   Social Media and Employee Voice: The Current Landscape. (n.d.). London, UK. Chartered Institute of Personnel and Development. Retrieved from https://www.cipd.co.uk/Images/social-media-and-employee-voice_2013-current-landscape-sop_tcm18-10327.pdf

[11]   Sessoms, G. (n.d.). How to get employees to voice their opinions. *Chron.* Retrieved from http://smallbusiness.chron.com/employees-voice-opinions-16072.html

[12]   Lytle, T. (2015, July 13). How to resolve workplace conflicts. *SHRM.* Retrieved from https://www.shrm.org/hr-today/news/hr-magazine/pages/070815-conflict-management.aspx

[13]   Marcic, D. (1997). *Managing with the wisdom of love: Uncovering virtue in people and organizations.* San Francisco, CA: Jossey-Bass.

[14]   Pearce, J. C. (2002). *The biology of transcendence: A blueprint of the human spirit.* Rochester, VT: Park Street Press.

[15]   Lewin, R., & Regine, B. (2000). *The soul at work: Listen . . . respond . . . let go: Embracing complexity science for business success.* New York, NY: Simon & Schuster.

[16]   ibid.

[17]   Chappell, T. (1993). *The soul of a business: Managing for profit and the common good.* New York, NY: Bantam Books.

[18]   Gilbert, J. A. (2011, February 14). Conducting a meeting—the civil way [Blog post]. Retrieved from https://organizedforefficiency.com/conducting-a-meeting-the-civil-way/

[19]   Lewin, R., & Regine, B. (2000). *The soul at work: Listen . . . respond . . . let go: Embracing complexity science for business success.* New York, NY: Simon & Schuster.

[20]   ibid.

[21]   ibid.

[22]   Pollard, C. W. (1996). *The soul of the firm.* New York, NY: HarperBusiness, and Grand Rapids, MI: Zondervan.

[23]   Sheridan, R. (2013). *Joy, Inc.: How we built a workplace people love.* New York, NY: Portfolio/Penguin.

[24]   Jackson, A. E. (2019). The secrets behind HubSpot's best places to work win. *glassdoor for Employers.* Retrieved from https://www.glassdoor.com/employers/blog/hubspot-bptw-2020/ Also see Huddleston Jr., T. (2014, August 22). Twitter tops all in culture and values, employees say [Blog post]. Retrieved from http://fortune.com/2014/08/22/twitter-tops-list-company-culture/

[25]   The Zappos Culture Book. (n.d.). Retrieved from https://www.zapposinsights.com/culture-book

[26]   Feintzeig, R. (2013, April 27). How to disarm a nasty coworker: Use a smile. *The Wall Street Journal.* Retrieved from https://www.wsj.com/articles/what-happens-when-coworkers-are-nasty-to-each-other-1377648431?tesla=y

[27]   Dutton, J. E. (2014). Build high-quality connections. In J. E. Dutton & G. M. Spreitzer (Eds.), *How to be a positive leader: Small actions big impact* (pp. 11–21). San Francisco, CA: Berrett-Koehler.

[28]   Gilbert, J. A. (2014, March 31) Catching divergence in companies [Blog post] (Retrieved from https://organizedforefficiency.com/catching-divergence-in-companies/). Modified and adapted from the original post.

[29]   Myatt, M. (2012, February 22). 5 keys of dealing with workplace conflict [Blog post]. Retrieved from http://www.forbes.com/sites/mikemyatt/2012/02/22/5-keys-to-dealing-with-workplace-conflict/#6376951715a0

[30]   Gilbert, J. A. (2014, March 31). Catching divergence in companies [Blog post]. (Retrieved from https://organizedforefficiency.com/catching-divergence-in-companies/). The five bullet points were modified and adapted from the original post.

[31]   Bedeian, A. G. (2002). The dean's disease: How the darker side of power manifests itself in the office of the dean. *Academy of Management Learning & Education, 1*(2), 164–173. https://doi.org/10.5465/amle.2002.8509359

[32]   Baillien, E., Notelaers, G., De Witte, H., & Matthiesen, S. B. (2010). The relationship between the work unit's conflict management styles and bullying at work: Moderation by conflict frequency. *Economic and Industrial Democracy, 32*(3), 401–419. https://doi.org/10.1177/0143831X10377929

[33]   Managing Conflict at Google [Video file]. Retrieved from www.youtube.com/watch?v=HsEJH8t08Q4

[34]   Lytle, T. (2015, July 13). How to resolve workplace conflicts. *SHRM.* Retrieved from https://www.shrm.org/hr-today/news/hr-magazine/pages/070815-conflict-management.aspx

[35]   Patterson, K., Grenny, J., McMillan, R., & Switzler, A. (2002). *Crucial conversations: Tools for talking when stakes are high.* New York, NY: McGraw-Hill. Information on the "STATE" model and priming example is from this source.

[36]   Gilbert, J. A. (2011, October 31). Dissension in the ranks [Blog post]. Retrieved from https://organizedforefficiency.com/dissension-in-the-ranks/

[37]   Comaford, C. (2014, March 12). How to stop workplace bullies in their tracks [Blog post]. Retrieved from http://www.forbes.com/sites/christinecomaford/2014/03/12/bust-workplace-bullies-and-clear-conflict-in-3-essential-steps/#38224af3188b

[38]   ibid.

[39]   Llopis, G. (2014, November 28). 4 ways leaders effectively manage employee conflict [Blog post]. Retrieved from https://www.forbes.com/sites/glennllopis/2014/11/28/4-ways-leaders-effectively-manage-employee-conflict/#b43dc345e15e

[40]   Asghar, A. (2019, February 19). A practical guide for defusing conflict [Blog post]. Retrieved from https://www.forbes.com/sites/robasghar/2019/02/19/a-practical-guide-for-defusing-conflict/#5f23667747b5

[41] Friedman, R., A., & Curall, S. C. (2003). Conflict escalation: Dispute exacerbating elements of e-mail communication. *Human Relations, 56*(11), 1325–1347. https://doi.org/10.1177/00187267035611003. Retrieved from http://www-personal.umich.edu/~lroot/ConflictMgtConceptMap/Friedman-Curall-ConflictEscalation-Email-2003.pdf

[42] Blanding, M. (2013, December 9). How cultural conflict undermines workplace creativity [Blog post]. Retrieved from https://www.forbes.com/sites/hbsworkingknowledge/2013/12/09/how-cultural-conflict-undermines-workplace-creativity/#37c7671214ff

[43] Strong Leaders Encourage Dissent, and Gain Commitment. (2005, November 21) [Blog post]. Retrieved from http://knowledge.wharton.upenn.edu/article/strong-leaders-encourage-dissent-and-gain-commitment/

[44] Roberto, M. A. (2005). *Why great leaders don't take yes for an answer.* Upper Saddle River, NJ: Pearson.

[45] Andersen, E. (2012, June 5). Courageous leaders don't make excuses...They apologize [Blog post]. Retrieved from https://www.forbes.com/sites/erikaandersen/2012/06/05/courageous-leaders-dont-make-excuses-they-apologize/#4441745b4ef8

[46] Kellerman, B. (2006). When should a leader apologize—and when not? *Harvard Business Review, 84*(4), 72–81. https://hbr.org/2006/04/when-should-a-leader-apologize-and-when-not

[47] Lazare, A. (2004). *On apology.* New York, NY: Oxford University Press.

Chapter 10

[1] Bible, J. D. (2012). The jerk at work: Workplace bullying and the law's inability to combat it. *Employee Relations Law Journal, 38*(1), 32–51. (p. 32)

[2] Torres, N. (2015, December 9). It's better to avoid a toxic employee than hire a superstar [Blog post]. Retrieved from https://hbr.org/2015/12/its-better-to-avoid-a-toxic-employee-than-hire-a-superstar

[3] Peck, M. S. (1978). *The road less traveled: A new psychology of love, traditional values, and spiritual growth.* New York, NY: Touchstone.

[4] Jaffe, D. T., & Scott, C. D. (1993). Building a committed workplace: An empowered organization as a competitive advantage. In M. Ray & A. Rinzler (Eds.), *The new paradigm in business: Emerging strategies for leadership and organizational change* (pp. 139–159). New York, NY: Jeremy P. Tarcher/Putnam.

[5] Dishman, L. (2015, December 28). The ten worst and best leaders of 2015. *Fast Company.* Retrieved from https://www.fastcompany.com/3054777/the-10-best-and-worst-leaders-of-2015

[6] Downs, A. (1997). *Beyond the looking glass: Overcoming the seductive culture of corporate narcissism.* New York, NY: AMACOM.

[7] Mawritz, M. B., Mayer, D. M., Hoobler, J. M., Wayne, S. J., & Marinova, S. V. (2012). A trickle-down model of abusive supervision. *Personnel Psychology, 65*(2), 325–357. https://doi.org/10.1111/j.1744-6570.2012.01246.x

[8] ibid.

[9] Weber Shandwick. (n.d.). The company behind the brand: In reputation we trust. Retrieved from http://www.webershandwick.com/uploads/news/files/InRepWeTrust_ExecutiveSummary.pdf

[10] ibid.

[11] Gilbert, J. A. (2012, April 11). Contemporary day Katniss [Blog post] (Retrieved from https://organizedforefficiency.com/contemporary-day-katniss/). The five bullets were modified and adapted from the original post.

[12] O'Reilly, C. A., & Pfeffer, J. (2000). *Hidden value: How great companies achieve extraordinary results with ordinary people.* Boston, MA: Harvard Business School Press.

[13] Tatley, K. (2015, July 13). Zappos–hiring for culture and the bizarre things they do [Blog post]. Retrieved from https://recruitloop.com/blog/zappos-hiring-for-culture-and-the-bizarre-things-they-do/

[14] Worrall, S. (2016, November 27). Here's what placebos can heal: And what they can't. *National Geographic.* Retrieved from http://news.nationalgeographic.com/2016/11/placebo-health-science-brain-suggestible-you-erik-vance/

[15] Treadway, D. C., Shaughnessy, B. A., Breland, J. W., Yang, J., & Reeves, M. (2013). Political skill and the job performance of bullies. *Journal of Managerial Psychology, 28*(3) 273–289. (p. 279). Treadway describes bullies as strategic individuals who carefully choose their targets to maximize their impact, and to escape the consequences.

[16] ibid.

[17] Hanson, B. C. (2011, July 13). Diagnose and eliminate workplace bullying [Blog post]. Retrieved from https://hbr.org/2011/07/diagnose-and-eliminate-workplace

[18] Ronda, L., Ollo-López, A., & Goñi-Legaz, S. (2016). Family-friendly practices, high-performance work practices and work–family balance: How do job satisfaction and working hours affect this relationship? *Management Research: The Journal of the Iberoamerican Academy of Management, 14*(1), 2–23.

[19] Bolman, L. G., & Deal, T. E. (2001). *Leading with soul: An uncommon journey of spirit.* San Francisco, CA: Jossey-Bass.

[20] Lewin, R., & Regine, B. (2000). *The soul at work: Listen . . . respond . . . let go: Embracing complexity science for business success.* New York, NY: Simon & Schuster.

[21] Huselid, M. A. (1995). The impact of human resource practices on turnover, productivity, and corporate financial performance. *Academy of Management Journal, 38*(3), 635–672. https://doi.org/10.5465/256741

[22] Pinchot, G., & Pinchot, E. (1993). *The end of bureaucracy and the rise of the intelligent organization.* San Francisco, CA: Berrett-Koehler.

[23] McNutt, C. (2017, March 9). Google tops the Fortune 100 places to work, once again. *Android Headlines*. (Retrieved from https://www.androidheadlines.com/2017/03/google-tops-the-fortune-100-best-places-to-work-once-again.html). Alphabet's Google Code of Conduct is available at https://abc.xyz/investor/other/google-code-of-conduct.html

[24] Feffer, M. (2015, June 1). What makes an employer a great place to work? *SHRM*. Retrieved from https://www.shrm.org/hr-today/news/hr-magazine/Pages/0615-great-places-to-work.aspx

[25] Murphy, S. (2016, June 30). Five overlooked ways to purposefully create optimism at work. *Inc*. Retrieved from http://www.inc.com/shawn-murphy/five-overlooked-ways-to-purposefully-create-optimism-at-work.html

[26] Boddy, C. R. (2014). Corporate psychopaths, conflict, employee affective well-being and counterproductive work behaviour. *Journal of Business Ethics, 121*(1), 107–121. http://dx.doi.org/10.1007/s10551-013-1688-0

[27] 50 Happiest Companies Award: CareerBliss Asks Employees to Rank their Workplace for 2017. (2017). *businesswire*. Retrieved from https://www.businesswire.com/news/home/20160929006123/en/50-Happiest-Companies-Award-CareerBliss-Asks-Employees

[28] Boyce, A. S., Nieminen, L. R. G., Gillespie, M. A., Ryan, A. M., & Denison, D. R. (2015). Which comes first, organizational culture or performance? A longitudinal study of causal priority with automobile dealerships. *Journal of Organizational Behavior, 36*(3), 339–359 (https://doi.org/10.1002/job.1985). The culture scale for this study was developed by Denison, D. R., Nieminen, L. R., & Kotrba, L. (2014). Diagnosing organizational cultures: A conceptual and empirical review of culture effectiveness surveys. *European Journal of Work and Organizational Psychology, 23*(1), 145–161. https://doi.org/10.1080/1359432X.2012.713173

[29] Cortina, L. M. (2008). Unseen injustice: Incivility as modern discrimination in organizations. *Academy of Management Review, 33*(1), 55–75. http://dx.doi.org/10.5465/AMR.2008.27745097

[30] Barge, J. K., & Oliver, C. (2003). Working with appreciation in managerial practice. *Academy of Management Review, 28*(1), 124–142. https://doi.org/10.5465/AMR.2003.8925244

[31] Quinn, R. E., & Thakor, A. V. (2014). Imbue the organization with a higher purpose. In J. E. Dutton & G. M. Spreitzer (Eds.), *How to be a positive leader: Small actions big impact* (pp. 100–112). San Francisco, CA: Berrett-Koehler.

[32] Freiberg, K., & Freiberg, J. (1996). *NUTS! Southwest Airlines' crazy recipe for business and personal success*. Austin, TX: Bard Press.

[33] Santoni, M. (2017, August 8). Southwest Airlines worker delivers Pittsburgh flyer's missing cancer medication. *TribLIVE.com*. Retrieved from http://triblive.com/local/allegheny/12597945-74/a-misplaced-suitcase-turned-into-an-inspiring-story-and-a-bit-of

[34] Marcic, D. (1997). *Managing with the wisdom of love: Uncovering virtue in people and organizations*. San Francisco, CA: Jossey-Bass.

[35] Pollard, C. W. (1996). *The soul of the firm.* New York, NY: HarperBusiness, and Grand Rapids, MI: Zondervan.

[36] De Pree, M. (1989). *Leadership is an art.* New York, NY: Bantam Dell.

[37] ibid.

[38] DuBois, S. (2012, January 25). Internal competition at work: Worth the trouble? [Blog post]. Retrieved from http://fortune.com/2012/01/25/internal-competition-at-work-worth-the-trouble/

[39] Sobre-Denton, M. S. (2012). Stories from the cage: Autoethnographic sense-making of workplace bullying, gender discrimination, and white privilege. *Journal of Contemporary Ethnography, 41*(2), 220–250. https://doi.org/10.1177/0891241611429301

[40] Gilbert, J. A. (2012, April 18). Control and the absence of consensus [Blog post]. Retrieved from https://organizedforefficiency.com/control-and-the-absence-of-consensus/

[41] Some information in "The Legacy of Bully Busters at Work" section was modified and adapted from the following blog posts:

    Gilbert, J. A. (2011, August 17). In your face activism [Blog post]. Retrieved from https://organizedforefficiency.com/in-your-face-activism/

    Gilbert, J. A. (2011, November 21). Modern day resistance [Blog post]. Retrieved from https://organizedforefficiency.com/modern-day-resistance/

    Gilbert, J. A. (2011, December 6). Rebel with a cause [Blog post]. Retrieved from https://organizedforefficiency.com/rebel-with-a-cause/

[42] Romm, C. (2015, January 28). Rethinking one of psychology's most infamous experiments. *The Atlantic.* Retrieved from http://www.theatlantic.com/health/archive/2015/01/rethinking-one-of-psychologys-most-infamous-experiments/384913/

[43] Namie, G., & Namie, R. (2009). *The bully at work: What you can do to stop the hurt and reclaim your dignity on the job.* Naperville, IL: Sourcebooks.

[44] Namie, G., & Namie, R. (2011). *The bully-free workplace: Stop jerks, weasels, and snakes from killing your organization.* New York, NY: Wiley.

A small portion of this book is from an unpublished manuscript by Jacqueline A. Gilbert entitled *Transcendent Management: The Journey From Bureaucracy to Spiritual Awareness at Work.*

Contributor Acknowledgments

The author wishes to acknowledge the individuals and entities who graciously granted permission to use their materials:

Dr. Elizabeth Allan for permission to use the "Hazing Continuum" which appeared in the StopHazing website

Dr. Jon D. Bible for permission to quote from the article "The Jerk at Work: Workplace Bullying and the Law's Inability to Combat It," which appeared in the *Employee Relations Law Journal*

Leslie Blanchard for permission to quote from her web article "My Worst Nightmare: What if I Accidentally Raise the Bully?" which appeared in the Huffington Post

Ariadne Brill for permission to use the "What Shame Teaches Children" table from the Positive Parenting Connection blog

Dr. David Foote for permission to quote from the "Leadership is not about Getting Things Done" blog post, which appeared in OrganizedforEfficiency .com

Graziadio Business Review for permission to quote from the article "Are Workplace Bullies Sabotaging Your Ability to Compete?" by John E. Richardson and Linnea B. McCord

Oisín Grogan for permission to use the "W.A.I.T. Why am I Talking" figure

How to Transform Workplace Bullies Into Allies, pages 247–248
Copyright © 2020 by Information Age Publishing

Harvard Business Publishing for permission to use the "Are you Falling into the Envy Trap?" assessment from the article "Envy at Work" by Tanya Menon and Leigh Thompson

Dr. Frances Henry for permission to use a portion of the "Strengthening Diversity in Your Organization: A Self-Assessment Tool" which appeared in the "Strengthening Diversity in Your Organization: A Self-Assessment Tool" web article

Bruce Holland for permission to use the "How Toxic is Your Culture?" figure that appeared in the "How Toxic is Your Culture?" web article

International Journal of Leadership Studies for permission to use the "Differences between Toxic and Community-Centered Organizations" and the "Descriptors of a Connective Community-Centered Organization" tables, along with quoted material which appeared in the article "Toxic Versus Cooperative Behaviors at Work: The Role of Organizational Culture and Leadership in Creating Community-centered Organizations" by Jacqueline A. Gilbert, Norma Carr-Ruffino, John M. Ivancevich, and Robert Konopaske

Dr. Andrea Sanders for permission to quote from the "Respect in the Electronic Media Part I" and "Respect in the Electronic Media Part II" blog posts which appeared on OrganizedforEfficiency.com

Springer Nature and Copyright Clearance Center for permission to use the "Diversity Management: A New Organizational Paradigm" figure which appeared in the *Journal of Business Ethics.* The article was coauthored by Jacqueline A. Gilbert, Bette Ann Stead, and John M. Ivancevich

CPSIA information can be obtained
at www.ICGtesting.com
Printed in the USA
LVHW100907240720
661397LV00003B/10